D0095273

TRACING YOUR
BRITISH ANCESTORS

TRACING YOUR BRITISH ANCESTORS

A Guide to Genealogical Sources

Gerald Hamilton-Edwards

BARNES
&NOBLE
BOOKS
NEW YORK

Copyright © 1966, 1967 by Gerald Hamilton-Edwards
All rights reserved.

This edition published by Barnes & Noble, Inc.,
by arrangement with Walker & Company.

1993 Barnes & Noble Books

ISBN 1-56619-113-0

Printed and bound in the United States of America
M 9 8 7 6 5 4 3 2

CONTENTS

ACKNOWLEDGEMENTS

I am grateful to many people for their help in the writing of this book, to a number of officials, secretaries of societies and individuals for information willingly given. Remembered with especial gratitude are Miss Joan Harris for her help in correcting proofs, Captain J. A. S. Trydell for his assistance with the index and bibliography, Lady Henriques for her information about the Jews and Huguenots in Stepney and Mr Alejandro Raimúndez for information about Spanish registration. I should also like to mention the help received from Mr Anthony J. Camp, Director of Research at the Society of Genealogists, Mr W. K. Ford, the Librarian there and Mr Donald J. Steel.

GERALD HAMILTON-EDWARDS

[1]

DISCOVERING WHAT IS
ALREADY KNOWN

Those of you who know Wilde's play, *The Importance of being Earnest,* may remember how annoyed Lady Bracknell was that Mr Worthing did not know the name of either of his parents. 'To lose one parent,' she declaimed emphatically, 'may be regarded as a misfortune; to lose both looks like carelessness!'

Few of us fortunately are likely to incur Lady Bracknell's displeasure through being in Mr Worthing's predicament. Nearly all of us know the names of our parents and usually quite a lot about them. Our grandparents, too, are usually familiar to us, though many do not know their christian names when it comes to the point, as we have always called them 'Grandpa' and 'Grandma'.

However, provided they were born in England or Wales or Scotland it is not too difficult a task to discover their full names and those of their parents and grandparents back to the time when civil registration began, which in England was in 1837 and in Scotland in 1855. Since those times there are general indexes in each country for all people who were born, married or died there.

But even this may be a very lengthy and slow business unless you go about it the right way. The first thing to do in this intriguing expedition into your past family history is to find out what is already known. You do not want to spend several years tracing back your family only to discover that 'Uncle Cuthbert worked all that out years ago'.

But before you make even these preliminary enquiries there

is one question you should ask yourself, namely, why you are doing it at all. The answer may be that you just want to get on record for your family and future generations of it some information about it before such knowledge is forgotten and lost. This is in itself a perfectly good and praiseworthy reason for wanting to trace and write up your family history.

You will notice that I have added 'write up', because if you fail to record your work, even in some simple form, such as a chart pedigree, you will probably only have succeeded in giving yourself some enjoyment and satisfaction and the value of your efforts will be greatly diminished. I shall later on have something to say on the best ways of recording your researches.

You may have other reasons. For instance your family may have played some small part at one time in a great national event and you may feel your work is a small contribution to history itself, as indeed it may be. For however humble and simple the lives of your ancestors may have been, their story is in itself a contribution to our knowledge of the past. Genealogists often discover in their searches interesting and delightful incidents which historians in their wider field might never come across, small incidents which reflect with great sincerity the life of the period.

Another question which you may like to have answered before you start on your task is, 'What are the chances of success?' This is a question which cannot be answered completely, because it depends so much on individual cases. Let me say straight away that any idea of tracing back to the time of William the Conqueror is almost certainly just a pipe dream. There has been a lot of nonsense talked by people claiming that their family came over with William the Conqueror. Naturally many of us are descended from the Normans who were present at Hastings or who came over later, when King William had established himself in England, but to prove it generation by generation from one of those who fought beside William at Hastings is a different matter. At the time of the Falaise celebrations in 1931, when a bronze memorial was set up in Falaise Castle to the honour of the Conqueror and his companions in arms, a number of people claimed to be descended from the knights who fought with him at Hastings. More recently the nine hundredth anniversary of the Battle of Hastings has produced a somewhat smaller number of claimants to such descents. But it appears that no living person is able to prove his descent step by step in the male line from a companion of the Conqueror at the battle of Hastings. This is the opinion among others of Mr G. H. White, editor of *The Complete Peerage*,[1] and also of the present Garter King of Arms, Sir Anthony Wagner[2]. As the latter explains, the Malets of Enmore came as near as anyone in being able to prove a direct descent in the male line from a companion of the Conqueror at Hastings, in their case from William Malet who fought at Hastings in 1066, but part of the descent in the early twelfth century is not clearly proved. As Sir Anthony has said 'could the early links but be made clear beyond all doubt the Malets would have the unique distinction of a proved male descent from a man who fought at Hastings'.

It is disappointing therefore that no man living today can prove satisfactorily a male descent from someone who fought at this famous battle. There are however a few families which can prove their pedigree beyond reasonable doubt to a holder of land in England at the time of Domesday. The Derbyshire family of Shirley are among those which have the rare distinction of being able to prove such a descent and Major John Shirley still owns the manor of Ettington in Warwickshire which his ancestor in the male line, Sewal, owned in 1086. This is probably a unique distinction. East Quantockshead in Somerset has been held since that time by only two families, the Paynels from 1086 to about 1200, and from that time by the Lutterell family, whose ancestor married the Paynel heiress.

There is one family which can even show a descent from pre-conquest times to the present day in unbroken male line. This is the family of Arden, which has a proved descent from

---

[1] See *The Genealogists' Magazine* Vol VI, pp. 50–57 (March 1932) and Vol IX, pp. 416–28 (September 1944)

[2] A. R. Wagner, *English Genealogy*, p. 60

Aelfwine, Sheriff of Warwickshire before the Conquest, down to Dr George Arden, who is 27th in direct descent. It is considered probable, though it is not proved, that Mary Arden, the mother of William Shakespeare, was of this family. The Berkeley family of Berkeley Castle has a strong probability of a pre-conquest descent in the direct male line, but one of its generations is doubtful and the identification of its earliest ancestor is conjectural. Many of the male lines of Norman and Angevin baronies have died out or are not known to exist because the inheritance has descended through the female line and a great number of peers today come from families which a few generations ago belonged to the middle or lower classes.

Descent from such early times as those mentioned above are quite exceptional and in general the person who can trace his family back to the seventeenth century is fortunate. It is quite likely he will get back no further than the mid-eighteenth century. Success in this matter depends on a number of factors. Sir Anthony Wagner, the present Garter King of Arms, in his *English Ancestry*, which is a shortened form of his *English Genealogy*, previously mentioned, both of which are recommended for reading, says that there are four main factors which govern the tracing of pedigree, namely, *status, record, name* and *continuity*.

By *status* is meant the position in the social structure. This may, of course, vary from generation to generation, but it will be apparent that it is easier to trace a prominent family than a more humble one. An hereditary peerage family is easy to trace as far back as the peerage goes, because the very essence of it is hereditary. But status is a wider term. It will be fairly easy to trace a professional family for instance which consisted mainly of clergymen, lawyers or officers in the army or navy. It will be less easy to trace a family lower down the social scale. But the pattern is often a changing one for, although class distinction was more marked in the past and people then, for instance, did not so often marry outside their own social circle, yet they did do so occasionally. Such a union was often the cause of rise or fall in status and, apart from marriage, it has always been possible in our country for men of ability to rise to high position. To realize this one has only to think of Cardinal Wolsey, said to have been a butcher's son, or Thomas Cromwell, a man of humble position who became Henry VIII's chancellor. This tendency to osmosis has long been apparent in England. In the eighteenth century there were numerous examples of men who rose to positions of wealth and influence. Josiah Wedgwood, the great potter, started with nothing and died worth half a million. The Lombe family, who were sons of a Norwich worsted-weaver and who bought Thomas Cotchett's silk-throwing factory in Derby, made a great fortune and Thomas Lombe was able to provide a dowry of £60,000 for one of his daughters when she married the Earl of Lauderdale. Sir Richard Arkwright came from a poor family. After he invented the water frame in 1771 his fortunes increased and when he rode into Derby as High Sheriff of the county he was accompanied by, among others, thirty javelin men dressed in the richest liveries ever seen on such an occasion. Sir Winston Churchill, in his *Great Contemporaries* has emphasized how much this country owes to the middle classes and has pointed out how many of the great names of his own generation came from such a background.

This rise and fall in social status has always been a feature of English life and there have been recent examples of men created peers whose immediate ancestry has been quite humble but whose more distant ancestry was found to be armigerous and recorded as such in one or other of the Heralds' visitations.

Record, the second factor mentioned, is of obvious importance. If the records have been lost or destroyed, as so many of the Irish records were in 1922 or the Devon and Cornwall wills at Exeter were during the last war, then a main source of information is gone. You may be unlucky in finding the very parish in which your ancestors lived has lost its parish registers. Fortunately this is not frequently so, for on the whole the British records have been well preserved and are one of our great heritages. It is really something of

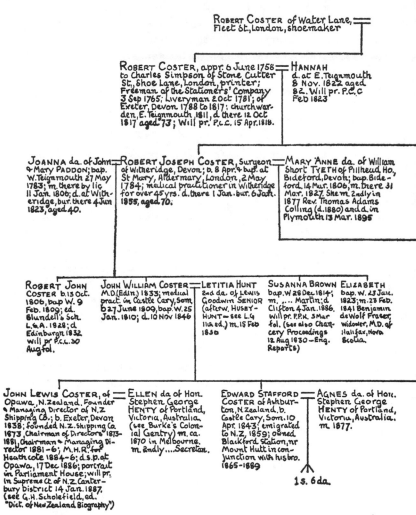

ROBERT COSTER of Water Lane, Fleet St., London, shoemaker

ROBERT COSTER, appr. 6 June 1758 to Charles Simpson of Stone Cutter St., Shoe Lane, London, printer; Freeman of the Stationers' Company 3 Sep 1765; Liveryman 20 Oct 1781; of Exeter, Devon 1788 to 1817; churchwarden, E. Teignmouth 1811, d. there 12 Oct 1817 aged 73; Will pr. P.C.C. 15 Apr. 1818.

HANNAH d. at E. Teignmouth 8 Nov. 1822 aged 82. Will pr. P.C.C Feb 1823

JOANNA da. of John & Mary PADDON; bap. W. Teignmouth 27 May 1763; m. there by lic. 11 Jan. 1806; d. at Witheridge, bur. there 4 Jun 1823, aged 40.

ROBERT JOSEPH COSTER, Surgeon of Witheridge, Devon; b. 8 Apr. & bap. at St Mary, Aldermary, London, 2 May 1784; medical practitioner in Witheridge for over 45 yrs. d. there 1 Jan. bur. 6 Jan. 1855, aged 70.

MARY ANNE da. of William Short TYETH of Pillhead Ho., Bideford, Devon; bap. Bideford, 14 Mar. 1806, m. there 31 Mar. 1827. She m. 2ndly in 1877 Rev. Thomas Adams Colling (d. 1880) and d. in Plymouth 13 Mar. 1895

ROBERT JOHN COSTER b. 15 Oct. 1806, bap W. 9 Feb. 1809; ed. Blundell's Sch. L.&.A. 1828; d Edinburgh 1832 will pr P.C.C. 30 Aug fol.

JOHN WILLIAM COSTER M.D. (Edin.) 1833; medical pract. in Castle Cary, Som. b 27 June 1809, bap. W. 25 Jan. 1810; d. 10 Nov 1846

LETITIA HUNT 2nd da. of Lewis Goodwin SENIOR (afterw. HUSEY-HUNT—see L.G llix ed.) m. 15 Feb 1836

SUSANNA BROWN bap. W 28 Dec 1814; m. .... Martin; d Clifton 4 Jan. 1886. Will pr. P.P.K. 3 Mar fol. (see also Chancery Proceedings 12 Aug 1830—Eng. Reports)

ELIZABETH bap. W. 23 Jun. 1823; m. 23 Feb. 1841 Benjamin de Wolf Fraser, widower, M.D. of Halifax, Nova Scotia.

JOHN LEWIS COSTER, of Opawa, N. Zealand. Founder & Managing Director of N.Z Shipping Co.; b. Exeter, Devon 1838; founded N.Z. shipping Co 1873, Chairman of Directors 1873-1881, Chairman & Managing Director 1881-6; M.H.R. for Heathcote 1884-6; d.s.p. at Opawa, 17 Dec 1886; portrait in Parliament House; will pr. in Supreme Ct of N.Z. Canterbury District 14 Jan. 1887. (see G.H. Scholefield, ed. "Dict. of New Zealand Biography")

ELLEN da of Hon. Stephen George HENTY of Portland, Victoria, Australia. (see Burke's Colonial Gentry) m. ca. 1870 in Melbourne. m. 2ndly .... Secretan.

EDWARD STAFFORD COSTER of Ashburton, N Zealand. b. Castle Cary, Som. 10 Apr. 1843; emigrated to N.Z. 1859; owned Blackford Station, nr Mount Hutt in conjunction with his bro. 1865-1889

AGNES da. of Hon. Stephen George HENTY of Portland, Victoria, Australia. m. 1877.

1 s. 6 da.

COSTER FAMILY PEDIGREE

COSTER FAMILY PEDIGREE: An example of a chart pedigree, showing the kind of details which should be included if known.

This pedigree is also a good example of the changes in social status which occur in so many families. The earliest known ancestor is a shoemaker. His son, after apprenticeship, becomes a liveryman of the

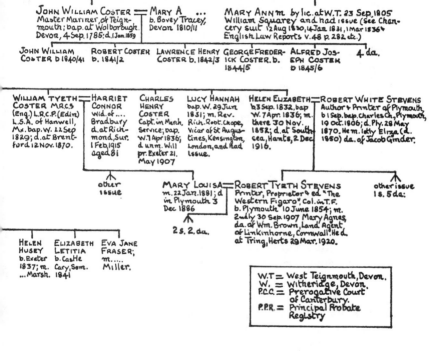

JOHN WILLIAM COSTER ══ MARY A ...
Master Mariner, of Teign-   b. Bovey Tracey,
mouth; bap. at Wolborough.   Devon 1810/11
Devon, 4 Sep.1785; d. 1 Jan 1859

MARY ANN m. by lic. at W.T. 23 Sep. 1805 William Squarey and had issue (See Chancery suit 12 Aug 1830, 14 Jan 1831, 1 Mar 1836 English Law Reports v.48 p.282 etc.)

JOHN WILLIAM COSTER b 1840/41
ROBERT COSTER b. 1841/2
LAWRENCE HENRY COSTER b.1842/3
GEORGE FREDERICK COSTER b. 1844/5
ALFRED JOSEPH COSTER b 1845/6
4 da.

WILLIAM TYETH COSTER M.R.C.S (Eng.) L.R.C.P.(Edin) L.S.A. of Hanwell, Mx. bap. W. 22 Sep 1829; d. at Brentford 12 Nov.1870.

HARRIET CONNOR wid. of .... Bradbury d. at Richmond, Sur. 1 Feb 1915 aged 81

CHARLES HENRY COSTER Capt. in March. Service; bap. W.7 Apr 1836; d. unm. Will pr. Exeter 21 May 1907

LUCY HANNAH bap. W. 29 Jun 1831; m. Rev. Rich. Robt. Crope, Vicar of St Augustines, Kensington, London, and had issue.

HELEN ELIZABETH b 3 Sep. 1832, bap W. 7 Apr 1836; m. there 30 Nov. 1852; d. at Southsea, Hants, 2 Dec 1916.

ROBERT WHITE STEVENS Author & Printer of Plymouth b 1 Sep. bap. Charles Ch., Plymouth, 19 Oct. 1806; d. Ply. 28 May 1870. He m. lstly Eliza (d. 1850) da. of Jacob Ginder.

other issue

MARY LOUISA m. 22 Jan.1881; d in Plymouth 3 Dec 1886
2 s. 2. da.

ROBERT TYETH STEVENS Printer, Proprietor & ed. "The Western Figaro", Col. in T.F. b. Plymouth 10 June 1854; m. 2ndly 30 Sep. 1907 Mary Agnes da. of Wm. Brown, Land Agent of Linkinhorne, Cornwall. He d. at Tring, Herts 29 Mar. 1920.

other issue 1 s. 5 da:

HELEN HUSEY b. Exeter 1837; m. ... Marsh. 1841
ELIZABETH LETITIA b. Castle Cary, Som.
EVA JANE FRASER; m..... Miller.

W.T = West Teignmouth, Devon.
W. = Witheridge, Devon.
P.C.C = Prerogative Court of Canterbury.
P.P.R. = Principal Probate Registry

Stationers Company and his elder son becomes a country doctor. The latter's eldest surviving son is also a doctor and marries into one of the county families of Dorset. His two sons migrate to New Zealand, where they marry sisters, the daughters of a well known Australian family. The elder brother founds a shipping company and becomes a member of the New Zealand Parliament.

which the nation can be rather proud, that it has preserved in the majority of cases its parish registers often intact from the seventeenth century and even in some cases from the time they were first ordered to be kept in 1538, and that the wills of quite ordinary folk like farm labourers or of soldiers who may have fought at Agincourt, have been preserved from even the fourteenth century.

Name, the third factor, has great bearing on traceability. Surnames fortunately came into almost universal use in England as early as 1400. A great many names came from trades, such as Baker, Butcher, Stewart, Le Despenser and so forth. Another group came from nicknames, which are not always so apparent, such as Basset, which means 'short' and Blount, which is 'blond', and, rather more obvious, 'Longshanks'. A further group derived from the place where a person lived. Many of these at first bore the French 'de', which signified this, such names as 'De Montford', 'De Montmorency' and 'De Bohun'. In the course of time the 'de' was frequently dropped and few survive today, except in the French-speaking Channel Isles. Names like 'Atlee' (At Lee) and 'Atfield' (At the field) are also topographical in derivation. In the course of time these names often became corrupted and it is not always easy to derive the name in its present form.

A rare surname is a great help in tracing a family. When it is very rare you can collect all references to it you come across with some possibility, but depending on the derivation of the name, that their possessors may be related. Obviously there is no reason for the many people who took their name from their trade to be related. But those derived from a place are more likely to be, though in the course of time this relationship will in many cases be extremely distant.

A common name can be a great bane. The name 'Smith' leaps to mind. This is the most common name in both England and Scotland and it is so because 'smith' was such a common trade. Apart from those descended from the village blacksmiths, many whose ancestors were goldsmiths, silversmiths or coppersmiths, received for brevity the shorter form 'Smith'. Even when other factors are favourable, when, for instance, the family remained in one parish for many generations, the disadvantage of a common name soon becomes apparent. In one parish you may find two John and Mary Smiths having children baptized at the same period and it may not be possible to distinguish between them. Since the civil registration came in, the wife's maiden name is given in all birth certificates, but in the parish registers in England and Wales this was not done.

If you are unlucky in having a fairly common surname, nevertheless an uncommon christian name may be very helpful. Up to the last century people were very conservative about the christian names they gave their children and this is a great help to genealogists. In England it was rare for a child not to be called after some relation of the earlier generations, so that christian names were perpetuated throughout the centuries. Usually in England the eldest son was named after the father.

This name pattern may be very important and if, in a family where the names are Richard, Henry and William, you suddenly find a Walter or Stephen cropping up, his relationship must be suspect and needs strong confirmation. New names do sometimes come into families through the wife, especially among the younger sons and daughters. Sometimes, too, they are named after a godfather or a patron or a popular hero, like the boys named 'Horatio' or 'Nelson' at the time of Trafalgar, or those called 'Eugène' after Prince Eugène of Savoy who fought with Marlborough during the War of the Spanish Succession. It was often customary for naval officers serving in a ship to ask their captain to be a godfather to any son born during the commission and he was often named after his godfather. Then there are people named from some national event. In the Stoke Damerell, Plymouth, registers there is an instance of a boy being christened 'Nile' because he was born at the time of that great victory. A number of boys were called 'Redvers' after Sir Redvers Buller during the Boer War, and in more recent times the author knows of a boy called 'Rodney' because his father was at the time serving in H.M.S. *Rodney*.

An excellent article on 'The Descent of Christian Names' by D. J. Steel, is to be found in the June 1962 issue of the *Genealogists' Magazine.*

Continuity, the last of the four factors mentioned by Sir Anthony Wagner, relates to the continuation of a family for some generations either in one place or in one occupation or trade. Even quite an obscure family, one, say, of farm labourers, who have never, to use a modern phrase, 'hit the headlines' in any way, may, if living continuously in one parish where the registers are well preserved, be traceable as far back as these registers stretch, perhaps to Elizabethan times. Existing wills will help to confirm and expand the information given in the registers. This assumes another factor, which is really contained in the 'record' factor, namely that the family were Church of England, or Church of Scotland if in Scotland. If they were Roman Catholics or Nonconformists, then the problem will not be so easily solved.

Continuity in the same calling or trade can also be of great assistance. Records of apprenticeship, where they exist, may establish parentage, for often the father's name and occupation is recorded. In a higher social sphere a tradition of service in the church may make the tracing of a family fairly easy, for in the past clergymen of the Church of England, or clerks in Holy Orders, as they are officially called, were frequently graduates and their matriculation at Oxford or Cambridge, the only two universities existing in England and Wales until the nineteenth century, should reveal their father's name and probably their birthplace and other information. The registers of both these universities have been published.

From what I have said you will be able to a certain extent to assess your prospects and if, having done so, you decide to go ahead with your researches, then you should consider your plan of action.

It is of course possible to have your pedigree traced by professional genealogists. The College of Arms is mainly concerned with matters concerning armorial bearings, but individual officers of the college will privately undertake genealogical research. The Society of Genealogists will also undertake such research or they will give you the names of professional genealogists who undertake such work, though they will not recommend any particular individual. Most professional genealogists work on a time basis at so much an hour, as this is really the only practical way in which they can do work. It must be appreciated that a genealogist may spend many hours in searching for some detail without any success. You should satisfy yourself before employing a professional that he is both reliable and competent. Not all genealogists doing such work professionally are competent and an occasional one may even be a charlatan. You need therefore to check the qualifications and recommendations of any professional help you consider employing.

However, if you do employ such help you will be depriving yourself of a great deal of the interest and excitement in tracing your ancestors and the aim of this book is to show you how you can do it yourself. Also you will save yourself much money, for professional assistance is bound to be expensive. There may, however, be occasional phases in your searches where you come up against a particularly difficult patch and in that kind of situation it might be worth your while to get professional assistance to tide you over your particular difficulty. If you, for instance, were having great difficulty in tracking down a particular will it might be desirable to seek the assistance of an experienced genealogist who would be more easily able to trace its existence, if existence it has. In some of the more specialized fields, for instance if you discovered an ancestor in the East India Company, you might prefer to employ an expert in East India Company records, who might more quickly be able to obtain results. But if you have the time and opportunities I recommend that you do it yourself, as in doing so you will learn so much about the records themselves and it will add greatly to the interest in tracing your ancestors.

Your first step then, in setting out to do your own searching, should be to make sure that no printed history of your family is already existing. It is true you will be lucky indeed if you find there is one, unless you come from a well-known family. Yet it is surprising how many such histories there are. There is a small bibliography of family histories by T. R. Thomson (2nd edition 1935) and there is a copy of it with MS additions at the Society of Genealogists. But the best way to make fairly sure there is no such history is to look in the British Museum Library catalogue, as in this catalogue any history of a family is entered under the name of the family at the beginning of that name, besides, of course, being entered under the author. As the catalogue is kept reasonably up-to-date this will ensure that you have covered all but very recent publications, apart from privately printed histories which have not been put on sale and are therefore outside the requirements of the copyright acts by which the library can claim a copy of every book published. Even so a number of these privately printed family histories have been given by their authors to the library to ensure their preservation. Next best to seeing the current catalogue in the library itself is to look in the recently published printed catalogue of the library, which is to be found in many large reference libraries. This gives publications up to 1955. It is also possible that among the very large collection of manuscripts in the British Museum there is something throwing light on your family and it is worth while searching the catalogues of these.

Besides actual printed family histories as such, there are great numbers of pedigrees in various publications, such as the various editions of *Landed Gentry* from 1840 onwards and numerous publications, such as *The Genealogist, Miscellanea Genealogica, et Heraldica* and *The Ancestor*. It would be a tall order to search through all these publications, or even their indexes, but fortunately this task is lightened for us by two valuable books, George Marshall's *Genealogists Guide*, the last edition of which was published in 1903, and J. B. Whitmore's supplement to it, *A Genealogical Guide*, published in 1947. In these publications it has been the aim of their compilers to record 'any descent of three generations in male line' which they have discovered in a very wide range of publications.

The next step, or perhaps a contemporary step, is to find

out all you can about the family from other members of it. Naturally you will turn to the older generations of them and do not be too diffident in the way you approach them. There is often a feeling that you are being rather a nuisance, especially when particular members of the family do not seem very interested in it. This is often from a sense of false modesty. You must positively badger them and if necessary become quite a pest. I myself was far too diffident when young and I realize now that I might have discovered much from people of the older generation now no longer with us. Very often there is one particular member of the family who has taken some interest in it and you should make careful notes of all he or she tells you, trivial though these details may seem at the time, as in this kind of detection little items fit together and it is surprising how pieces of information which seem unimportant at the time later turn out to be just the piece of information you need to confirm something.

Of course there are certain forms of information much more important than others. You should try to collect, or at any rate see and make copies of, any family documents, such as wills, marriage settlements, deeds of family arrangement, birth, marriage and death certificates. If you are lucky you may even find someone who has an old family Bible in which entries of baptism, marriage and burial have been made, as was the custom in the past, and naturally such a discovery is particularly fortunate. The information from it may allow you to construct a pedigree running back for several generations. It was the custom for the bride in past times to be given a family Bible on her marriage, in which she could enter the details of her own marriage and the baptisms, marriages and burials of her children. The eldest son would receive the family Bible of the father, and if he in turn was the eldest son of an eldest son, the entries in the Bible might go back for many generations. Family Bibles of younger children would not be so helpful, as they would only cover recent generations.

Besides visiting and questioning members of the family, it is quite a good idea, before doing so, to send out a questionnaire to all the members who are likely to know anything about it. This can be either printed or duplicated. It will show that you are in earnest and will be more likely in consequence to win their co-operation, especially if accompanied by a tactful covering letter expressing hopes that they will do all they can to help! You will also get your information in a more systematic form, and you will be saved repeating the questions to many people. A suggested form of questionnaire is given at Appendix A, but this of course may need modifying in accordance with a particular family's requirements.

This notice, having been sent out, will no doubt irritate, intrigue or bore the various members of the family, according to their individual characters, but will also stimulate some interest in the family, cause members of it to chat among themselves, with no doubt caustic remarks about your own sanity or peculiarity (What does he want to dig up all that stuff for? Much better left in the dust – all those old family quarrels and scandals!). In time you will get replies, some helpful, others less so, but the sum total will help you to build up quite a useful picture of the family background and will no doubt reveal information of which you had no idea. Often those members of the family who start off by saying they know absolutely nothing about it in the end provide a considerable amount of information. Remember that family traditions are always valuable, however absurd or exaggerated they may seem. There is nearly always some basis of truth in them, though they may have been much distorted in the course of time. Maiden aunts are inclined to push the social scale up a bit. 'He was something in the City,' they will tell you proudly, but that 'something' may turn out to have been some minor clerkship in a city firm, not that managing directorship of a world famous firm, the name of which has escaped their memory, but which their tone so emphatically implied.

Your preliminaries are now concluded and in the next chapter I will discuss the methods of keeping your information.

⌈2⌋

KEEPING YOUR RECORDS

A little forethought on the way you are going to record the
information you discover will pay dividends in the future.
When I started looking into my family history I rather hap-
hazardly noted things down in an ordinary exercise book.
As the material grew and I had to go into further books, I
realized it would have been better to have had some kind of
loose leaf note book, so that I could bring together notes
referring to individuals or periods, as invariably when searching for one piece of information I came across something
relating to another period or another person. My collection
started off and for some time continued unsystematically,
so that in time I found myself with some forty exercise books,
the contents of which are contained solely and imperfectly
in my memory.

I am now keeping my material far more systematically and
I hope, on reading this, you will be led to do the same.
Although a little more trouble, in the long run it certainly
pays you handsomely.

There is no accepted system of indexing and filing
genealogical information of which I know, but there is a
very useful booklet by Dr J. E. Holmstrom, called *How to
take, keep and use notes*, published by Aslib in 1947, which
deals with the marshalling of information in a general way.
The pamphlet is primarily concerned with collecting
methodically information for use by writers and other research workers, but much of it is applicable to the kind of
research done by genealogists.

Dr Holmstrom recommends the use of the 8″ x 5″ card and cabinet, dismissing the smaller sizes as too small for use in gathering the type of information with which he is mainly dealing. For genealogists, however, who are frequently concerned in collecting small pieces of information, such as a single entry from a parish register, the smallest size has certain advantages. I recommend using both the 5″ × 3″ and the 8″ × 5″ sizes, using the former for small details such as I have suggested and the larger for longer material, such as extracts from wills and cumulative information about individuals from various sources. It is true you have the disadvantages of two separate arrangements, but I think the advantages outweigh the disadvantages.

In compiling the family history, if a larger card or slip is set aside for each member of it, his or her surname, followed by christian names, clearly shown in block capitals along the top of it, this can be followed by standard details, such as date and place of birth, marriage and death. The lower half can contain additional information about his or her career and life which has been gleaned from various sources.

As Dr Holmstrom has pointed out, the larger size cards are the same size as the octavo pad, so that such pads can be conveniently used instead of cards. I personally prefer using slips of paper to cards, as they take up less room and, if reasonably strong, are quite suitable for ordinary purposes. It is convenient to have at any rate the larger slips in book form and this can be done by buying the full size quarto exercise book (10″ × 8″) and asking a printer to cut it in half, wideways, or 'landscape', as the trade call it, with his guillotine. This gives you two booklets of 8″ × 5″. When you have filled up the booklet you can then separate the pages and file them in your cabinet in the correct place. I prefer narrow gauge lines on the cards or slips as these give you a bit more information on each. I have found an extract from a normal length will can be very conveniently recorded on such a slip, going over the page to use the back if necessary. Dr Holmstrom also suggests making envelopes by cutting in half old 10″ × 8″ envelopes. These are the kind of envelopes in which you will have received brochures for Dutch bulbs, mergers of firms in which you may have a few shares, booksellers catalogues, sales of goods in which you have no interest from establishments of which you have never heard and other such matters which flow into your letter box. Apart from the satisfaction in making use of this otherwise often irritating literature, you can accumulate in these pockets newspaper and other cuttings, bits from relations' and other correspondents' letters and other matters which otherwise stray.

The most suitable way in which your material should be arranged in the trays needs careful thought. Dr Holmstrom suggests following a recognized classification in general outline and recommends the Universal Decimal Classification, which is an extension of the Dewey Decimal Classification used in most public libraries. For a genealogical collection, however, no classification is really detailed enough. Perhaps some librarian-genealogist will one day confer a boon on his fellow genealogists by developing and compiling a suitable one. The Library of Congress scheme is fuller than most, but the Dewey, with its simpler notation, seems more useful and practical. At any rate the main headings of this classification can be followed and, as genealogical material is particularly concerned with information about *people*, an alphabetical arrangement within the main headings of most of the material is a natural one. In fact, for the ordinary private collection, an alphabetical arrangement throughout, with cross references where necessary, rather like the dictionary catalogue found in many libraries, may prove most suitable. Third- or fifth-cut guides can be obtained on which the surnames or Dewey group can be inserted.

To be logical, as you are using two runs of slips, the 8″ × 5″ and the 5″ × 3″, you should make cross-references from the two series where necessary, but in practice, as it is you who will be making use of the collection, it is hardly necessary to do this. You will naturally look in each series of trays for information. Remember, this is your hobby, so do not make yourself a slave to your own system.

Early on you will find it useful to get out a chart or tabular pedigree, as this helps you to see things clearly. Here again it is advisable to adopt some consistency from the beginning. You want your pedigree to contain as much information as possible without losing its clarity. This obviously means you cannot include a great deal of detail. The amount will vary according to its importance. For instance, it is much more important to include the place of baptism, marriage and burial in entries before 1837, because these details cannot easily be found. Similarly, the existence of a will and where it was proved, prior to 1858, is very important.

Abbreviations must be used as much as possible. It is well to look at a publication like *Burke's Peerage* or *Landed Gentry* to see what abbreviations are used. Do not use 'b' for 'baptized', but 'bap', as 'b' should be reserved for 'born', which is already more or less an accepted practice. Always repeat the surname with each male entry. This may seem tiresome but leads to greater clarity. It is best not to repeat the surname with females. Use the equals sign for signifying marriage, inserting it between the names of the man and woman in question. From this sign draw your line showing descent. It is advisable to bring this line down to a point just above the level of the next generation, then horizontal just above the names. This is not only the clearest but allows the space above to be utilized. Ideally it would be nice to be able to show each generation in the same line, but this is not often practicable and lines may have to be brought round below or taken over, with suitable indication marks, to other pages. As long as it is quite clear whose children the next generation are, that is sufficient. Making a pedigree is a skilled job and only by guidance from experts and a certain amount of experimenting will you find the best arrangement. Study the lay-out of pedigrees in such works as Cussans' *History of Hertfordshire* or Ormerod's *History of the County and City of Cheshire*. Although these works were published in the last century the pedigrees they include are examples of good lay-out and also of the amount of detail which can fairly succinctly be included.

Personally, in making a pedigree, I work on the plan of exhausting in the early lines of descent those without issue or whose issue it is not intended to include, showing lower down those who have their issue inserted, and so on, generation by generation. The lay-out of a pedigree is bound to be to a certain extent a compromise, for you cannot show everything you would like to, and you do not want the pedigree to be too large and unwieldy. But British people are supposed to excel in compromise.

You will soon find you want several copies of your pedigree. With brief-size paper and carbon and a ball pen you can get, with fairly thin paper, three or possibly four good copies, but it is a better plan to do your pedigree with indian ink on a transparent paper, or on linen paper or 'Ethulon', which is a plastic material something like linen paper. The advantage of using a transparent paper or other material is that you can have as many or as few copies as you want reproduced by one of the dye-line processes, which are the same methods by which architects have their plans reproduced. The Rapidograph or Mars pens are very useful in making these pedigrees, as they flow easily with a jet black ink and you do not have to blot frequently or wipe off the edge of the ruler when ruling lines. It is also useful to use a transparent plastic ruler of about fifteen inches in length as you can see through it exactly where your lines are coming.

You need only have made the number of copies actually required at the time, as another advantage of the transparency method is that you can always have further copies made from the transparency and this can often be done while you wait or at any rate within a few hours. Most towns of any size have at least one place where dye-line prints are made and your local library or a stationer who sells mathematical instruments or stencils will no doubt be able to tell you where to find such a place.

Another advantage of this method is that it is easy to add further details to your pedigree as you find them and it is also not too difficult to make erasures and corrections. This method is a great time-saver. It means that early on you can get out a pedigree and send copies of it to members of the family and others who may be able to help you. If you join the Society of Genealogists, which it is well worth your while to do, it is a good idea to send a copy of your pedigree to them as soon as possible, as it is possible that some other member may be interested in the family and may be able to give you information.

As regards the family, it will further help to stimulate their interest. It is surprising how people will tell you they know nothing, but when confronted with an actual pedigree will begin informing you of its inaccuracies and omissions. Your transparency can include drawings of any authorized armorial bearings, if the family should possess them, and also, a very useful adjunct, a sketch map of the district in which the family lived.

The photostat is another useful, though more expensive, way of reproducing your pedigree. It has the disadvantage that you cannot add to it, so should only be used, if at all, when you are satisfied your pedigree is as complete as you want it to be.

Photography can be used for cutting down the long hours spent in copying material. A simple photographic process not requiring a camera, which can save much time and ensure the avoidance of errors, is that known as reflex printing. There is now a type of paper on the market which does not require a yellow filter, so that the process only consists in laying the photographic paper, sensitive side downwards, beneath a piece of glass and above the matter to be copied, exposing it for a few seconds and then developing and fixing it in the ordinary way. A useful book describing the process and other copying methods is *Document Photography* by H. W. Greenwood (Focal Press 1947). The *Library Association Record* of May and June 1942 contains an excellent and concise account by C. S. Minto of the reflex process in its simplest form, while Dr Holmstrom also describes the method in his pamphlet.

For photographically-minded genealogists the use of a 35

mm. camera with suitable auxiliary lenses can be a great time-saver. Many pages of a book can be photographed in a few minutes, while tombstones and monumental inscriptions can also be quickly and accurately recorded.

[3]

CIVIL REGISTRATION

Having collected all the preliminary information you can from the family and other ready-made sources, you now start out on your adventure with your first practical investigations.

Naturally all possible aid must be taken from the civil registrations of births, marriages and deaths. Sometimes people have rather a shock when they learn that such registration only started in England and Wales in 1837 and that prior to that time there was no direct means of a person proving his birth, marriage or death except through church records, such as parish registers of baptism, marriage and burial, which are after all only records of religious ceremonies. The College of Arms did make an attempt as early as 1747 to institute a general register of births for the whole country, but mainly, it is said, through lack of publicity, the scheme eventually fell through.

In Scotland civil registration was introduced even later, in 1855, and in Ireland, although there was a registration of protestant marriages from 1845, the complete civil registration did not come in until 1864. As, however, Scotland and Ireland will be dealt with in later chapters, this one is concerned only with the registration in England and Wales.

These registers are kept at Somerset House, in the Strand, London, where there are general indexes covering the whole of England and Wales in one alphabetical arrangement for each quarterly volume. There are also district registers, kept in the District Registry of Births, Marriages and Deaths in each locality. If you are absolutely certain that your ancestors came from an area within the district registry it would be easier and quicker for you to search the local indexes, for these are far smaller and often contain perhaps five years or more in one index. However, if there is any doubt of the district in which your forebears were born, then it is necessary to go to the General Register at Somerset House.

You will have to work out, from the information you have accumulated, in which years to search for information. For instance, you may know the date of death of your grandfather, but not know his age and therefore when he was born. You can get his age from his death certificate in the General Registry and from this you can work out his approximate date of birth, remembering that the ages given by the informant at the time of death are by no means always accurate.

If your grandfather or other ancestor died after 1866 you will not need to get a copy of the death certificate, as the age is given in a column in the index. You will have to pay the search fee of 1s. 6d. to look in the indexes of deaths and, having found the required age and worked out the date of birth, you then go downstairs again to the official and pay another 1s. 6d., having first filled in the form for application for a birth certificate, showing the five years you wish to search for your fee. It is best to cover two years either side of the date of birth you have worked out, but start searching in the index at the most likely year.

Covering, as they do, the whole of England and Wales, the indexes contain a great number of names and therefore each year is divided into quarters, marked on the back with the last month of the quarter. To cover one year you have, therefore, to search in four volumes. People are often surprised at the size of these indexes, which must be about two feet by eighteen inches and even the more modern ones weigh about eleven pounds each and the earlier ones, being parchment, weigh approximately twenty-one pounds. Bearing in mind that you have to search twenty of these volumes for a five year period, pulling them out from their shelves and lifting them on to racks provided for the purpose, you will soon appreciate that genealogy is sometimes physically as well as mentally exhausting. After a few hours of searching there you will feel quite overwhelmed with fatigue. Discard, therefore, all heavy overcoats and similar trappings and approach the task in an athletic mood. I often feel that the correct dress for this work should be shorts and an open neck shirt! But we are a conventional race and few come there so sensibly habited.

You can get a general search ticket for 30s., which enables you to search the indexes unrestricted for a whole day. However, I do not recommend this, as, with careful working out of dates it will cost you less to pay the individual fees and you may, for the reasons given above, not feel like going on all day at this heavy task.

You may also feel somewhat depressed on your first encounter with these indexes to discover the number of people, not only of your surname, but also of the same christian name or names. It is sometimes, in fact, quite hard to identify an individual, especially if he has a common surname and a common christian name also. The area in which his birth took place will help, but there are cases where identification has been extremely difficult and has had to be supplemented from other sources, such as wills. Certainly people with unusual surnames have a great advantage and even an unusual christian name, as already mentioned, can be a great help, though it is unfortunate that earlier on people so seldom had more than one christian name.

However, assuming that you find in the index the entry which you are convinced is the right one for your particular ancestor, you then take the form down with the details filled in from the index and hand it to the official, paying a further 3s. 9d. for the certificate. It is one of the annoyances to genealogists that it is necessary to obtain an actual certificate to get the information on it, as though you needed it for some legal purpose. Perhaps some day the authorities may be persuaded to allow genuine research workers to take copies of the entries without further payment for at any rate the earlier entries, say of a hundred years ago or more, in the same way that the census returns can now be consulted without fee at the Public Record Office up to and including the 1861 census. In Scotland there are more considerate facilities of this nature.

The birth certificate gives the following information: Place and date of birth; sex and names of the child; name and occupation of the father and the name and maiden name of the mother and finally the name, description and address of the informant.

The marriage certificate gives the place and date of the marriage, the names, ages, occupations, addresses and marital status of both bride and bridegroom, together with the names and occupations of both bride and bridegroom's fathers, also the names of the witnesses. These latter may be very useful, as they are so often relatives. In the case of a marriage in church, the name of the officiating minister is also given. He is occasionally a relative, as, if there was a clergyman in the family, he was often called upon to perform the ceremony. The certificate also shows whether the marriage was by banns or licence.

The death certificate in England is not very informative. It only gives the place, date and cause of death, the name, sex, occupation and age of the deceased and the name, description and address of the informant. You will see that it does not even indicate whether the deceased was married or single. Nevertheless the small amount of information available from the certificate may prove useful in certain cases, but it is well to remember that if one only wants to discover the age and the rest of the information is known, then after 1868 the index will give you this and save you the expense of a certificate.

You can obtain these certificates by post and if you live far from London you may have to do this. But it is better to go personally if you can, as, apart from saving the search fees additional for a postal search (6s. 3d. instead of 1s. 6d. on each one), you will be able to follow up clues on the spot, which the official searching for you will never do. For instance, in searching for one relative you may in the indexes come across another brother or sister, born within the five years you cover. You may not want a certificate at the time, but you can make a note of it in case you want to get one later. Similarly, if you do not find the entry within the five years you search, you can have an additional search either side of the period, paying the additional fee.

There are certain other records at Somerset House in the General Register Office. These are the records of births and deaths at sea since 1st July 1837; certain army returns of birth, marriage and death of soldiers and their families as recorded in army registers, some extending back to 1761, similar R.A.F. records since 1920, and the consular returns of birth, marriage and death of British subjects in foreign countries which were recorded at the British consulates since July 1849. It is possible, however, that some or all of these records may shortly be transferred to the Public Record Office.

You will see from the information given above that searching at Somerset House will take some days, as you have to wait for the certificate which will give the information for the next step. You can either get these the next day personally, which is the quickest procedure, or else fill in an envelope with your name and address and have it posted to you. This may take some days, as they give priority to those being fetched, which they ensure are ready the following day.

At some period you will reach beyond the civil registration period and then you have to turn to other records. If you are lucky, though, you may find a great-grandfather or even a great-great-grandfather who was married just within the registration period, perhaps even in July 1837, the month in which the registration began. This will give his and his wife's father's name and occupation and so will take you back another generation.

[4]

CENSUS RETURNS

At this stage it may be necessary to consider whether you should next examine the census returns or the parish registers. If you find, after the results of searching the civil registration that your family seem to have been established fairly firmly in one particular parish, then it might be best to search that parish register straight away. But even in that case it would be advisable to search the census returns also to gather the additional information which may be contained in them. In other cases, that is, in cases where it is not at all certain to what locality the people earlier belonged, the census returns may prove invaluable and certainly must be consulted. Remember, once civil registration is left behind, place is far more important than exact date, as there is no index covering the whole country, as in the civil registration, and to search the nine thousand odd parish registers would be an impossible task, taking several lifetimes.

It is unfortunate, from the genealogist's point of view at least, that no census was made in England until the nineteenth century. In 1753 a proposal came before Parliament to take a census, but it met with great opposition. Opponents of the idea said it would reveal England's weakness to possible enemies. Others opposed it on religious grounds, fearing it would provoke the wrath of God, quoting the Second Book of Samuel, the 24th Chapter. Parliament rejected the proposal and there was in consequence no census until 1801. The censuses since then have been made every ten years, except in 1941, during the Second World War. Those before 1841 however, if they had survived in detail, would have been of no use to genealogists, as they gave only the numbers in each household. The census of 1841 was the first to give the name of every person in the household with their approximate age (to the nearest five years below), their sex, occupation and whether they were born in the same county or not. It did not, unfortunately, give the relationship of each person to the head of the household, as the 1851 and later censuses did, but this can often be estimated with success. You will find, as you progress in your searches, that you must from time to time make intelligent guesses and your ability to do this is a great asset, but any such conjectures must, of course, be confirmed later with further evidence.

The 1851 census was far more valuable than that of 1841. This took each house, street by street, and gave the address, the names of all the people in that house the night of the census on the 30th March that year, their condition (single, married, widow, etc.), their exact age, their occupation and, perhaps most valuable of all, their exact place of birth. It also showed the head of the household and the relationship of each person to him, i.e. son, daughter, visitor, servant, apprentice. An annoying exception to the place of birth is of those born outside England and Wales, when the column will probably only say 'Scotland', 'Ireland' or 'France' etc.

The main problem in using the census returns is in finding the exact residence of the person concerned, but this usually works out to be easier than it sounds. You will probably find that one of the family was born somewhere around 1851, and this will show the address where the parents were living. Local directories may also be useful, though these often only gave the householders. There is a good collection of such directories in the Guildhall Library, London, and usually the library in the locality concerned has some local directories. In the larger towns, such as London, there is an index of streets to the returns, so that you can discover easily in which volume of the returns your family will be found. In the case of smaller towns and villages there is probably no index, but at the beginning of each book will be shown the parish and the streets and area covered. If your ancestor was born in a village you may only be able to discover the name of the village in which he lived and no address, but it is not a very long job to search the census of a whole village, which may only extend to three or four books. One's eye gets quite quick at picking out the name of the head of the family in each household. Apart from getting the genealogical information you will probably learn quite a bit about the village in question, the main occupations of the inhabitants and so forth, and this should prove very valuable to you when you come to write up your family history. It will enable you to make it much more interesting if you can work in a little historical background rather than make your history just a bare recital of family facts. Learning about your ancestors and the places where they lived is one of the fascinations in this family research, which makes it a living thing, not at all the dry-as-dust affair that so many people who know nothing about it are inclined to term it.

There is always an element of luck in genealogy and the census returns may give you an unexpected piece of information which will be of great value. You may find, for instance, that there was an elderly maiden aunt or great-aunt living with the family. Such a relative may take the pedigree considerably further back. Take, for instance, someone aged eighty living then. The returns will give her birthplace and you will know she was born approximately in 1771. I say 'approximately' because you must be wary of taking these ages as absolutely correct. Sometimes these aged relatives were forgetful or did not want to reveal their real age. Sometimes the information was supplied by another member of the family or household, such as a niece-in-law, who would be unlikely to be very certain of the age of her husband's aunt, and may not have been very conscientious about finding out. On the whole, however, the returns seem to have been carefully made and are therefore particularly valuable. You will be able to go to the parish registers of the places of birth indicated and perhaps find the family has been in that parish for generations. I know of someone who was lucky in this way and was able to trace his family back to the middle of the sixteenth century in a matter of a few weeks and then, by use of wills, in which he was also fortunate, to get them back into the fifteenth century. But you must not expect such good fortune or you are likely to be disappointed, for such luck is exceptional.

You will of course keep carefully all the details you discover in the census return, including the visitors and servants, if any, for these can also prove valuable. For instance, families often got servants from their parents' or wife's parents' homes, and the birthplace of the servant may indicate where the family itself came from. Apprentices, who are often found living in the house of their master, were sometimes relations, and their birthplace may indicate a useful source.

Recently the 1861 census returns have been made available to the public. This, being ten years later, is not so valuable as the earlier one, but in cases where the whereabouts of the family cannot be found in 1851 but is known for 1861, then this return will prove particularly useful. The information in it is similar to that given in the 1851 return. Unfortunately this return is in a far poorer physical condition than its predecessor.

All these returns are to be found in the Public Record Office in Chancery Lane and there is now no fee for inspecting them, but it is necessary to get a ticket to search there, a reasonable precaution to try to ensure that the people who search there are responsible people who will respect the value of these records and treat them with care.

The information you glean from these returns will give you, if moderate fortune attends you, a considerable amount of further information about your family. Even with people of fifty years of age it will show you where they were born at the turn of the century and indicate further places of search for you. In the ordinary way this will be the parish registers and this valuable archive will be dealt with in the next chapter.

[5]

PARISH REGISTERS

If your forbears belonged to the Church of England your next step will be to examine the parish registers of the place where they lived and the locality around. If they did not belong to the established church then it will be necessary to a great extent to look elsewhere. Roman Catholic and Non-conformist records will be examined in the next chapter.

An English vicar or rector is in a very secure and un-assailable position. So long as he carries out certain minimum duties, such as holding services even to a very attenuated extent and baptizing, marrying and burying his parishioners as these services are required, and so long as his moral be-haviour remains above the level which might bring con-demnation and sentence from the ecclesiastical courts, no one, not even his bishop or his archbishop, can remove him from his living once he has been inducted. He is like a judge of the high courts in that he is almost irremovable. He may conduct high or low church services. He is under no legal obligation to visit the needy or sick, nor need he lend the vicarage gardens for the Mothers Union annual fête.

Personally I rather rejoice in this independence of the clergy and hope that no alteration will be made in their position, as has been suggested in a recent report. It allows them to perform their duties in a manner free from care and in a way which they feel suits them best and is best suited to their individual character. Occasionally there may be a failure. There may even be a scoundrel – and how some elements of the Sunday press will relish that! We shall read all about his

39

disreputable and scandalous behaviour and forget all about the thousands of quiet unobtrusive clergy who go about their way conscientiously and who are often beloved and appreciated by the parishioners whom they serve, but never strike the headlines in the newspapers.

Another reason I favour this independence of the parish priest is that, largely because of this independence, it has bred a thoroughly individual type, sometimes even eccentric, and this is all to the good. We do not want a world all made up of types. The stage loves to portray clergymen in a certain cast, somewhat simpering, good-natured and ineffective characters who plough their way through life in a dreamy spiritual world of their own and never appreciate the realities of existence. But the stage is more wrong in such type-casting than in almost any other of its miscast types. Clergy produce probably a richer variety of types than any calling and this is largely due to their freedom from arbitrary control and its consequent opportunities for developing uncoerced characteristics.

What has all this to do with genealogy, you may ask! Well, genealogy brings you into contact with all sorts of people and I personally have enjoyed very much the variety of clergy which it has produced for me in my searches. There are the gaunt impressive types, who stand over you in the vestry watching your every movement as you examine the registers, exclaiming triumphantly, as you make some note, 'Ah! You've found another!' and marking it down in a red notebook so as to make sure you pay the full fees. There are some who show such a reluctance to produce their registers that you feel as though you had asked the Public Record Office to produce the original Domesday Book for you to finger through. There are round-faced hospitable ones, who ask you back to lunch, lavishing kindness on you, a stranger, from their meagre stipends, which makes you feel overwhelmed that such good-hearted benevolence should exist. Then there are the ones who have taken a great interest in their parish history and regard their registers as one of their treasured possessions. They can sometimes help you a great deal with their local knowledge. It is always best to visit the parish and look at the registers yourself, but before doing so make sure, firstly, that the parish registers have not been published, as many have been, and, secondly, that the registers are still in the hands of the incumbent, and not at a county record office. If the incumbent searches the register for you, then it is preferable to ask him to extract all entries of the name or names you seek between the dates you require, rather than to ask if a certain baptism is there. This will ensure your discovering any brothers or sisters baptized there. The same applies to marriages and burials. Very often in the earlier volumes of the registers the baptisms, marriages and burials are all in the same volume and so, by asking for all entries of the name you will get any marriages and burials also.

Incumbents are not legally bound to make searches on your behalf, but they may agree to do so. They are also not legally bound to supply certificates on application by post nor to allow the registers to be photographed, but they are required to allow searches to be made at all reasonable times.

Many incumbents are helpful and often look further than you ask them. Naturally you must be prepared to pay the statutory fees for the search you have requested, which can mount up to quite a lot. Baptisms and burials are at present three shillings for the first year and one shilling and sixpence for each year thereafter. Thus if you want the baptisms or burials for a hundred years searched it will cost you £7 11s. 6d. Marriages are less expensive, only one shilling and six pence for the first year and ninepence for each subsequent year. But probably you will be able to arrange your search to avoid long periods. Besides this many incumbents are willing to agree to a lower fee if you are having many years searched. There has been quite an amount of correspondence in the press from time to time about these fees. They certainly seem somewhat illogical. For instance, in a small country parish in the seventeenth or eighteenth century a year may only be a page of the register, while in a large town parish in the early nineteenth century it may be as much as twenty pages. So the town priest has to search twenty pages but the country priest only one. In theory an incumbent could also charge for his time in searching, but few do so. In any case these fees fall rather heavily on someone just engaged in a hobby and not doing it for profit.

Assuming, however, that you are able to visit the parish yourself, you should make arrangements in advance with the incumbent, as it is not always convenient for him to let you search at a specific unannounced time. One of the conditions of such searches is that it should be supervised, which means that the vicar has either to be there himself or arrange for some other responsible person to be there. This procedure must not be resented by you, as these are precious documents and there have been too many cases of registers being mutilated by unscrupulous people, some even having been known to tear a page out to save copying it. Some incumbents, when they see that you appear to be a reliable person, will perhaps after a time leave you alone, but I always appreciate the one who does not do so, as I feel he is carrying out his instructions and has some regard for the value of his records.

One appreciates especially on cold wintry days, those parsons who take you to the vicarage and leave you to browse through the registers in a comfortable warmed room, with perhaps a cup of tea thrown in half-way through the morning or afternoon. But one should not trespass on their hospitality and I always try to make up for any I receive in some other way, and not accept it as a matter of course.

When you search the registers yourself, apart from its being more satisfactory and satisfying, as you can then follow up any additional clues which may arise during your search, the rector or vicar is usually prepared to compromise on some set fee, such as ten shillings for the morning's or day's search. After all, there should be a difference when you do the work yourself instead of the incumbent, but it is part of the illogicality of fees laid down that they do not take this into account. Many incumbents, when you do the searching, will not charge you a fee at all. I have known them say that the fees are only applicable for their doing the search and not applicable when you do it yourself. They may perhaps legally be wrong in this and they may be entitled to the full fee whether you do the search or they, but it is a reasonable attitude and one which is appreciated. In such cases I usually offer a small sum to the church funds and this is, I feel, a tactful and acceptable way of dealing with the situation. Some vicars, without charging, may draw your attention to their restoration fund, which you then promptly augment.

You may find a hiatus in the parish registers during the Civil War in the seventeenth century. Also, during the Commonwealth in 1653, it was enacted that the births, marriages and deaths should be registered by 'some able and honest person' in a special book 'of good vellum or parchment'. This person was not the parish priest and this was really an attempt to set up a civil registration. You will notice it was the birth and death which was to be registered, not the baptism and burial. Unfortunately very few of these books survive. Fortunately in quite a number of cases the order was disregarded and the incumbent of the parish continued to record the baptisms, marriages and burials in his parish registers as before. But in other cases you may find an annoying gap, usually just at the period when you least want it!

It must also be borne in mind, when searching the earlier parish registers, that until 1st January 1752 the year began on the 25th March, the Feast of the Annunciation, so that before that date any dates in January and February and in March up to 24th came after December. People who have not realized this have been bewildered to discover a child born for instance in December 1750 baptized sometime in January or February 1750. Sometimes these dates are now written, in the form, '25th January 1734/5,' signifying that the date was 25th January 1734 in the old style, but 25th January 1735 in the new style.

Apart from seeing the registers personally, there are other advantages in going to the parish. You have, for instance, a chance to look around the church. There is always a possibility of some memorial inside it and then there are the monumental inscriptions on the tombstones outside. Unfortunately, each year these are becoming less decipherable and today any prior to about 1800, unless they are on slate or else in a very sheltered part of the churchyard, are often impossible to read. It is worth enquiring if the inscriptions have ever been copied, as some parishes have copies of them made in the past and these can of course be very valuable, for the information on a stone is often far more informative than the bald entry of burial in the register.

Some stones which seem at first almost indecipherable can, after careful examination, be worked out. Sometimes they become quite clear when you look at them from a different angle. You can also clean the stone a little and it is worth while on such expeditions to arm yourself with a stiff, but not too stiff, brush. I hope none of you will have the experience which happened to one genealogist, who was carefully brushing the surface of a stone when the vicar came along. He was very nice and said he did not mind as long as it did not damage the stone. 'Oh, no,' the searcher assured him, 'I am very careful to rub gently,' and he gave an additional rub to show how gentle he was, but at that moment the whole face of the stone fell forward. However, the vicar had a sense of humour and they both laughed, so all ended happily.

Apart from the churchyard you may pick up local knowledge by wandering around the village. You may even hear something of your forbears over a glass of ale in the local pub. Names persist in localities even in these days of movement. A furniture remover recently told me that half his work was spent moving people back to the place in which they were born, after they have retired. It is a very human instinct to return to your native land in your old age. Some 'oldest inhabitant' may be able to give you some first- or second-hand information about your ancestors, if they were not there too far back. In the 1930's I heard in a Devonshire village something of the character of my great-grandfather who had been a doctor there and had died in 1856, some eighty years before. An old man did not remember him personally, but he had 'heard tell on him' and of his cheerful bedside manner. Not many counties are as fortunate as Gloucestershire, where Ralph Bigland, who was Garter King of Arms from 1780 to 1784, copied or had copied nearly all the inscriptions in most of the parishes in the county. They are contained in two huge folio volumes published at the end of the eighteenth and in the nineteenth centuries. Bigland was working at a time when the stones outside in the churchyard could be read even back to the time of Queen Elizabeth I. Would that all counties had had a Ralph Bigland!

It is best for you to take your extracts from the registers on the 8″ × 5″ slips I have suggested for the larger items. It is quicker this way, rather than attempting to use the smaller 6″ × 3″ slips for each individual entry. You can transfer each individual item to a smaller slip when you get home and, although this may seem rather a trouble, it is in the long run worth doing, as you then automatically bring together all your information about a particular individual.

When you go to your parish you must be prepared for disappointment. You probably optimistically hope to trace back for many generations, and you may be lucky enough to do so. But it is surprising how much people moved about even in the past. Even the poorer people, although they probably did not move very far, seem to have moved about in the county, perhaps as work took them to neighbouring or more distant parishes. The higher class people may have moved further afield, unless they belonged to the county families and had a seat firmly fixed in the county. If you find your line dies out in the parish, then you may have to look around in the neighbouring parishes, but it depends on the individual circumstances. It is quite a good idea to look at an old map and see where the road from your village led to and where was the nearest inn. Villagers would often walk up the road in search of refreshment and change and many a village lad met his future bride through first contacting her father or brother in the neighbouring 'local'.

If the name is a rare one, then it may be better to search the wills of the period, both in the local courts and in the Prerogative Courts. It also depends on the status and occupation of the family. If they were farmers or farm labourers then you may find them in the neighbouring parishes. Perhaps a son married a farmer's daughter from a nearby parish and he later took over the farm. Then there is always the difference between the movement of the farmer and the farm labourer. The labourer may move to a place where there is work in bad times. The movement into the towns in the late eighteenth and early nineteenth centuries must be borne in mind. You will find yourself learning a good deal of social history in your trail of searches and clues.

When you get home after your day's search in your ancestor's parish you will return with perhaps varying emotions and certainly quite tired. Your forbears' village may not have fulfilled the image of it which you had built up in your mind. It may have been excessively modernized, so that little of it is left which your grandfather or great-grandfather would have recognized. Nevertheless it is bound to be interesting to you and no doubt you will have learnt a certain amount about it, even if not as much as you hoped.

Naturally a good map of the locality in which you discover your ancestors is invaluable. The 6″ to the mile and 25″ to the mile Ordnance maps of the earliest date available are desirable, but even more useful may be a copy of the tithe map for the parish, or of that part of it which covers your particular home. By the Tithe Commutation Act of 1836 tithes were changed to fixed charges on land and this necessitated a detailed survey, apportionment and valuation. This resulted in the best and most complete land record since Domesday was made. Each parish had its copy of the tithe map, which, in conjunction with the tithe apportionment lists, showed each field and house with its boundaries and the name of the owner. A second copy was sent to the Diocesan Registry and the third copy went to the central office of the Tithe Redemption Commission, now at 33 Finsbury Square, London, E.C.4. The parish copies have often been lost. The diocesan copy is more likely to be extant and probably now in the County Record Office. At the central authority you may be reasonably certain of finding a copy, their records being fairly perfect. A photostat copy of one of these together with the apportionment list applicable can be most valuable to you in your searches and enable you to visualize more easily your forbears' way of life.

If the registers of the parish are missing or partly missing, its bishop's transcripts may survive. These are copies of the original registers which the incumbent had to send in annually to the diocesan registry. Many of them have now been transferred to the county record office or offices within the old diocesan boundaries. Here they can be consulted in comfort and usually without any fee. Those still in diocesan registries can be seen on application to the registrar and a fee may be required.

Unfortunately many of these transcripts have been lost or have survived in poor condition. The forwarding of them each year was an additional and irksome task and less conscientious incumbents were often careless in this duty. Furthermore their preservation in the registry was often in conditions far from ideal. The result is there are many gaps in these transcripts, particularly for the earlier periods, and those surviving, being on sheets of paper, are often torn or in a fragile condition. In copying them important details may have been omitted, although there are rare cases where details have been added which are not in the original registers.

For all these reasons, except the last mentioned, it is advisable to examine the original registers where they exist. Ideally it might be best to see both originals and transcripts, and where they are both in the custody of the county record office it may be quite convenient to do so.

[6]

NON-PAROCHIAL REGISTERS

It must be admitted at the start that the search for parentage of people not members of the established church is far more difficult. In the days when toleration of religious beliefs was not an accepted code, people who would not conform to the established church suffered many disabilities and even persecutions, and it was only their strong belief that their faith and conduct were right which sustained them.

After the breach with Rome in Henry VIII's time the Roman Catholics in England were hounded and persecuted and their religion, so to speak, went underground. Services and confessions were held in secret and the many priest holes in old houses in England confirm this. As a result Catholic registers were only able to be kept *sub rosa* and it is not surprising that few survived. Most of those that did were not included in the non-parochial registers which were handed over to the General Registry in accordance with the Act of 1840, as the Roman Catholic church requested to be allowed to retain them. It is necessary therefore to ascertain from the Roman Catholic authorities whether any registers survive in the area where the people in question lived. The Catholic Record Society began publishing records in 1905 and have published some forty-eight volumes, which include a number of registers of baptism, marriage and burial. The baptisms often include the names of godparents. Those marriage registers which exist are mainly prior to 1754, because after the Hardwicke Marriage Act came into operation 25th March that year most Roman Catholics were married in the Church of England to ensure the legality of the marriage, though they may also have had a Roman Catholic marriage ceremony, which possibly went unrecorded. For the same reason many Noncomformists were married in the parish church because before 1806 this was the only legal way in which they could be married and it was necessary for such purposes as proving inheritance that the proof of marriage should be unassailable. For the same reason a number may have been baptized in the established church, though these were far fewer than the marriages. When it comes to burial, many of these sects had their own burial grounds and kept their own registers.

The Congregationalists are a very old body of Non-conformists and date from Reformation times. These earliest Congregationalists, or Independents, as they were often called, felt themselves unable to accept the idea of the sovereign being head of the established church and they also disagreed with the idea that anyone could be a member of the Church, and insisted that 'only people who were in earnest about their christian discipleship and made open confession of their faith should be counted as members'. In Stuart times, when the kings tried to re-establish the Roman Catholic religion, the Congregationalists increased. Historically the name 'Puritan' is applied to all these early Independents and the Pilgrim Fathers belonged to the Independents.

The Congregationalists suffered under many acts of Parliament when Charles II was restored. Among them were the Corporation Act of 1661, which prevented them from holding office, the Act of Uniformity of the next year and the Conventicle Act of 1664 which forbade all religious meetings but those of the Anglican Church. The Five Mile Act of the next year brought even further disabilities, for this forbade Nonconformist ministers to teach in schools or to live within five miles of a corporate town. In 1673 the Test Act was passed, which ordered that all people holding office under the crown should take the sacrament according to the Anglican rites.

During the eighteenth century there was a gradual relaxation of these severe measures and they came to be more honoured in the breach than in the observance. Great Con-

49

gregationalist preachers, like George Whitefield, stirred the conscience of many established church leaders. Although we sometimes think of the eighteenth century as one of great materialism and corruption, yet there were other elements stirring and a movement to humanitarianism and tolerance was spreading. By the nineteenth century many of the measures against Nonconformists had disappeared, though the Test Act did not go until 1828, in which year the Corporation Act was also repealed.

Unfortunately many Nonconformist records have been destroyed. The National Union of Congregational Churches, founded in 1832, did a certain amount towards their preservation, more particularly in establishing, the year before, the Congregational Library, where many of the surviving records are today housed. The Congregational Historical Society has since 1901 published in its Transactions a number of early records.

The Congregational registers which survived were handed over under the 1840 Act to the General Register House and are now in the Public Record Office. Where they do survive the information in them is often fuller than that of the parish registers of the Church of England. For instance, a baptism of a child of John Harrison in Mount Street Independent Chapel, Plymouth Dock (now Devonport) in 1827 gives the dates of baptism and of birth, the maiden name of the wife and their abode. The additional information of the mother's maiden name is particularly useful at a time when this would not have been recorded in the parish registers. But in general there are few registers before the late eighteenth century and these often have long gaps with no entries.

The Methodists are of later origin. The church came into being through the work of two brothers, both Anglican clergymen, John and Charles Wesley, who were dissatisfied with the lassitude and lack of driving force in the established church of their time. The Wesley brothers went around the country preaching, often meeting with great opposition. They never intended their followers to form a separate church but this gradually came about. Even in Wesley's lifetime the ministers of his following began to baptize, marry and bury their followers, though many other followers continued to be baptized and buried and particularly to be married in the established church.

But after the death of the two Wesley brothers, Charles dying in 1788 and John three years later, the Methodists began to form themselves into churches. There were also several offshoots from the main body, known as Wesleyan Methodists, such as the Methodist New Connection, formed in 1797, the Primitive Methodists (1807), the Bible Christians (1815), the Protestant Methodists (1827), the Wesleyan Methodist Associates (1835) and the Wesleyan Reformers (1849). After the end of the eighteenth century, however, there was a gradual progress towards unification again and today there are just the two bodies, the United Methodists and the Methodists.

In 1818 a Methodist Registry was opened for recording centrally the baptisms being performed in the various chapels throughout the country, and this register is now one of those in the Public Record Office. Wesley's own chapel in City Road, London, had its own graveyard and the registers of this ground start in 1779. Many other Methodist burial grounds have kept records, which are now at the Public Record Office. Besides the three large volumes of the Metropolitan Register there were 856 Methodist registers of baptisms, and burials handed over to the General Registry under the Act of 1840. These are now also at the Public Record Office. Marriages were not recorded in Methodist registers until after the Marriage Registration Act of 1837.

The official archives of the Methodist movement are kept in the Methodist Book Room, City Road, London. Information about individual Methodists who were active in the movement and about Methodist ministers can be gathered from the movement's magazine, which began as the *Arminian Magazine* in 1778, successively changing its title to *The Methodist* (1798–1821) and *The Wesleyan Methodist Magazine* (1822–1913). Nearly always there are obituaries of ministers. There is an index to these memoirs and to local histories from 1778–1839 published in the *Proceedings of the Wesley Historical Society*, Volume 7 (1909–10). The various branches of Methodism have also published their magazines.

The Quakers realized early the importance of keeping records of their baptisms, marriages and burials, and their records are on the whole well kept and also often well indexed. They date from their foundation by George Fox in the seventeenth century.

The Quaker records were handed over to the authorities in accordance with the 1840 Act, but before they did so they made digests of the information in them. These are held and carefully indexed at the Friends House, Euston Road, London, N.W.1. The digest entries are arranged geographically in the Quarterly Meeting areas, each of which had separate volumes for baptisms, marriages and burials. The form of dating is that peculiar to the Quakers, that is, January is 'First Month' and Sunday is 'First Day' and so forth. In each volume the entries are alphabetical as far as the initial letter and within each letter the entries are chronological. There are some eighty-five volumes, which contain approximately the following number of entries: births, 260,000; marriages, 40,000; deaths, 310,000. There is a description of these registers by J. S. Rowntree, *The Friends' Registers of Birth, Death and Marriage, 1650-1900*. The Scottish records are included in the digest at the Friends House, London, but the records of the Irish Friends are at their depository at 6 Eustace Street, Dublin. All these digests continue up to 1837 in England and Wales. There is a useful account of the archives of the Quakers by R. S. Mortimer in the *Amateur Historian*, Volume III, page 55.

As mentioned, in general Roman Catholic registers were not deposited under the 1840 Act. This was also so with the registers of the Jewish synagogues, as the Jews, like the Roman Catholics, asked to be exempted from the requirements of the Act, feeling that their registers were better kept with their own communities. There were also a number of Welsh Nonconformist chapel registers not deposited. These can only be consulted through the bodies concerned.

[7]

WILLS AND ADMINISTRATIONS

Wills to the genealogist can be the most valuable and also at times the most frustrating of aids to information. The first difficulty is in finding them and then, when you have done so, you are often disappointed at the meagre information which they reveal.

On the more optimistic side, wills can reveal an enormous amount of information and one of their intriguing merits is that they may reveal all sorts of ancillary information which you never suspected and which you might never have lighted upon through other sources. Then in some cases inventories survive. These were lists of the goods of the deceased made by the administrators or executors after the person died. From these you can often glean a great deal about their lives. John West, in his delightful and informative book *Village Records*, published in 1963, has shown how you can even conjecture and reconstruct the house in which your forbears lived by means of these inventories.

A will, being a very personal document, adds body to the bare bones of your pedigree. You feel as you read through the winding legal phrasing that you are getting nearer to your ancestor and his ideas and thoughts. Sometimes there are strong human touches and often humour. I remember being much amused at the will of a late eighteenth century woman, who left her glasses to her sister Anne 'but if they do not suit her, then I leave them to my sister Mary'. I wonder what the ophthalmic surgeons of today would say about that kind of amateur prescribing!

Since 1858 wills and administrations in England and Wales present no difficulty, for from that time forward they were proved either in the Principal Probate Registry at Somerset House or else at one of the District Probate Registries which were set up at that time. But wherever they were proved, the printed will and administration calendars at Somerset House and at the District Registries list them. In other words you have an index in exact alphabetical order of all wills proved and administrations granted in England and Wales from 1858 to the present day. At Somerset House you can see either the original or a copy of any will or the details of any administration for the fee of one shilling. You may by now already know the date or approximate date of death of the person whose will you want to see, but in any case it is not a long job to look through, say, ten years of these calendars. In fact, if you do not know the date of death of someone and you are fairly certain he is likely to have left a will or enough estate to have had an administration if he died intestate (and most people do leave something, even if only a few pounds), then it is quicker to search the calendars here than to search the indexes to the deaths in the General Registry, as the indexes of death are divided into four quarters, while in the probate calendars you only have to search one index. The indexes of wills also give you far more information about the deceased and may save you from having to get a death certificate. They give you his description, address and place of death, his former place of residence if the will describes him as of somewhere else, the date of his death, the names of his executors or administrators and their address and description. The main item they do not give you which the death certificate does, is the age of the deceased. As far as intestates are concerned the information in the calendar is about as full as that given in the administration act, so there is really no need to see it.

Having found the will in the calendar, you can then, as mentioned above, see either the original of it or a copy, according to whether it was proved at the Principal Probate Registry in London or at one of the district registries. Recently there has been some relaxation of the rules which governed your copying extracts from wills, and now you are allowed to make short extracts, provided you write in pencil. But you can get a photostat copy of a will for two shillings per page. A long will might be rather expensive, but you need not have a photostat of the whole will. You can have photostats of the pages you require, as often much of a long will is taken up with legal repetitions.

When we turn to wills prior to 1858, and these are the ones the genealogist will be principally concerned with, the situation is very different. Before that date the proving of administrations and wills was in the hands of the church. This may come as a surprise to you, but it is all bound up in our history and, just as the only way of recording your birth, marriage or death prior to 1837 in England and Wales was through the baptism, marriage or burial registers in the church, so the recording of wills was left to the church. From early times a will was regarded as a rather sacred document and that is why in these early wills we nearly always find them starting with the words 'In the name of God, Amen', and continuing with hopes of salvation for their soul through the merits of Jesus Christ.

In theory, if a man died leaving a will and having land or property all in one archdeaconry, then his will would be proved in the particular archdeacon's court. If he had property in two or more archdeaconries in the same diocese, then his will would be proved in the bishop's court. If he had property in two or more dioceses, then his will would have to be proved in one of the archbishops' courts, the Prerogative Court of Canterbury or the Prerogative Court of York. Where a person had property in both provinces, although Canterbury appeared to have the right of prior probate, such wills were usually proved in the York province also.

Already you can see the picture getting complicated, for you would not know whether a man had property extending over two archdeaconries or two dioceses, so already your field of search is being extended. But this unfortunately is by no means the end of the story. Although a man having property in a particular archdeaconry *could* have his will proved in that archdeaconry, there was no bar to its being proved in a higher court and it often was. It is noticeable that up to the end of the eighteenth century people of any substance at all tended to have their wills proved in the Prerogative Court, particularly that of Canterbury. 'Men of substance' does not mean necessarily great landowners or local squires, but it includes people like farmers and tradesmen. Probably the wills of farm labourers and employed workers would only be proved in the archdeacon's court, for there were some additional expenses in proving in one of the higher courts, but their masters and employers might well do so. This may have been done, as is often maintained, because there was greater security in proving in a higher court. Perhaps the archdeacon's court was not always too efficiently run and there was more chance of a will getting lost in one of the smaller courts. But there is another possible contributory cause. Executors and the family may have felt there was more privacy in proving in a higher court, which was probably more distant. For people who proved their wills in the local archdeacon's court there may have had doubts about this. Junior clerks in the smaller courts, knowing the local people, may have been inclined to gossip about the contents of the wills. 'She never left Bob a penny – and him the eldest too – left it all to that "mummy's darling" Geoffrey!' Before 1858 proved wills were not normally open to inspection, but, even if they were, a person would have possessed an unusual curiosity to make an expensive and long journey to London, for instance, to see a will for no other purpose than idle inquisitiveness and even a trip to the local diocesan registry would not, in those days, be lightly undertaken if one lived the other side of the county from it.

After the end of the eighteenth century it is noticed that people did tend far more to prove wills in the archdeaconry courts. Perhaps by then they had become more efficient and were regarded as more reliable and discreet.

Then there are the 'peculiars'. These add further to the difficulties of finding where a will was proved. These 'peculiars', sometimes 'royal peculiars' were courts having special jurisdictions over certain areas. Thus if a person happened to have property in one of these districts, his executors would not be allowed to prove his will in the local archdeacon's court or even perhaps in the bishop's court, though he would always be able to prove it in the prerogative court. The origin and existence of these peculiars goes right back in our history and it is a subject in itself. In general one may say that they were a means of giving some extra emoluments to some offices and thus adding to the perquisites of some perhaps poorly paid positions. The King might grant a peculiar to some favourite, in the same way that the Stuart kings angered the nation by granting monopolies to certain favourites, so that only they could make or sell certain goods.

One such peculiar, as an example, is that area around Hurst and Wokingham, now in Berkshire, which was once part of Wiltshire, a little island of this county surrounded by Berkshire, to which geographically it should obviously have belonged. This was because that area was a peculiar of the Dean of Sarum, or Salisbury, and anyone happening to live in that area and have property in it had to have his will, when he died, proved in the Dean of Sarum's Court. This of course set up all sorts of confusion. Sometimes the peculiars were merely attached to a particular parish, where the rector or vicar benefited from the particular additional fees coming from this source.

It will be realized that the absence of any central index of wills and administrations means that the finding of a particular will may involve considerable research. The more obvious places are the archdeacon's, bishop's and archbishop's courts covering the locality of the person's home and death. It is not too difficult to check whether his locality lay within the jurisdiction of a peculiar and then you will, of course, search for the will or administration in that court. But sometimes a will is eventually found in the most unlikely place. A man might die in Devonshire but his will might be found proved in the archdeaconry court of Norwich, because one of the executors lived in Norfolk and found it more convenient to prove the will in his nearest probate court.

In 1964 valuable consolidated indexes of wills and administrations covering the period 1796 to 1857 used by the Estate Duty Office were transferred to the Public Record Office. These indexes (in the Inland Revenue Section 27) are particularly useful in two ways, firstly because they cover wills and administrations in all the courts of England and Wales, not merely the P.C.C., and secondly because they are indexed in a more detailed way, as explained below, and not merely to the first letter, as with the P.C.C. Wills. For these reasons no doubt genealogists and other research workers will use them more and more as their existence becomes known.

The indexes fall into two sections, those covering the period 1796 to 1811 and those covering the period 1812 to 1857.

In the period prior to 1812 the indexes are divided into three groups, namely (1) The P.C.C. Will Index (PRO Reference No. I.R. 27/1–16), divided into yearly parts, indexed in alphabetical order of surname in the year and month in which the will was proved, (2) P.C.C. Administrations Index (I.R. 27/17–20). Each volume contains details of administrations for a number of years, the entries being alphabetical, though not completely chronological. (3) The County Courts Indexes (I.R. 27/67–93) which cover both wills and administrations in the county courts, each volume containing entries for a number of years and of more than one court.

After 1811 there are only two groups, namely the wills indexes and the administrations indexes. Each group covers both P.C.C. and county courts.

The will indexes between 1812 and 1857 (I.R. 27/140–323) are divided into four annual parts, covering the names A–D, E–J, K–R, and S–Z. They give details of all wills proved each year in whichever court they were proved.

The Administrative Indexes from 1812 to 1857 are divided into two parts, namely (i) P.C.C. (I.R. 27/21–66) and (ii) County Courts (I.R. 27/94–139).

In the earlier period before 1812 the indexes are arranged

under the first letter and the first vowel, thus there are five divisions, for the five vowels, within each initial letter. This means that the consonants following the initial letter are disregarded and it is the first vowel which fixes the name's position in the group. This may sound a little complicated but it is quite easy to follow when used a little. An example will make this clearer. Taking the names Carpenter, Chapman, Chaundy, Cheney, Chitty, Christian, Church, Clarke, Cross, Crozier, Cruse, Crawshaw, Creasey, those in the CA group would be: Carpenter, Chapman, Chaundy, Clarke, Crawshaw; those in the CE group would be Cheney, Creasey; those in CI, Chitty, Christian; those in CO, Cross, Crozier and those in CU, Church, Cruse.

From 1812 onwards the names included together are usually indicated by three letter groups, depending on the frequency of the names, for example HIG to HIK; HIL to HIM. In all cases with this index the existence of a will or administration proved or granted in England and Wales can be found in a matter of minutes, contrasted with the fifteen or twenty minutes taken to search each initial letter in the P.C.C. indexes at Somerset House. The disadvantages in consulting this index at the moment are that it is not on the shelves of any of the rooms at the Public Record Office and thus has to be applied for, volume by volume as required, and that this index is not in the same repository as the wills themselves. Thus it is necessary to search for the existence of a will or administration in one place and see the will or administration in another place. Even so these indexes are a great time-saver, especially if they are combined with other work at the Public Record Office. It is possible at some later date that these disadvantages may be obviated. The P.C.C. wills at any rate might be moved to the P.R.O. and room may be found on the open shelves for the Estate Duty indexes. Wills proved and administrations granted in the provincial courts will, of course, have to be sought in the appropriate repository, probably the local record office.

These indexes are particularly valuable not only because they cover the whole of England and Wales, and therefore direct a person straight away to the court in which the will is proved, but also because they give more detail than the normal calendar before 1858, namely the name of the testator, his residence, the names of the executors of the will and the court in which the will is proved. Copies of the wills themselves also existed in this office and this is fortunate, as it means that copies of those wills of the period covered which were destroyed during the Second World War at Exeter have been extracted and eventually will be available at the County Record Office at Exeter. It is understood that the remainder of the wills in this office are being or have been destroyed on the grounds that other copies exist elsewhere. I hope it is correct that copies in every case do exist elsewhere. It seems a great pity in any case that these second copies of wills should be destroyed, as it is only too possible that individual wills have been lost in the various depositories throughout the country. However, it would appear that the Lord Chancellor has approved the destruction of these wills, presumably because their great bulk is causing housing difficulties.

Indexes of wills proved in the Prerogative Court of Canterbury (P.C.C. for short) have been printed, mainly by the British Records Society, up to 1700, and the Administrations have been covered to the mid-seventeenth century. Also there have been a number of indexes published, by this and other societies of local courts.

An invaluable guide through the morass of difficulties in finding these wills is A. J. Camp's *Wills and their Whereabouts*, a thorough revision and extension of B. G. Bouwens' work of the same title. This was published by the Society of Genealogists in 1963. It is a county by county survey, showing where the wills are to be found, and giving details of the various courts, the wills and administrations of which are now mostly transferred to the county record offices and other archive depositories. It also contains useful notes on testamentary procedure and hints on making will extracts, adapted from the notes made by B. G. Bouwens in his original work.

The situation today regarding the homes of the various wills is far better than in the immediate past, when they were in the custody of the various district probate registries, the officials of which, concerned with the day to day registration and probate of modern wills, were not always interested in these earlier wills and did not appreciate their value as historical and genealogical documents. Some no doubt were reasonably conscientious about their custody, but Bouwens records hearing of at least one registry where, when it was being closed, the wish was expressed that 'all the old stuff might get lost' and, as he remarks, 'the wish may be father to the deed'. Now that a great proportion of them have been transferred to other depositories, mainly to county record offices, they have come into the hands of people who appreciate their value, trained archivists who are anxious to make them available to research workers, and they can in consequence now be consulted in far more favourable and often more comfortable conditions.

It should be noted that during the period of the Commonwealth all the wills were proved centrally. This period is covered by the British Record Society indexes and this, among other advantages, is a very useful indication of the distribution of surnames in the middle of the seventeenth century. While one regrets the action of the Commonwealth government in instituting the civil registration of births, marriages and deaths, one rejoices in their action in instituting a central registration for wills and wishes it had been continued. There were, however, disadvantages. In times when travel was difficult it seems many wills failed ever to be registered.

It is hoped, however, that you will be successful in tracking down some of your family wills. As already suggested, it is best to take down details of wills on the 8″ × 5″ slips. The details you should record are as follows: (1) Name, as the heading. (2) Exact description of the person making the will, as given in the will itself. (3) Any note regarding place of burial, etc. (4) Bequests, amounts, to whom and any special provisos. (5) Any details of land held, being careful to note exact description and parish if mentioned. (6) Names of any trustees and conditions of trust. (7) Note of any family heirloom or articles to which there seems to have been special importance attached, such as tools of trade, which may indicate occupations. (8) Names of executors and any guardians of children. (9) Date of will. (10) Witnesses. (11) Details of any codicils, following the above pattern. (12) Details of probate. (13) Exact name of court in which proved, with reference. Below is given an example:

COSTER, Edward
Of the parish of St Martin Orgar, City of London 'oylman'
Bequests – to Daughter, Elizabeth Row
mentions late daughter, Mary Hardy
Grand-daughter, Elizabeth Mary Hardy
Executors, friends Wilfred Reed of Lower Thames St,
'oylman'; John Sawyer of St Martin's Lane, Cannon St,
gent., and the testator's wife, Jane Coster.
Dated: 28th February 1787
Witnesses: Joshua Stafford Snr. Joshua Stafford Jun.
Proved: P.C.C. (66 Holman) 18 Feb. 1794 by Wilfred
Reed and John Sawyer, surviving exors.

You will appreciate that from the above quite an amount of information about the family is gleaned. One of Edward Coster's daughters had evidently married someone called Row, and another daughter, who was dead in February 1787 when the will was made, had married a Mr Hardy and had a daughter living at that time. The wife was alive when the will was made but was dead before it was proved in 1794 because the executors who did so are described as 'surviving executors'. You also obtain the occupation of the deceased, namely 'oylman' and this will suggest other sources, because, as he was working in the City of London he may have been a freeman and a member of a city livery company. Thus the freedom rolls and the city livery company records may provide further information, including the important one of the name and occupation of the testator's father. If he in turn was a freeman, then you get his father's name and occupation and so on. In earlier times it was not possible to practice certain trades in the City unless you were a freeman, and the freedom rolls of other towns, where they have survived, are also very valuable in tracing parentage.

If you are searching for a name which is fairly uncommon and you have traced it down to a particular district, you should systematically make extracts of all wills and administrations of the name in that area. Then you can sit down and have the enjoyment of fitting it all together, rather like a jig-saw puzzle.

Inventories, as already mentioned, where they survive, are often very helpful in piecing together something of the man's life and occupation, as if, for instance, he was a farmer it will indicate his farm stock, the value of his grain and so forth, or if the deceased was a tradesman or craftsman of some sort, this will probably be revealed by the inventory, probably listing his tools and materials. Inventories are often available for wills proved in the archdeaconry and diocesan courts. The inventories for the great collection of wills in the Prerogative Court of Canterbury were in 1964 transferred to the Public Record Office and are being indexed, but are not yet available for the public to see. W. G. Hoskins in his work *Local History in England* points out that these inventories contain an enormous amount of information of every kind about the upper strata of the population and emphasizes how necessary such information is for a good local history. 'The continued refusal to allow students to use these records,' he wrote, 'is a thoroughly disgraceful piece of administrative shuffling and ought to be remedied at once.' No doubt his and similar protests have been instrumental in getting these valuable records transferred to the Public Record Office so that they may be available for consultation. The indexing of this vast collection is a great task and will take a considerable time. But when it is completed it will be a most valuable tool to genealogists among others. It will in fact form an index to many of the P.C.C. wills, because where there is an inventory there should also be a will, though the reverse is not necessarily true and there may be a number of wills which have no inventory.

This search for wills may be just one of those occasions mentioned in Chapter 1 when you may prefer to employ a professional genealogist. As also mentioned in that chapter, the Society of Genealogists do this kind of research themselves or they will provide you with a list of professional genealogists. Some of these advertise in the Society's magazine and elsewhere. A professional genealogist has the advantage that he or she is experienced in this rather specialized and difficult field and may be useful to you in your initial search for wills, even if you continue with it later on. But as mentioned earlier, if you can spare the time it is better for you to do it yourself, because you will learn personally much more about your ancestors and will probably enjoy the searching and atmosphere of pursuit which attaches itself to the work, rather like a detective gradually unravelling clues.

After you have searched the wills, parish registers and census returns you have searched what may be termed the normal and direct sources. Your next step will be to examine more specialized records, which will depend on what you have discovered so far. The succeeding chapters will mainly deal with these.

⎡8⎤

MARRIAGE LICENCES

Marriage was often by banns, that is, notices of intention to
marry called out three times during the Sunday services
in the parish church or churches in which the bride and
bridegroom lived, in one of which the two people intended
to marry. When for some reason the people concerned wanted
to dispense with this requirement they could do so by being
married by licence. Such an occasion might be when the
couple wanted to be married quickly because the future
husband was perhaps going abroad with his regiment. But
licences cost more money than banns, so that nearly always
the poorest classes if possible were married by banns.

Probably for that very reason it became to a certain extent
what would today be called a 'status symbol' to be married
by licence. It was thought rather ordinary or common to be
married by banns and so in the past everyone who could
afford it was married by licence, even though there was
plenty of time to have the banns called in the parish church.
There was probably another reason why banns were disliked
by the upper classes. They did not enjoy having their names
called out in church for all and sundry to hear. They felt this
revelation of their intentions in such a personal matter as
marriage was rather vulgar and they had no wish to see the
village yokels gaping with curiosity at hearing about their
squire's daughter's matrimonial future. Such things were considered private family affairs and not the concern of the
villagers.

Of course there were others who thought differently and

many a good country squire might have been happy to feel that the villagers, who were probably mostly his tenants and employees, took an interest in his daughter's marriage, but even so he would probably have followed the convention and had them married by licence.

Of course, as always happens in history, the habits of the upper classes were copied by those of lower social status and so all down the classes people got married by licence if possible, until it came down to the man who really could not afford the higher fees, the ordinary workman, who would perhaps in any case have been thought presumptuous at marrying by licence and laughed at by his fellow workers as having ideas above his station.

So it was not merely the upper classes, as is sometimes thought, who were married by licence, but most farmers, yeomen, merchants and clerks in city offices did so and it was generally only the great mass of what have in the past been called the lower classes who had their banns called out.

All this is very useful to the genealogist, for not only is it a little easier to trace a marriage if it was made by licence, but also some additional information will be gleaned about the bride and bridegroom.

There were several kinds of licence. If both people lived in the same diocese, then they could get the licence from the bishop of that diocese, but if they were in different dioceses, then they had to go to the archbishop's office for it. These came from the archbishop's vicar-general and so were known as vicar-general licences. But it might happen that the two people wanting to get married lived in two ecclesiastical provinces, in which case they had to go to the office of the Master of Faculties of the Archbishop of Canterbury as Primate of all England and so these were known as Faculty Office Licences. There were also certain deans and chapters, archdeacons and holders of peculiars who had the right to grant these licences. You will probably already be noticing a similarity to the method for obtaining probate of wills, and the various jurisdictions were in fact similar.

The actual licence was given to the people who were being

married, but the allegation, which was a kind of statement made by the bride and bridegroom, was kept at the diocesan registry, together with the bonds, which were assurances by the bondsmen, who went surety for the couple about to be married. These bondsmen were usually friends and sometimes relatives.

Information from the allegations and bonds varies in different dioceses, but the allegation usually gives the name and status of the bride and bridegroom, that is, whether the man was a bachelor or widower and the woman a spinster or widow, and it often gave the occupation of the bridegroom. It would also indicate the place or possible places where the marriage could take place. If one or both of the people were under age, then the name or names of the parents giving their consent would be given and this is, of course, particularly valuable information.

These allegations and bonds were kept in the diocesan registry, where some still remain today. Their consultation may be hedged with difficulties and in some dioceses you can only have them consulted by an agent, usually the diocesan registrar, who is generally a solicitor. This involves fees which may be rather high. In other cases you are allowed to consult the indexes yourself and the necessary documents will be produced, again for a fee which is not always light. However, most dioceses have now handed over their records to the local County Record Office, which becomes also the Diocesan Record Office. Here the records are under the care of trained archivists and are available for consultation, usually without any fee and the staff are very helpful.

A number of marriage licences have been published by the Harleian Society and other bodies, such as county record societies. Others have been indexed in manuscript and some copies exist in typescript. The Society of Genealogists, for instance, has many MS copies. The Devon and Cornwall Record Society has TS indexes and copies of marriage licences for Devon and Cornwall from 1631 to 1762, extracted by Dr Mann and also an earlier series by Vivian, indexed by Mann and Pershouse, for the period 1523 to 1631. There are copies of these in the Society of Genealogists.

There is often at the registry a calendar of the licences, arranged chronologically under the various licensing authorities, such as the archdeacons surrogated for the granting of licences. This means going through them page by page, but in some cases there is a rough index, to the first initial letter, of the licences. This index may only cover a portion of the period. Towards the end of the eighteenth century the authorities seem to have got more index-conscious and sometimes these indexes start around 1780. But even then they are usually only under the bridegroom's name and they may also prove rather unreliable, even though they do save time. It is hoped that soon all the marriage licences for the different dioceses may be properly indexed and that this source of information, so valuable, not only to genealogists, but to all searchers seeking biographical and sociological information, may be more easily available.

[9]

SOME PRINTED SOURCES

In the first chapter brief reference was made to the necessity for making sure that your family has not already been written up. Therefore you will by now, I hope, have made certain that there is no printed history of it available and no MS or TS account of it lurking among the old papers of relatives. But there are a number of other printed sources which may have some reference to your family and contribute to part of its history. The chances of your finding such printed assistance may not be great, but you should at any rate make sure that no one has already done part of your work for you.

Naturally the finding of printed material of major importance will depend on the status of your family in the past. This may have varied at different periods, for, as I have pointed out in the first chapter, one of the refreshing aspects of British history is that people of ability and character have always been able to rise in the social scale. Equally it must be admitted and realized that families as easily fall in the social scale. There is a lot in that old Lancashire proverb 'There's nobbut three generations between clog and clog'. There have been so many examples of industrialists during the nineteenth century making great fortunes, which have been quickly dissipated by their sons, brought up in a different social environment far from their father's industry, perhaps put into the army with a commission in a crack and expensive cavalry regiment to raise the social strata of the family.

Therefore, whatever your family's position today it need not have been in that position years ago. Consequently it is not to be ruled out that your family has links with the peerage, even if this does not seem likely to you. One of the best-known peerages is the *Complete Peerage*, edited by G. E. Cokayne and others, in thirteen volumes, which has only just been completed. This is a monumental and accurate historical account of every holder of a peerage as far as can be gathered throughout our history. But to the genealogist it is only useful when information is wanted about the actual peer or his wife, as the antecedents and the children, other than the successor, are not included.

One of the most useful peerages for the genealogist is Collin's *Peerage of England*, and the most useful edition of it is that edited by Sir Egerton Bridges and published in 1812. It can be found in a number of larger reference libraries. This gives a very full account of the peerage families, attempting to trace their origins as far back as possible and giving the descent of younger sons and daughters and often their descendants to several generations. The ninth volume contains a reasonably full index, which is, of course, particularly valuable. There are, as may be expected in a great work like this full of factual matter and one compiled in days when means and methods of research were more limited, a number of errors and some of the early generations of families are suspect, but on the whole the work is reasonably accurate for its period. This peerage, as its title implies, does not include Scottish and Irish peerages, but as far as Scotland is concerned there is *The Scots Peerage* by Sir James Balfour Paul, a former Lyon King of Arms, the nine volumes of which are a mine of information, dealing with the peer's antecedents and a great number of collaterals. The last volume is an excellent index to the whole work.

The two principal current peerages are *Burke's Peerage* and *Debrett's Peerage*. Debrett's is the older, having been first published in 1803, and, perhaps for that reason, always seems to be referred to by the press as the ultimate authority on matters concerning the peerage. One connects it with old saws like 'if your name's in Debrett don't say "serviette" ', and so forth, but from the genealogist's point of view Burke's peerage is far more useful, as it shows the pedigree of the peer and his family as far back as it is known. Some people at first find the manner in which the descents are shown confusing, but once the ingenious lay-out is mastered it becomes very clear and concise.

It is really a pity that there should be these two peerages in what is a limited field and if only they would pool their resources, retaining the more-satisfactory Burke style of lay-out, then perhaps they could produce a really outstanding work, combining to include a full index, which at present is such a dire need to make the work really complete. The index could be a separate volume and it would not be necessary to produce one with every issue. An index of the editions at ten year intervals or even twenty year intervals would be a great assistance.

Another valuable publication, already mentioned earlier, is *Burke's Landed Gentry*, which has been published at various intervals since 1836. Its first edition, which was not arranged alphabetically, was called *The History of the Commoners* and is in four volumes. There has been an index to the families in it, but not a full index to everyone mentioned in it though each volume has an index. The second edition, published in three volumes between 1846 and 1849, contains an index of some 311 pages, with references to some 100,000 names. This makes it a particularly useful edition. From the second edition until the ninth edition (1898) the title was *The Landed Gentry of Great Britain and Ireland*, but in 1899 the first separate edition of *The Landed Gentry of Ireland* was brought out, subsequent editions of the Irish volume being 1904, 1912 and 1958. The main work after 1898 became known as *The Landed Gentry of Great Britain* and this had an Irish Supplement in 1937 and an American Supplement in 1939.

The peerages of both Burke and Debrett contain baronets, and there is also the *Complete Baronetage*, edited by G. E. Cokayne, published in five volumes from 1900 to 1906. This, like the *Complete Peerage* is mainly useful for the holders of the title and their wives and does not otherwise give the history of their families. *Walford's County Families*, published at various intervals between 1864 and 1920, is a useful work often overlooked. It, however, does not give the ancestry of the families, but only details of living people belonging to such families, usually the head of the family. It is somewhat similar to the modern *Kelly's Handbook to the Titled, Landed and Official Classes*, 1880 to date, published originally (1875) as *The Upper Ten Thousand*, Walford gives more genealogical detail, mentioning usually the eldest son or heir. It is perhaps more confined in its scope, but both publications include all county magistrates.

If you are fortunate enough to have a prominent individual in your pedigree you will get much reliable information about him from the *Dictionary of National Biography*. The present edition of the main work of this great reference tool, known for short as the D.N.B., is in twenty-two volumes, taking its scope from the beginning of England's history up to 1900. It is particularly inclusive of literary and clerical people, but is often criticized for its failure to include distinguished engineers and business men. This fault is not so prevalent in the supplements, known as the *Twentieth Century D.N.B.* published at intervals since 1900, the last volume of which brings the work down to 1950. Unfortunately, for financial reasons, although these supplements are better balanced in the fields of activity they cover, they are not so inclusive as the main work and for that reason many distinguished people who would have been in the main work have not been able to be included in them.

This work really supplants most of the earlier biographical works, drawing upon and correcting them as necessary and including many more people. There is however one work which is not as well known as it deserves to be and which has brief notices of many people who died between 1851 and 1900 not included in the D.N.B. This is *Modern English Biography* by Frederick Boase, which, with its supplements, runs into six volumes and contains over 30,000 biographies. It was originally published between 1892 and 1921 and was reprinted in 1965. It has a good subject index which includes lists of pseudonyms. It fills a gap before such works as *Who's Who* came into existence, though there is also *People of the Period*, which is useful to a limited extent.

The best way to make use of *Who's Who* in genealogy is to use the *Who Was Who* volumes, which cover all those who have been in *Who's Who* and who have died between the years covered by each volume. These cover from the beginning of the work in 1897 to 1960 and in recent years have been published for every ten-year interval.

Kelly's Handbook, mentioned above, includes some people not to be found in *Who's Who* and vice versa. There is today a plethora of *Who's Who* in particular fields, such as Art, The Theatre, Sport, Librarianship, Municipal Government, but as these are nearly all of recent date their value to the genealogist is not great.

If you discover that any of your family owned property or were in any way prominent in some particular locality, then the county histories of that locality should be examined. Some counties have been far more fortunate in their historians than others. One could wish that all counties had had such works as Blomefield's *Norfolk* or Bateson's *Northumberland*, Ormerod's *Cheshire* or Cussan's *Hertfordshire*. Ralph Bigland's history of *Gloucestershire*, which fulfils the genealogist's dream, has already been mentioned.

One of the greatest works in this field is the *Victoria County History*. Unfortunately in so many of the counties the work has never been completed, but counties are at present in many cases making valiant efforts, some far more than others, and hardly a year goes by now without at least one volume of the work being published by some county or other. This is a very full and excellent work, tracing the history of each manor in each parish, and it is well indexed, so that where the work has been completed, as, for instance, in Hampshire and Berkshire, it is a valuable work to consult.

[10]

PERIODICALS AND NEWSPAPERS

One of the most useful genealogical tools is the *Gentleman's Magazine*, which was first published in 1731 and continued into this century, though for genealogical purposes it is only useful to 1868, after which it ceased to give those valuable notices of birth, marriage and death, which it had done from its commencement.

Do not be misled by its title into thinking that these notices only refer to the upper classes. Even from its earliest times it included notices of merchants and other middle-class citizens and, as it developed, these notices increased. They are to be found at the end of each monthly issue and there are also longer obituary notices of more prominent people. Naturally, distinguished people, nobles and outstanding personalities are given fuller notice. One nearly always finds the clergy well covered and not only do you get the marriages and deaths of most of these but you can also trace their appointments in the preferments lists. Notices relating to officers in the Army and Royal Navy are plentiful. The volumes are not much use in tracing persons in the lower social strata, such as farmers, artisans or labourers, though these may be mentioned, particularly in obituary notices, if there was something of special interest in their lives or if they lived to a great age.

Each volume of the magazine is indexed under various headings and for the genealogist's purpose the most useful of these is, of course, the index of names. Unfortunately this index is a poor one in that it only lists the surnames and gives no christian names or even, until the nineteenth century, initials. This means one has usually to look up every reference to the surname in the hope of finding one you want. This may not be a very heavy task if one is dealing with a rare surname, but when you come to such common names as Smith, Jones or Robinson, you will appreciate that the task is a formidable one.

In addition to the indexes for each volume there are cumulative indexes, from 1731 to 1786 and from 1786 to 1819, but unfortunately these again only list the surnames, so when confronted with 'Smith' you have before your eyes a sea of volume and page numbers. For many years genealogists have been hoping for a comprehensive index of the whole work. The College of Arms have a slip index, not open to the public, and some years ago there was a project in conjunction with the Society of Genealogists for this to be typed, so that copies could be available at the society and in other places. This, however, fell through, but since then the Church of the Latter Day Saints, generally known as the Mormon Church, have made a typescript copy of this index. Unfortunately there is no copy of this at the Society of Genealogists, but it is hoped that there may be one there at some time in the not-too-distant future or at any rate a microfilm of this index may be available there.

The Mormons' interest in genealogy is a religious one. They are anxious to trace their forbears so that they can baptize them by proxy into their church. Their genealogical researches are therefore prompted by a motive which differs from that of the ordinary genealogist. This American religious body has spent very large sums of money in having records in Great Britain and in Europe copied, often by microfilm, and their genealogical library in Salt Lake City, Utah, which is their headquarters, contains a vast amount of genealogical material which has been gathered from all over the world. They are using many modern methods, including punched card and electrical sorting machines, to assist in the vast work of indexing the material which they have on hand and as this becomes sorted and indexed, in as far as it is made available it should be of great value to all genealogists.

Meanwhile there are partial indexes which are very useful. There is Edward Alexander Fry's *Index to the Marriages in the Gentleman's Magazine, 1731-1768*, published in 1922, and there is the *Index to the Biographical and Obituary Notices . . . 1731-1780*, published by the British Records Society in 1891, revised by Mr Fry. Another useful help is *Musgrave's Obituary*, published by the Harleian Society, which lists many deaths in the eighteenth century of which notices appeared not only in the *Gentleman's Magazine* but also in other contemporary publications, such as the *London Magazine*.

In the earlier volumes of the *Gentleman's Magazine* the editor probably depended largely on sources which were sometimes rather inaccurate and doubtful, but, though the entries must be accepted with caution, yet there are often little pieces of information in them which are quite correct and which are amusing and help to infuse your skeleton pedigree with life. Some relate to runaway marriages at Gretna Green or elsewhere, such as the notice in June 1795 'at Gretna Green, Mr Wm Coster, clothier, of Salisbury to Miss Savage, a natural born daughter of Edward, late Duke of Somerset, about 19 years of age, with a fortune of 5000l.' In those more calculating days they were fond of mentioning a bride's dowry. The magazine is rich in local colour and history and you feel, as you turn over the pages that you are seeing almost at first hand the life of the time.

The *Gentleman's Magazine* also used current newspapers for its notices of birth, marriage and death. You will see on its title page a number of newspapers listed and these were no doubt the ones on which it drew. Sometimes the notice in the newspaper is fuller than that in the magazine and it is worth while tracking it down. This is not as difficult as it sounds if you live in or can visit London. The British Museum Library has a fine collection of early newspapers called the *Burney Collection*. One advantage of this collection is that the papers are arranged chronologically and not by separate newspapers. Thus you find the various papers together for the same day or week. In the eighteenth century there were a number of newspapers, many of them weekly or bi-weekly, but some were dailies, such as the *Daily Courant*, the *Daily Journal* and the *St James's Evening Post*. The provinces were not so well supplied, but there were papers like the *Bath Chronicle* which in the eighteenth century covered notices not only of local people but also of people throughout the country. It also covered lists of arrivals in the city, but these were mainly people in the social world.

The two older universities have good collections of early newspapers and there is a useful *Catalogue of English Newspapers and Periodicals in the Bodleian Library, 1622-1800*, published in 1936, by R. T. Milford and D. M. Sutherland.

There are articles on the genealogical value of early English newspapers by Mr C. D. P. Nicholson in the *Genealogists' Magazine* in the March 1929 and successive issues. From these you will see the kind of additional information you may obtain from a newspaper entry. It must be observed, though, that the majority of these entries relate to comparatively well-known people and many entries of lesser people in the *Gentleman's Magazine* have no notice at all in the newspapers. There is a useful article in the *Amateur Historian* by G. R. Mellor on 'History from Newspapers' (Volume II, 97, 1955) and another article in the *Proceedings of the Leeds Philosophical Society*, Volume VIII (1957), by Donald Read on 'North of England Newspapers (*c.* 1700 – *c.* 1900) and their value to Historians'.

Notices of marriage and death were always more numerous than those of birth and in the early issues of periodicals like the *Gentleman's Magazine* only very prominent people had notices of the birth of a child. Even *The Times*, which later became such a medium for the announcement of such events, from the time it began in 1788 until well into the nineteenth century had very few notices of birth. This paper, however, has the advantage over other papers in having been indexed from its commencement, first by *Palmer's Index* and later by its own official index. These indexes do not include the notices of birth, marriage and death, but they do include obituary notices (very sparse in early numbers) and such wills as were reported.

The number of periodicals relating to particular counties is very great. Many counties have record societies in the publications of which are often information about families connected with those counties. Many of them, like the Devon and Cornwall Record Society, have also fine MS collections.

The *Annual Register* began life in 1758 and has been published every year since then. It is very useful for providing information about events in any particular year but from a genealogical point of view it is not nearly as useful as the *Gentleman's Magazine*. Its lists of births, marriages and deaths are far more limited, referring only to well-known people. Their obituary notices include many people who would not be found in the *Dictionary of National Biography*, but they are still more exclusive than those for whom obituaries would appear in *The Times* of more recent years.

There are also many periodicals devoted to particular interests, such as the *United Services Magazine*, which began life as the *United Service Journal and Naval and Military Magazine* in 1829 and was later known as *Colburn's United Service Magazine*. It contains notices of birth, marriage and death and obituaries, sometimes quite extensive, of officers of the Navy and Army. Unfortunately, as so often with these magazines, it is not indexed, so you need a good idea of the date of the event to be able to find it without lengthy search. Fortunately it is not difficult to find the date of death of an officer in either service as you can search the army or navy lists and see when the name disappears and probably find the exact date in the report on deaths since the last publication. There is also a very useful MS index to naval obituaries which appeared in the *Naval and Military Gazette* in the Admiralty Library at Earl's Court, London. It must be emphasized that this only covers naval obituaries.

If you happen to be dealing with a surname which is not further down the alphabet than 'Alexander', then there is a particularly useful index by Joseph Foster, that prolific and painstaking collector and writer to whom genealogists owe so much. It is unfortunate it never reached completion as its compiler intended. It includes notices of all marriages in the *Gentleman's Magazine* and the *Historical Register* and also all marriages in *The Times* from 1865 to 1880. It also includes marriages from Westminster Abbey registers. It was published in *Collectanea Genealogica* 1881–85 as 'Marriages of the Nobility and Gentry, 1650–1880'.

E. L. C. Mullins' *Texts and calendars: an analytical guide to serial publications*, published by the R. Hist. Society in 1958, is particularly useful in giving lists of the publications of societies like the British Records Society, Harleian Society and of the various county record societies.

[11]

RECORDS OF CLERGYMEN

Before Durham University began life in 1832 and London University some four years later, the only universities in England and Wales were the two ancient foundations of Oxford and Cambridge. As, in the past, many clergymen had a university education it is a comparatively easy matter to trace the parentage of the clergy, because the matriculation registers of the university concerned will give the father's name and usually the place of residence when the son was born, and these registers have been published for both Oxford and Cambridge. The Oxford registers, called *Alumni Oxonienses*, edited by Joseph Foster, are in two series, the earlier in four volumes covering the matriculations from 1500 to 1714, and the second covering from 1715 to 1886. There are also two additional volumes, published in 1893, also edited by Foster, called *Oxford Men and their Colleges*, the second volume of which gives the matriculations from 1880 to 1892. These registers often give brief biographical details beyond the university career, particularly for clergy, the dates of their successive livings and of their death. Ordination papers too are particularly valuable in the case of non-graduate clergy, as these include a certified copy of the ordinand's baptismal entry. Today they are usually held by county record offices.

The Cambridge registers, the *Alumni Cantabrigienses*, are also in two series, the first, edited by John Venn and J. A. Venn, covering from the earliest times to 1751 and the second, edited by J. A. Venn alone, from 1752 to 1900. The biographical details given in the Cambridge *Alumni* are rather fuller than those in the Oxford one, particularly in the second series. They may, for instance, include the name of the wife. Both these publications try to link up the person with any other relations at the university and sometimes you can trace a man's pedigree back several generations if his forbears were also university men.

It should be remembered that clergymen are officially described as 'clerks in holy orders' and this is frequently abbreviated to 'clerk', so that if you come across someone so described he was probably an ordained member of the Church of England and not a 'pen-pusher' in an office. Information can also be found about clergy from Crockford's *Clerical Directory*, first published in 1858, and from earlier clergy lists. A useful book, as far as it goes, is Joseph Foster's *Index Ecclesiasticus*, which gives clerical appointments for the period 1800 to 1840.

Information about ministers of other denominations is more difficult to trace. There are lists of such clergy for many of them, but they do not go back very far in most cases. The Methodists have indexed the biographical notices of their ministers from 1778 to 1839 of whom obituary notices appear in their Arminian and Methodist magazines, as mentioned in Chapter 6. The Congregational Union of England and Wales have obituaries of their ministers in their Year Book and these are often quite full, but they do not go back far. Information about Jewish rabbis and Huguenot ministers will be dealt with in a later chapter and likewise records of Scottish and Irish clergy will be referred to in later chapters on those countries.

Roman Catholics suffered for many years under disabilities and were not allowed to conduct services. Information on some of their priests can be traced in the publications of the Catholic Record Society and there have been biographical dictionaries of some of the orders, such as H. N. Birt's *Obit Book of the English Benedictines from 1600 to 1912*, published in 1913, and W. Gumbley's *Obituary Notices of the English Dominicans from 1555 to 1952*. In general, information about Roman Catholic priests is best sought through the authorities of that church.

[12]

LAWYERS, DOCTORS AND OTHERS

In England and Wales men in the legal profession divide into two groups, barristers and solicitors. A solicitor cannot be a member of the bar and a barrister cannot be enrolled as a solicitor.

To become a barrister you must be admitted through one of the inns of court, which are today, Lincoln's Inn, which is particularly linked with Chancery practice, the Middle Temple, the Inner Temple and Gray's Inn. When men enter these inns certain particulars about them are recorded, including their parentage, usually a description of their father's occupation or status and his place of residence. All the inns, except the Inner Temple have published fairly complete admission registers, so that information from these is easily obtainable. In the case of the Inner Temple it is necessary to write to the Librarian for information. It is believed this inn suffered some loss of its records during the Second World War, but at any rate certain periods of their admissions survive. Only admissions of an early period have been published by this inn.

Solicitors are more elusive people. It is possible some details are recorded on their enrolment, but these have not been published. This is a pity as, while barristers are usually university graduates and therefore traceable through the matriculation records, solicitors even today are not always so and in the past were seldom so. Their names and the place where they practised can be traced through the law lists and by going through these you can usually discover when a solicitor died, and you would normally expect, in view of his profession, that he would leave a properly drawn up will, but this is not always the case. Not all solicitors seem to practice what they preach.

In earlier times young men were apprenticed to attorneys in the same way that others were to other trades, so that in the eighteenth century period when there was a tax on apprenticeship indentures, you will be able to discover details of them in the Society of Genealogists' index of apprentices.

Judges of all courts are appointed from the barristers, so that their parentage is traced from the same sources, and judges of the higher courts, being prominent people, are easily traceable in such works as Foster's *Judges of England*, but many of them in any case will be found in the *D.N.B.*

Magistrates, or justices of the peace, are laymen. They are appointed by the Lord Chancellor and their record of appointment will be among the Lord Chancellor's records, .but many county record offices have lists of J.P.s for various periods and they can also be traced during the nineteenth century from directories of their locality. Some information about officials of the various law courts may be traced in such works as the *Royal Calendar* which exists from the late eighteenth century.

Medical men, if they are graduates in medicine, can be traced through the university records, which will give their parentage. It may be more difficult to trace others.

The medical world in earlier times had divided itself into two main divisions, the physicians and the surgeons. The physicians were of higher status, often university men with degrees in medicine or members of the College of Physicians. The surgeons until 1745 were in London linked with the barbers in the Surgeons and Barbers Company, one of the livery companies. After that date their status began to improve, particularly after 1800 when the Royal College of Surgeons was founded. Nevertheless even in the early nineteenth century surgeons stood well below the position of physicians. The term then did not indicate the function they have today. They did not specialize in surgery but had the simpler functions of a general practitioner of medicine and dentistry, the setting of bones, pulling out teeth and serving as general medical advisers and apothecaries. Socially they stood somewhere between the tradesman and the professional man. Even physicians were not regarded socially as much above attorneys. There were no doubt those among the upper classes who would have exclaimed disdainfully, as Bertram did when being forced to marry Helena in *All's Well that Ends Well*, 'She had her breeding at my father's charge, a poor physician's daughter my wife! – Disdain rather corrupt me ever.' It must also be remembered that the law about medical practice and medical practitioners was far more lax in the past and men could practise and call themselves doctors with little or no medical qualifications. A young boy might be apprenticed, as the poet John Keats was, to the local surgeon for five years. If this was during the early and mid-eighteenth century his parentage may be found in the apprentices index already mentioned. If he was a member of the Royal College of Surgeons or of the Royal College of Physicians, then information about him may be traced from their records. Many doctors in early times were Licenciates of the Society of Apothecaries (L.S.A.) and that body, from the late eighteenth century, has detailed records of people admitted. These records, which are now in the Guildhall Library, London, are very useful, as they give not only the name and occupation of the father, but also other details, such as the names of referees and include a certificate from some-one verifying that the applicant is over twenty-one years of age. As sometimes the applicant obtained his reference from his local vicar or rector, this often indicates where he came from.

Monk's Roll of Physicians should not be overlooked, though this only covers a few better-known medical men. Medical directories began to come out in the early nineteenth century and these will tell you where a practitioner was in practice and in the volume of the year after he died you may even find a short obituary of him. Some of the later directories give a brief account of those entered, at least indicating their qualifications.

Many English doctors qualified in Scotland or Ireland or abroad. Leyden in Holland was at one time a popular place to do so and a list of English students there has been published. All four of the Scottish universities are of old foundation. Glasgow and Aberdeen have each published some details of their matriculations, Glasgow being the fuller. It must be remembered that Aberdeen was divided between King's College and Marischal College and it is necessary to look in the records of each. St Andrews has only partial lists of matriculations and Edinburgh has not published any of its matriculations, but only lists of graduates. In some cases the information in the matriculation registers is disappointing and one will not necessarily discover the names of the parents from them. Many English medical men qualified in Ireland at Trinity College, Dublin, and the matriculation registers of this college have been published.

Medical men in the Army and Navy and in the East India Company service can be traced in the records of these services. As in civil life, surgeons in the services in the past had a lower status. In the Navy they were not commissioned officers but only warrant officers and their status in the Army was not much better until the mid-nineteenth century.

The sources for information about other professions are very varied and extensive. It is only possible to give here briefly some of these. Tradition is a strong thread in many occupations and in none, perhaps, is it stronger than in the theatrical profession. One thinks of the Forbes-Robertsons, the Terrys, the Keans, the Lanes, the Gielguds and the Redgraves. Theatrical families, as you can see looking through *Who's Who in the Theatre*, tend to marry among themselves, so that you get a great number of links between them all. A lecture by Dr J. M. Bulloch on 'Theatrical Families' is published in the *Genealogists' Magazine* in Volume 6, p. 337 (Dec. 1933).

The well-known *Dictionary of Music and Musicians* published originally in four volumes under the editorship of

Sir George Grove, now, in its fifth edition, expanded to nine volumes, will give information about distinguished musicians. A valuable work on architects is H. M. Colvin's *Biographical Dictionary of English Architects 1660–1840* and in an allied field mention may be made of an article on 'County Masons' in the *Genealogists' Magazine*, Volume 9, p. 274 (Dec. 1952) by Frederick Burgess. From the eighteenth century details of careers of men who served in the customs and excise services, either in London or throughout the British Isles, may be gathered from the establishment records at the Public Record Office. These begin in 1683 but there are a number of gaps. The run is good from 1700 to 1763, after which there is a gap until 1770 when they continue to 1829, the period from 1813 to 1829 being a good one. A good article on these records by Rupert C. Jarvis is in the *Genealogists' Magazine* for September 1948 (Volume 10, p. 221).

When the History of Parliament now being compiled is completed it will be a great source of biographical information. The recent volumes by Sir Lewis Namier and John Brooke covering the House of Commons 1754–1790 are an indication of this. Two of the three volumes are devoted to biographies of all the members of that period. There are earlier collective biographies of members, such as Joshua Wilson's *The Present House of Commons* dealing with the house at the time of Trafalgar in 1805.

Artists are covered by Samuel Redgrave's *Dictionary of Artists of the English School*, first published in 1874, and by M. H. Grant's *Dictionary of British Etchers* and his *Dictionary of British Sculptors*. Authors are covered by a number of publications and their career can be traced to a certain extent by noting their publications in the British Museum catalogue.

[13]

NAVAL ANCESTORS

In a seafaring nation like Great Britain most families can expect to find one or more ancestors of its line in the Royal Navy and such ancestors can usually be traced with some success for, as those who have served in one or other of the forces will well know, these services have a habit of wanting returns in triplicate of all sorts of details and this paper-work, irritating at times, comes in good stead when you want to trace something about someone. Unfortunately in the past they were not always as thorough or as demanding as the present day service departments.

Nevertheless service records are prolific and the Navy has as good records as any service. Naturally it is easier to trace information about an officer than a rating, but even so in the MS records far more can be discovered about a rating than about a man in a comparable position in civilian life.

The main MS sources are among the Admiralty records in the Public Record Office, but before dealing with them I will first mention some of the printed sources. These in general refer only to officers.

Earliest among them is John Charnock's *Biographia Navalis, or, Memoirs of the Officers of the Navy from 1600*, which was published in 1794 in four volumes. John Campbell's *Lives of British Admirals*, also in four volumes, was published in 1779 and, as its title implies, is confined to Flag Officers. *The Naval Biography of Great Britain*, by James Ralfe, published in 1828, is a rare work which includes some officers not in other works. John Marshall's *Royal Naval*

Biography, which, with its supplements, runs into twelve volumes, covers all officers who reached the rank of commander and who were living, or had only recently died, during the period from 1823 to 1830. All these works give details of the officer's career, particulars of any actions in which he may have taken part and often his parentage.

The most comprehensive printed work is W. R. O'Byrne's *Naval Biographical Dictionary*, published in 1849 and including every officer of the rank of lieutenant and above, serving or retired, who was living in the year 1845. It includes notices of nearly 5,000 officers. O'Byrne mentions in many cases the father of the officer and frequently any other relatives who were serving or had served in the navy. In addition, the original MSS of this great work are easily accessible, being in the British Museum MS Department (Additional MS 38039–54) and these MSS, include in most cases the completed forms which were sent out to the officers concerned, together with any letters the officer may have written and these often give far more information than is contained in the printed volume.

The Sailor's Home Journal, afterwards the *Naval Chronicle* edited successively by W. R. O'Byrne and by his brother Robert, during the years 1853 to 1863, contains many obituary notices of naval officers which supplement the information in the dictionary.

O'Byrne brought out a second edition of his work and this was more comprehensive because it included also all Royal Marine officers, surgeons, chaplains and pursers. Unfortunately it was never completed but only reached the name 'H. S. C. Giles'. It is difficult to come across copies of this edition, but there is one in the British Museum Library and in certain naval libraries and clubs.

An officer's career can be traced through successive navy lists. Steel's *Navy List* was first published in 1772. It was succeeded in 1814 by the official *Navy List*, while Joseph Allen's *New Navy List* was published for many years during the nineteenth century. In 1954 the National Maritime Museum published *The Commissioned Sea Officers of the*

Royal Navy, the three volumes of which include brief dates of promotion of officers from the earliest times until 1815.

A useful list of MS and printed lists of naval officers is contained in R. Sims' *Manual for the Genealogist, Topographer, Antiquary and Legal Professor*, 1856.

Turning to MS records, the Admiralty Records at the P.R.O. seem at first sight rather overwhelming. They are described in Volume 2 of the 1963 edition of the *Guide to the Public Record Office* and they are listed in the *Public Record Office Lists and Indexes XVIII* (H.M.S.O. 1904) to which there is a supplementary typescript list on the shelves of the Round Room at the Record Office. A very useful little book is Gerald Fothergill's *Records of Naval Men* published in 1910. It is designed to be read in conjunction with the official list and explains the type of information found in the various records.

In seeking the parentage of an officer one of the best sources is the series of Lieutenants' Passing Certificates, as from 1789 onwards, with a few earlier ones from 1777, the Navy Board copies of these have filed with them the baptismal certificate which the candidate had to produce to prove that he was at least twenty years of age. In the Round Room at the Record Office there are two MS indexes to these certificates. One was compiled by Miss E. H. B. Fairbrother and covers the years 1777 to 1832 and includes the information from the baptismal certificates. The other, compiled by Miss P. Schrader, covers the years from 1789 to 1818.

Adminstration of the Royal Navy was, prior to 1832, divided between the Admiralty and the Navy Board, each jealous of their own particular provinces, which to a considerable extent overlapped. Because of this dual control we find also a series of Passing Certificates in the Secretary of the Admiralty's records, but these do not contain the baptismal certificates and are only useful for the other information contained in them should the Navy Board copy be missing.

If your ancestor was prominent in any sea action you will be able to trace information about him in various reports and letters, such as the Admirals' Despatches or Captains' Letters in the Secretary's Department. There is also a possibility he may be mentioned in one of the naval histories, in particular in Sir William Clowes' *Royal Naval History*, the eight volumes of which contain reference to hundreds of naval officers and men. There is no general index, but each volume is well indexed and does not take long to consult.

If a forbear was unfortunate enough to be wounded or court-martialled, then his misfortune is, in your search for information about him, your good fortune. An instance of the former in my own family may help to illustrate the kind of information you may find in these cases.

Thomas Ambrose Edwards, when a lieutenant, was wounded in 1807. At that time officers and men did not automatically get a pension for wounds. The wounded man had to submit a petition, or 'memorial', to the King, asking that a pension might be granted to him. In order to back his claim he would give an account of his career and show how he came to be wounded. Thomas Ambrose Edwards therefore submitted such a petition in 1810, which came before the Prince Regent.

'Your Memorialist,' it reads, 'entered the Service as a Midshipman on board His Majesty's Ship *Hyaena*, commanded by the Honble. C. Boyle, in the Year 1798, and accompanied Captn. Boyle into the *Cormorant*, which ship was wrecked on the Coast of Agypt [sic] in 1800, when your Memorialist was made a Prisoner by the French and was severely afflicted with the Ophthalmia while in Egypt. Your Memorialist, on being liberated, joined *La Diane* and continued in her until that ship was paid off in 1802.

At the commencement of the present War, Your Memorialist joined the *Pompee*, Sir W. Sidney Smith, and after the capture of the Island of Capri, was sent to a signal Duty on shore; the *Pompee* being ordered home your Memorialist was directed to leave the Island of Capri and join her, and was proceeding from Malta to Gibraltar, on board the transport ship *Monarch* when she was attacked off Tunis on the 11th Augt. 1807 by the French Privateer *Prince Jerome* and later engaged in a severe action of half-an-hour during which Your Memorialist received a Grape-shot and a Musket ball in the left thigh, that broke and splintered the bone, and occasioned a considerable contusion of the thigh, with lameness.

In June 1809 your Memorialist was promoted to the rank of Lieutenant and appointed to the *Pandora* Sloop of War, and when assisting the embarkation of Troops at Deal on the 18th July 1809 he was thrown from the bow of a boat on the beach at Deal and, falling on the side that was before wounded, he received a violent contusion that occasioned the wound to break out and which has not since healed and ultimately rendered your Memorialist incapable of doing his duty, and obliged him to be invalided from the *Pandora*. A Certificate from Captn. H. H. Spence to this effect is enclosed, and as your Memorialist, owing to the wound and hurts he has received in His Majesty's Service is (and will be always) afflicted with extreme lameness, so as to render him unable to serve on board a Ship, he humbly hopes his case will be taken into consideration, and a Pension allowed to him.

And your Memorialist as in duty bound will ever pray.

THOMAS AMBROSE EDWARDS
No 1 Charlotte St.,
Bloomsbury Square.
Decr 27th 1810.'

The memorial was presented to the Prince Regent in Council at Carlton House on the 8th February 1811 and was referred by His Royal Highness to the Lords Commissioners of the Admiralty. They on the 14th March following reported that they found the allegations to be true and that 'the College of Surgeons by whom the Memorialist had been surveyed, have reported to us that the Injury his Thigh-Bone has received is in its effect of equal prejudice to the habit of Body with the Loss of a Limb'. Their Lordships, therefore, recommended 'a Pension of Two Shillings and six pence a day be settled on the Memorialist'.

Courts martial will often reveal details about the person tried. Usually information of at any rate part of his career comes out and often the statement in mitigation will give an outline of the accused's service. Often, too, letters written to the Admiralty after an officer had been sentenced may reveal much. In one such letter or petition to be reinstated after dismissal a young midshipman revealed that he had four brothers in the 'Service of the Army and Navy, one an old and wounded officer, a Lieut. in the Navy...two in the regular Army and another younger than himself still in the Navy' and that there had been another 'who had lost his life in the service of his country'. This last stated fact, in this particular case, revealed something which was not known from any other source.

Probably the next most valuable direct source of information to the Passing Certificates for officers are the various returns of services. That of 1817 includes all officers serving. It is of particular value because from it can be gleaned the whole of the officer's naval career to that date. Where the baptismal certificate is missing from the passing certificate, as it sometimes is, especially if the officer was examined abroad, then his place of birth can be discovered from the muster rolls of any ship in which he was serving before his promotion to lieutenant. His place of birth is also mentioned in some of the returns of midshipmen's services.

The ship's musters list all the officers and ratings on board and in the case of the ratings give the birthplace. Midshipmen and Volunteers (later Cadets) were not commissioned officers and were therefore technically ratings and thus their birthplace was given. So, by tracing back an officer's career to when he was a midshipman you can then, through his ship's muster, find the place of his birth. It must be mentioned, however, that many of these places of birth are inaccurate and also that there are examples of forged baptismal certificates among the passing certificates. There are stories of how men sat outside the dockyards when the midshipmen were taking their examinations for lieutenant, prepared for a small fee to issue bogus baptismal certificates to show that the mid-shipman was over twenty years of age, as required by the regulations. Ages as stated on returns are also often wrong. Both Nelson and Collingwood provide examples of false ages in their records.

Among other useful returns are the 'List of Acting Lieutenants, Masters, Mates, Midshipmen, whose qualifications have been admitted at an examination' of 1816 and 1818, which contain the place of birth and age of those who passed in those years. The 'Return of Midshipmen's Services' for 1814 also gives the place of birth.

The 'Register of Lieutenants Soliciting for Employment' from 1799 onwards is another example of a valuable source, for this gives the applicant's address. It must be remembered that in earlier times the Navy was not a continuous service as today and officers were commissioned anew each time a ship was commissioned. In theory they were civilians in between commissions, when they were left on shore.

The 'Bounty Papers', which cover the period 1675 to 1822, give the name and address of the relation to whom the bounty is to be paid in the case of seamen killed in action or dying, and also certificates of baptism of the next-of-kin and often parents' marriage certificates to prove relationship. These series include both officers and men.

Most of the records, it will be noticed, belong to the period starting towards the end of the eighteenth century. Early records are less prolific. Nevertheless they are quite consider-able and the difficulty lies more in tracing where the information is. These earlier records are seldom well indexed. There is, however, a great deal of information about the Navy of the Restoration period and this is mostly due to the diarist Samuel Pepys who, it will be remembered, was Secretary of the Navy. The collection itself is at Magdalene College, Cambridge, and is not accessible to the general public, but there is available Dr Tanner's *Catalogue of Pepsyian MSS*, really a calendar of these papers, which cover the proceedings of the Admiralty and the Navy Board from 1673 to 1679. Pepys' 'List of Commissioned Officers' is particularly valuable in giving the name with the rank and ship of almost every officer who was serving between the years 1660 and 1688. These names have been included in the *Commissioned Sea Officers* published by the National Maritime Museum referred to earlier.

The 'Captains' Letters' in the Secretary's Department cover a very wide range and are often very valuable. You never quite know what you are going to find in them and it is a rather exciting kind of lucky dip. I found, for instance, a letter written by the same Thomas Ambrose Edwards who was wounded, writing when a captain to ask for an appointment for his youngest midshipman brother Nathaniel Frederick. Applications for appointments of relations were quite common in days when influence was used quite openly.

These captains' letters are kept in bundles or groups of years and then alphabetical under the captain's name. They are indexed.

'Lieutenants' Letters' often contain applications for appointment to ships and they usually give the home address of the officer. There are similar series for officers of the Royal Marines.

The series of letters entitled 'Promiscuous' may be on almost any conceivable subject, from an irate uncle seeking the whereabouts of his nephew to a creditor that of his debtor. They are in bundles arranged alphabetically and chronologically. The letters from the Royal Naval College, Portsmouth, beginning in 1773, are useful in giving reports of the scholars' progress, usually mentioning the parents' name and giving the date and reason for discharge.

Another valuable source is contained in that whole and voluminous series of letters, papers and registers covering Greenwich Hospital. The old Greenwich Hospital stood roughly in the same relation to the Royal Navy as Chelsea Hospital does to the Army, but the naval hospital was wider in scope, covering both in and out pensioners, the school and apprenticeship of children of seamen, and such matters as the children at Clarence House, Paddington Green. They are invaluable for information about anyone admitted to this foundation, whether officer, seaman or child.

All the 'Secretary's In Letters' series can best be consulted through either the digests, which are subject indexes commencing in 1762 and more detailed after 1792, or by the indexes proper. A useful account of the subject headings and catch letters and abbreviations used in the digests and indexes is given in Fothergill's textbook. A word of warning must be given to the impatient. The consultation of these letters is a slow business. The indexes and digests are not themselves on the shelves of the Record Office and have to be applied for, as for any other document or register. There is thus the inevitable delay in awaiting its arrival, perhaps half an hour, and then, after its consultation, the application for the actual bundle and a further delay. Once the rhythm has been set in motion it is not so bad, as one can be working on one matter while waiting for other material, but you cannot hope, for instance, to do much in one day unless you write in advance asking for the documents you require. The Record Office staff are very helpful and co-operative and will even answer queries by post which do not involve much research, but you cannot expect them to give time to anything approaching an extensive search. They do keep lists of searchers who are willing to undertake such work on payment, should you wish to employ one rather than do the research yourself.

It is always useful in genealogical research to have a background knowledge of the social circle with which you are dealing. Clowes' History has already been mentioned. A shorter useful book is Michael Lewis' *The Navy of Britain* and his *England's Sea Officers* is valuable in its specialist field. But one of the best books to read about the social life of the Navy during the period indicated is the last mentioned author's *Social History of the Navy, 1793–1815* published in 1960. Drawing considerably on Marshall's *Royal Naval Biography* and O'Byrne's *Naval Biographical Dictionary*, the author has made a valuable analysis of the social background of the naval officer of the period. From this one gleans such information that 29 per cent of the officers from the

landed-gentry families reached the rank of post-captain; and
that, though few working class men could hope to attain

AN OXFORDSHIRE YEOMAN MAKES HIS WILL: "IN THE NAME OF GOD
AMEN the Fourth day of February in the Fourth yeare of the reigne
of our Sovereigne Lord and Lady William and Mary by the grace
of God of England Scotland France and Ireland King and Queen
Defendors of the Faith et Anno Dni 1692 I Nicolas Good of Great
Hazeley in the County of Oxon yeoman being somewhat infirme in
body but of sound and perfect mind and memory blessed bee God
for the same and considering our fraile Estate under the condicon
of mortallity how that in the midst of life wee are in death Have
thought good to make and accordingly I doe make this my last
Will and Testament in manner and forme following hereby revoking
and making void all former Wills whatsoever by mee heretofore made
AND first and principally I commend my Soul into the hands of
Almighty God my Creatour and most mercifull Father haveing an
assured hopes by the meritts death and passion of my Blessed Lord
and Savour Jesus Christ without any other meritts or meanes whatsoever to have full pardon and free remission for all my Sins and
after this life to enjoy everlasting life and happiness in his heavenly
Kingdome And my Body I comitt to the Earth from whence it
came to bee buried in such place and in such decent manner as my
Executrix herinafter named shall thinke fitt and convenient And for
such Worldly Estate wherewith it hath pleased God of his great mercy
and bounty to blesse mee which I doe acknowledge with all humble
thankefulnes to have received by his providence and blessing and
whereof it hath pleased him to give mee the Disposition that the same
shall bee disposed off And accordingly I doe hereby give Devise be-
queath and Dispose of the same as followeth ...'

This will, with its elaborate preamble and pious hopes of salvation,
is typical of the wills of the 16th, 17th and early 18th centuries. The
testator goes on to leave to his 'Loving Wife Elizabeth the use of all
and singular my household goods...' for her lifetime, and leaves
the residue to his daughter 'Elizabeth Good of Rycott Lane in the
said County of Oxon Spinster' and appoints her his sole executrix.

Nicolas Good signs by making his mark, as does one of the three
witnesses whose names are at the bottom on the left. Below the
testator's mark is the notification in Latin of the probate with the
name of the registrar, Ben: Cooper, beneath it. This shows that the
will was proved on 10th April, 1694 in the court of the Archdeacon
of Oxford by Elizabeth Good, the daughter and sole executrix.

This is a particularly well-written and clear will of the period.
Many of them are far more difficult to read.

MS WILLS. OXON 129, BODLEIAN LIBRARY
OXFORD

commissioned rank at all, of those that did so over 13 per cent reached post rank and even 2 per cent reached flag rank. It also makes clear those intricacies of entry into the Navy before 1794, when there were 'Captain's servants' who were actual servants and 'Captain's servants' who were protégés of the captain, young gentlemen belonging to the quarter-deck,

PART OF A SCOTTISH SAISINE OF 1697: William Edward and Marjorie Rattray his wife take seisin of property in Coupar Angus.

This saisine records that it was registered at Perth 23rd August 1697 and that in the presence of the Notar Public and other named witnesses there appeared personally on the ground of the land in question 'ane discreet man John Sanders ballie substitute of the regalitie of Coupar ballie in that pairt of Mr John Ogilvie ballie depute of the sd regalitie be the precept of Seisine underinsert speciallie constitute,' and also was present William Edward in Coupar for himself and on behalf of his spouse Marjorie Rattray, and William held in his hand a disposition by the said John Ogilvie 'to and in favor of the said William Edward and Marjorie Rattray the Longest Liver of ym two in Lyfrent during all the dayes of yr Lyftyme And the aires Lawllie procreat or to be procreat betwixt them Which faylzeing the aires or assigneys of the sd William Edward Whatsomever in fie Heretablie and Irredeemablie Without any kynd of Reversione Whatsomever...'

It then goes on to describe the particular piece of land in detail, mentioning the other lands with which it was bounded. This often gives valuable information as it frequently shows who previously held the lands, sometimes mentioning any relationship which may have existed between the present and previous holder. In this case the lands are 'ALL AND HAILL that his tenement of land with houses biggings yeard and kill and frie ishue and entrie yrto Lyand on the Eist syde of the toune of Coupar boundit with that croft called St Catherines Croft sometyme perteining to the deceast Agnis Halyburton and now to John Ramsay Lawll sone to the deceast George Ramsay of Gallway on the Eist and South the Lands somtyme to Alexander Campbell of Ballgershoe and now to the said William Edward on the West and the heighway that Leads from the toune of Coupar to New Calsay on the North Pairts...'

The Saisine later describes how William Edward and Marjorie Rattray or their 'certaine Actourney in their names' took 'reall actuall and Corporall possessione' of the property by the delivering to them 'of earth and Stone of the ground of ye saids Lands', thus fulfilling the traditional requirements of the law.

PART. REG. SEIS. PERTH, SCOTTISH RECORD OFFICE
EDINBURGH.

who after 1794 were to be termed 'First Class Volunteers' and later still 'Cadets'.

The excellent account of lower deck life is also useful. The genealogist can learn, for instance, that there is a 23 per cent chance a seaman ancestor during the French Wars was a volunteer and that 15 per cent of a ship's complement were foreigners.

The author also emphasized the point made earlier of the unreliability of ages in naval records. He records how Admiral Sir George Elliot related that 'a crown-piece handed to the porter at the Navy Office as one went in to be examined produced a certificate showing one to be of any age one liked to mention'.

The book also brings out the importance to the genealogist of the captain of a future officer's first ship, for he is likely to be at any rate a friend of the family and possibly a relation, for this was an age when influence or 'interest' was widespread and of paramount importance.

The records of the Royal Marines are now at the Public Record Office. They were only transferred there in 1960 and it is unfortunate they were not handed over earlier as it appears a number of their records, notably some of the 'Description Books' (Adm. 158), have been lost. However, the material surviving is good and fairly comprehensive. They are described briefly in the 1963 edition of the *Guide to the Public Record Office*.

The information in the Royal Marine records is similar to that found for the Army. The 'Attestation Forms' (Adm. 157), 1790–1883, give the age, birthplace, trade and physical characteristics of each recruit, with details of his enlistment and attestation. There are also summaries of service and details of discharge. These are arranged alphabetically under the year of attestation or of discharge.

The 'Description Books' (Adm. 158) referred to above are probably the more convenient source for the genealogist. There are 283 volumes of them surviving, covering the period 1750 to 1888. These are in book form and summarize in alphabetical order the information given in the attestation forms. Rather less valuable, because of their later date, are the more modern 'Registers of Service' (Adm. 159), which cover from 1842 to 1905 in 79 volumes. These give similar information to that found in the Attestation Forms and some additional information.

Recently the Royal Marines appointed an official Corps Historian, who has his office at Eastney Barracks, Southsea, Hants, and is helpful in providing any information he can about the Corps. He is usually able to provide a record of officers' services of more recent times and it may be advisable to discover from him what he has available before visiting the P.R.O.

$\lceil 14 \rceil$

ARMY RECORDS

As in the case of the Navy, the main bulk of the Army records are held at the Public Record Office and, like the Admiralty records, they are very extensive. Regimental records, however, are now held at Army Record Offices in various parts of the country.

As with the senior service, the tracing of an officer's career is naturally easier than that of someone in the ranks. There are no collective biographies of army officers as a whole, like Marshall's *Royal Naval Biography* or O'Byrne's great work. Had a work been produced, say, about 1820, it would have included all those who had survived Waterloo and would have been most valuable. There are, however, a great many regimental histories, varying greatly in quality. The best of these are very good and often give accounts of officers' services. An early series of regimental histories are those edited by F. Cannon, but many later histories are more accurate and more comprehensive. There is also the work of the Institute of Army Historical Research, which publishes a journal, the volumes of which contain a great amount of information about regiments and their officers and men.

The Regiment or Corps is the key to information in the Army. An officer can be traced fairly easily through the army lists. There are MS lists among the army records at the P.R.O. from 1702 onwards (W.O. 64) and the lists have been printed annually since 1754, though there is an isolated issue of 1740. There is also Charles Dalton's *English Army Lists and Commission Registers, 1661-1714,* in 6 volumes and his *George*

I's Army. The 13 volumes of Sir John W. Fortescue's *History of the British Army* are well indexed and contain references to hundreds of officers and men.

The earlier printed Army lists are not always indexed, but by the end of the eighteenth century they are regularly so and it is therefore not a long task to trace an officer through the successive volumes, noting his promotions and finally his disappearance from the lists. This may be because of his death, in which case you will find a notification of it in the pages of casualties. He may, on the other hand, have sold his commission, in which case you may find a reference to that also.

To trace an officer this way you naturally want to use a library where there is a good run of the lists on open access. The P.R.O. has a nearly complete set of them. The Society of Genealogists has a good run of them and some of the military clubs, like the United Service or the Army and Navy clubs, have good runs, and also the National Army Museum, Sandhurst.

At the P.R.O. there are valuable returns of services for officers at various periods. These do not unfortunately start very early, but the 1828 returns of officers retired on full pay and half-pay and the 1829 active list full-pay returns are especially valuable for the detailed information they give.

The 1828 (half-pay) return (W.O. 25) gives, among other details, the age on first appointment, the date of the latter and the regiment in which commissioned; the successive promotions and dates, whether placed on half-pay by reduction or by the purchase of a half-pay commission, etc., if desirous of further service; the total length of service on full pay and half-pay; whether married and, if so, the date and place of marriage, and the general place of residence during the last five years.

The 1829 (full-pay) return (W.O. 25 and W.O. 76) gives all the above details with some important additional ones, namely, the place and date of birth; whether first commission obtained by purchase or otherwise, details of any campaigns in which the officer has taken part; an account of service abroad; if married, details of place and date and name of wife and indication if she is still alive, names of legitimate children, with their date of birth and place of baptism; total service, divided into time abroad and time at home.

In both the above return you get the signature of the officer making it.

The returns of services of officers retired on full pay and half-pay of 1847, being more recent and referring only to retired or half-pay officers, is not for those reasons so valuable. Nevertheless it may prove very useful in filling in gaps and in giving a succinct account of an officer's service.

This return gives the following information: Name, rank and regiment; full christian names and surname; age at time of the return and on entering the service; dates of the various commissions held; date of last retirement or entry on to the half-pay list and cause of retirement (whether arising from reduction, the decision of a medical board, at own request or in consequence of regimental proceedings); if under sixty, whether fit to serve again or under any disability and also whether engaged in any employment which would interfere with serving permanently or temporarily on full pay and also, if under sixty, the number and ages of family and how many of them are capable of maintaining themselves; finally, the place of residence, parish and nearest post town, and the officer's signature.

In the early nineteenth century the War Office issued instructions that officers were to report their marriages and these reports give the officer's age on marriage, the name and age of the bride, the place and date of the ceremony and the names of the officiating clergyman and witnesses. These returns are to be found in W.O.25 at the P.R.O.

There are also card indexes there for the half-pay returns of 1828 and for the Reports of Officers' Marriages from about 1810 and there is a card index in progress for the Records of Officers' Services from 1829 onwards (W.O. 25 and W.O. 76).

Another valuable source of information about officers' careers is the Commander-in-Chief's Memoranda (W.O. series 31). In earlier times there was no Royal Military Academy to enter by competitive examination or possibility of being selected from the ranks to go to an O.C.T.U. Officers had to be recommended by persons in influential position and approved by the colonel of the regiment into which they aspired to obtain a commission. They could be recommended for a commission either with or without purchase. There has been much nonsense talked about the purchase of commissions. Some people seem to think that you were just able to go along to some army agent and buy a commission, like buying a pound of tea at the grocer's. The purchase of a commission was only part of the procedure. It was really a kind of payment down as an indemnity, rather like the caution money at Oxford and Cambridge colleges. It was returnable to you when you gave up your commission in that you could then sell it to some other approved purchaser. The same happened when promotion occurred. You had to pay the difference between the purchase money of that rank and the value of your own commission. Higher ranks were more expensive, of course, and also prices varied according to the regiment. A cavalry commission was more expensive, as being more exclusive, than an infantry regiment, and such famous regiments as the Life Guards or Horse Guards, which formed the Household Cavalry, were the most expensive of all. Promotion was, of course, dependent on vacancies, and the sad thing was when a perfectly efficient and otherwise eligible officer could not raise the money for his next step in promotion and had to let it pass and see the officer below him buy it and step up above him. The system had many faults, but not nearly as many as some people allege it had. There were always ways of granting promotion to really outstanding officers without purchase and there are many examples of people like Major-General James Wolfe, who reached high rank without either influence or wealth.

Genealogically, however, these Commander-in-Chief's Memoranda are most interesting. You will often find in the bundle concerned the letters of recommendation and will learn from them a great deal about the young man anxious to obtain a commission. You will discover, for instance, the names of the people who recommended him. These will probably be friends or at least acquaintances and their letters will also often indicate where the applicant was living. There will also be a letter of application, probably with the applicant's home address, mentioning the regiment in which he desires to be commissioned, and possibly giving reasons why. Perhaps he has had relatives who have served in it, and these may be mentioned by name.

By the end of the eighteenth century the price to be paid for commissions in the various regiments had been regulated. There were, in fact, printed forms and the future officer had to declare and certify 'upon the Word and Honour of an Officer and a Gentleman, That I will not, either now or at any future Time, give, by any Means, or in any Shape whatever, directly or indirectly, any more than the Sum of ... being the full Value of the said Commission as the same is limited and fixed by His Majesty's Regulation.' The colonel of the regiment also, in making his recommendation, had to state, 'I veritably believe the established Regulations with regard to Price is intended to be strictly complied with, and that no Clandestine Bargain subsists between the Parties concerned.' These Memoranda papers (W.O. Series 31) begin in 1793.

When an officer sold his full-pay commission and purchased a half-pay commission he went on to the Half-Pay Register. If he died while still holding such a commission, there would probably be some small balance of pay due to him and this had to be disposed of, so that in the Half-Pay Warrants you should find details of this, giving probably the date on which the officer died and either the name of the executors or, if the officer died intestate, the person to whom Letters of Administration were granted. These wills or adminstrations were nearly always proved or taken out in the P.C.C. and further useful information may be derived from consulting them.

The records of applications for cadetships at the Royal Military Academy, Woolwich, or at the Royal Military College, Sandhurst, when later on they were established, usually had baptismal certificates with them to show the applicant's age.

Officers' records are mostly at the P.R.O., but those of other ranks will be in one of the Army Record Offices throughout the country. Since the Second World War there has been much reorganization of the Army and, with the reduction of regiments, many have been amalgamated and the regiments have been grouped into brigades, such as the Home Counties Brigade, the Lancastrian Brigade, the Wessex Brigade and the Light Infantry Brigade. This has also meant the amalgamation of many regimental record offices. A list of the present record offices, indicating the regiments which the particular office includes, will be found in *Whitaker's Almanack*, indexed under 'Army Record Offices'.

A great deal of information can be discovered about a man who served in the ranks of the Army. The first need is to discover in which regiment he served. This is not as difficult as it sounds. Usually there is some idea in the family, some old cap badge retained or some tradition remembered. These regimental records usually start towards the end of the eighteenth century, though the Royal Artillery has muster rolls going back to 1719 and quite a number of units and regiments have records from the mid-eighteenth century.

These muster rolls are arranged by ranks, officers, sergeants, corporals, drummers, privates, casuals, etc., and within each group they are entered in the order in which the men joined. From 1790 onwards they are usually in bound books. The muster will usually show on the man's first muster on joining, his place of birth and age on enlistment and sometimes an indication of his trade.

Starting from a somewhat later date are the Description Books, which give fuller information about each man, not to help future genealogists, but so that he could be traced if he ever deserted. They give usually the date and place of enlistment, age, perhaps the trade, height, colour of eyes and hair and description of his complexion. Some of these Description Books go back to 1795. It is quite a remarkable thing that you may be able to discover the colour of your ancestor's eyes and hair, an ancestor who was serving perhaps at Waterloo as a private soldier.

The Chaplains Returns usually cover only stations abroad. They record details of birth and baptism, marriage and death and burial of men in the Army and their families between 1796 and 1880. These records are, however, at the General Register Office, Somerset House. There is a comprehensive index of these returns covering the whole period. A small fee is charged for search in it.

There is also at the General Register Office a series of registers of regiments stationed both at home and abroad, which has records of births, baptisms, marriages, deaths and burials both of officers and other ranks, and their families. These registers go back to 1790 and there is an index of births and baptisms but not for the marriages, deaths and burials. Here again these can be consulted for a small fee.

There are Records of Service for the Royal Artillery at the P.R.O. which cover both officers and men for the period 1756 to 1917. These records give the name, description, place of birth, trade, length of service, details of promotion, discharge or death.

There are also a series of returns of Widows' Pensions for the period 1735 to 1912; pensions for Wounds and Superannuation, 1814 to 1920 (P.M.G. 9); Pension Returns of the Royal Hospital, Chelsea (W.O. 116), 1842 to 1883; Miscellaneous Pensions, 1795 to 1856 and some other similar returns. The Casualty Returns, 1809 to 1857, are valuable where you know an ancestor was killed in battle. As in the case of the Navy, the courts martial records can give much information about ancestors who have gone astray. They cover the period 1684 to 1847.

⌐15⌐

THE EAST INDIA COMPANY

This great company, sometimes known as 'The Hon. John Company' founded in 1601 as a trading company, became one of the greatest administrative units the world has known. Its trade grew and grew and many of our great families of today owe their rise in the social world to the wealth which their ancestors in this company brought back with them when, after their profitable years abroad, they retired to England.

The returning 'nabobs' became a feature of English life in the eighteenth and early nineteenth centuries. They often entered Parliament and usually settled in pleasant and large estates, suitable to their new fortunes and status, often regarded by their older-established neighbours as *nouveau riche* but gradually living this down and becoming absorbed, through the osmotic trend which has always been a feature of English society, into the aristocracy or landed gentry. One can think of families like that of the Kennaways of Escot, Devon, whose ancestor, Sir John Kennaway, concluded with the Nizam of Hyderabad a treaty of alliance against Tippoo Sultan, for which service he was in 1791 created a baronet. He married a daughter of James Amyatt, sometime M.P. for Totnes and Southampton and a former free merchant and sea-captain in the service of the company. These Anglo-Indian families frequently intermarried and this was notably so in the military service, as can be seen from that valuable work by Brigadier V. C. P. Hodson, *Officers of the Bengal Army*, of paramount use from a genealogicial point of view.

The East India Company's records are among the finest in the world. This material is now available in the India Library in the Commonwealth Office in King Charles Street, Whitehall, which is a true gold mine for the historian and researcher.

In 1771 an official was appointed by the company to take charge of the records and from that time forward they are remarkably good. But even the earlier records, though they had no single official responsible for their preservation, have been well looked after and much work has been done and is being done towards publishing them. It is interesting that, although India and Pakistan are today republics, both these countries, especially India, have done much work on these records and the publishing of them.

The company was a trading company and its ancillary forces, its army and navy, only came into existence as forces for protection against attack by natives or by some other country. As early as 1606 this 'civil service', as it became called from about 1750, was organized in grades, such as merchants, factors, writers and cadets. The careers of these early civilians can only be traced through the *Court Minutes, Original Correspondence, Factory Records, Consultations* and so forth. But from the mid-eighteenth century more information can be discovered from the *Writers' Petitions*, beginning in 1749 and continuing until 1805. In the early years they may be scanty or missing but in general they should give you information regarding parentage and place and date of birth. From 1806 to 1856 similar information can be obtained from the 70 volumes called *Committee of College Reference*, the college being the old East India Company College, now Haileybury College. There is a two-volumed index covering the whole period from 1749 to 1857.

Persons applying for a writership had to submit a certificate from a teacher stating that the applicant was competent in the elementary general principles of mercantile accounts and had also to forward a copy of a baptismal or birth certificate the former duly certified by the incumbent and the two churchwardens. A number of the company's civil servants had in addition to provide a bond in the sum of £500 with two people as securities. These could be friends or possibly relations and so are a useful clue. Registers for the civil servants abroad exist from 1741 and are indexed. There are also bonds starting in 1788 for those employed at home, such as the clerks at East India House in London.

Apart from the MS returns relating to the three main stations of Bengal, Madras and Bombay, which in the case of Bengal start in the early eighteenth century, there are the three printed volumes by Dodwell and Miles covering the period 1780 to 1838 for the three stations and the *Register of Bengal Civil Servants, 1790-1842*, by H. T. Prinsep, and a *Record of Services of Madras Civilians, 1741–1858*, by C. C. Prinsep.

There are good records of officers who served in the company's army from 1790, when applications for cadetships are recorded in a series of 147 volumes called *Cadet Papers*. These contain among other details certificates of baptism and are well indexed in ten volumes, so the parentage of a military officer is not difficult to ascertain in the period from 1790 to 1860, during which some 20,000 young gentlemen entered the company's army service. From 1809 the papers record, or should record if properly filled in, the school at which the applicant was educated and also the profession, situation and residence of the parents or next-of-kin. It is interesting to note that in the twenty-five years from the time this detail was recorded, that is, from 1809 to 1834, Charterhouse sent more young men into the service than any other of the principal English public schools, followed closely by Westminster and then, in order, Rugby, Eton, Winchester, Harrow, Blundell's, Shrewsbury and Merchant Taylors.

There are numerous sources through which an officer's career can be traced, though it may require patience and considerable labour. However, if you are fortunate, you may find your officer among the limited number in some MS volumes called 'Service Army Lists' in the Military Record Department. This series, which appears to have been compiled about 1839 in England from details forwarded from

India and then continued to 1859, will give you details of the officer's career and service. They are divided into the three main presidencies, Bengal having 48 volumes, Madras 29, and Bombay 16, each presidency being well indexed. There are also numerous MS army lists for the eighteenth century and printed ones by the time the nineteenth century had begun. Then there are the valuable series from 1803 of *East India Registers* which, among other matters, contain lists of army officers.

Prior to about 1790, when the cadet papers start, the appointment of military officers can only be traced through the *Court Minutes, Despatches* or *Proceedings.* Although this is cumbersome and lengthy, nevertheless the material is mostly there, and these are among the records which the Republic of India are continually publishing.

Embarkation Lists, from 1753 to 1860, give details of all ranks embarking for India and also details of civilians, such as free merchants and their wives.

Lord Clive's Fund gives useful information about recipients of this bounty, such as widows or orphans of officers and others. Beginning in 1770 it often discloses information of families not otherwise easily discovered.

The Medical Services of the company have been well covered by a published work, which largely saves any further research. This is Lieut.-Colonel D. G. Crawford's *History of the I.M.S.*, 2 vols., 1914, and his later work, *Roll of the I.M.S., 1615 to 1859.*

The Veterinary Service has a volume of certificates covering the period 1826 to 1859.

The company had both a naval and a merchant navy service. Genealogical details of sea-officers in these services are less easy to trace. There are three volumes of baptismal certificates of some officers, covering the period 1780 to 1830, mentioned in Section III of the *List of Marine Records*, under 'Miscellaneous'. Fuller details of the marine records will be found in the *List of Marine Records of the late East India Company*, published in 1896. From about 1702 ships' logs are fairly complete and there are some accounts of earlier voyages from 1605. The logs often contain lists of officers, crew and passengers on board. A printed list, *Register of Ships employed in the Service of the Hon. the United E.I.Co.*, compiled by Charles Hardy was published in 1798 and his son Horatio C. Hardy compiled two supplementary volumes, which bring the work down to 1812. From then onwards the *East India Register* gives similar information. C. R. Low's *History of the Indian Navy, 1613–1863*, should also be consulted.

There were certain employees of the company known as 'Uncovenanted Civilians', who were only available for subordinate appointments, and were sometimes known as 'Monthly Writers'. There are various lists of these, the earliest being in 1774 of some of them employed under the Calcutta Committee of Revenue. Another, of 1783, is in the *Bengal Public Consultations* of the 29th May that year.

From the earliest times of the company until 1834 no one was allowed to go to India unless he had the company's permission, nor could he live there without a licence. A considerable body of such people were the 'Free Merchants', that is, people trading in India who were not employees of the company. Naturally there were many anxious to go out there, as fortunes were to be made fairly easily in the early days, so permission was a privilege not casually granted. Applications appear in the *Court Minutes* and permission may be granted in these records and an announcement made in the *Despatches*. Free merchants had to obtain securities, and the names of the people acting as such will also be given in the *Court Minutes*. In later times lists of persons in India not servants of the company are shown in a special series, commencing in Madras in 1702, in Bombay in 1719 and in Bengal in 1794. The *East India Register* from 1803 to 1837 contains similar lists. There are also twenty-five volumes (1766–1829) covering Europeans who were not employees of the company and who had been accused of misconduct.

There is a large series of more than 800 volumes, entitled 'Home Miscellaneous', covering a multitude of matters. A detailed catalogue of these, with a good index, was compiled by S. C. Hill and published by the India Office in 1927.

From early times chaplains at the various factories or stations forwarded home copies of their baptismal, marriage and burial registers, so that even where the originals have been lost, as those of St Anne's, Calcutta were during the time of the 'Black Hole' and siege, certified copies are available. These cover the periods, Bengal from 1713, Madras from 1698 and Bombay from 1709. There are also Roman Catholic registers for Bengal and Madras from 1836 and Bombay from 1842. A great many of the registers have been published and also many of the inscriptions on European tombs in India. In addition to this there are many MS copies of registers and monumental inscriptions at the Society of Genealogists, where there is also a monumental card index of information about people in India, compiled by Lieut.-Colonel H. K. Percy-Smith, covering military, naval, merchant marine and civilians.

The wills and inventories of early company servants are often recorded in the *Consultations,* and in the *Factory Miscellaneous* series there is a volume for the years 1618-1620 and 1657–1725. In the Ecclesiastical Record Department at the India Library there is a MS alphabetical list of wills and administrations covered by the Mayor's Court for the following years: Bengal, 1704–1779; Madras, 1753–1779; Bombay, 1728–1783, and there is also a register of all wills proved in the three presidencies for the following years, namely, Bengal from 1728; Madras from 1736 and Bombay from 1723 onwards. Then there are records of grants of probate and of administration as follows: Bengal, wills from 1780; administrations from 1777; inventories from 1780: Madras, wills and administrations from 1780; inventories and accounts from the same date. Bombay: wills and administrations from 1783; inventories and accounts from 1798. Each of the presidencies has an index and it is therefore a simple task to trace a particular name.

There are many printed sources, particularly for the later period, the late eighteenth century and nineteenth century. One can only indicate a small number in this very large field. There is, for instance, S. C. Hill's *Bengal in 1756,* and his list of Europeans and others in the English Factories in Bengal at the time of the siege of Calcutta in that year, a most detailed and useful list, giving sources of information and references. There is Prebendary H. B. Hyde's *The Parish of Bengal* and *The Parochial Annals of Bengal;* the valuable *Guide to the India Office Records, 1600 to 1858,* by Sir William Foster, the *Court Minutes of the East India Company,* published in a number of volumes covering the period from 1601 to the mid-seventeenth century. Then there are the many periodicals, like the *Asiatic Journal,* which began publication in 1816, the earlier *Asiatic Annual Register,* unfortunately unindexed, which covered the first dozen years of the nineteenth century and last, and undoubtedly the most valuable and already frequently referred to in this chapter, the *East India Register and Army List,* which was issued twice yearly from 1803 to 1860 and covers such matters as casualties, notices of births, marriages and deaths, lists of Europeans not in the company's service and shareholders of East India stock, with their place of residence. As previously mentioned, it also gives lists of ships with the names of owners, commanders and principal officers.

For fuller details of these records you should consult an excellent article on 'India Office Records' in the *Genealogists' Magazine* for March 1933 by V. C. P. Hodson, whose work has already been referred to and who is an expert on East India Company records.

The Central Library at Poplar, London E.14, has some records relating to the East India Company's hospital there, which was demolished in 1866.

You will see that, if you had an ancestor in this great and unique company, there is plenty of material for you to search for information about him and, as so large a number of families were connected with this company, the chances are that you will sooner or later come across one of your own ancestors so connected.

[16]

JEWS, HUGUENOTS AND
OTHER IMMIGRANTS

The Romans invaded and conquered Britain in 55 B.C. and occupied it for many years. But they eventually returned to Rome, though no doubt some soldiers, having married British wives, stayed behind and became farmers and there must be diminutive portions of Roman blood in British descendants living today. The Anglo-Saxons invaded, conquered and stayed, eventually intermingling with the Britons, so that today we regard ourselves as an Anglo-Saxon race, though the Norman conquest in 1066 brought in its turn much French blood into our veins.

The Normans were the last invaders, but England has long been the refuge for the persecuted and homeless and among these one particularly remembers the Jews and the Huguenots.

The Jews for many generations in England suffered oppression and restrictions on their liberty and it was not until the last century that their final disabilities, such as their right to stand for parliament, to be Lord Mayor of London, or to be even a freeman of that city, were finally removed.

From earliest times there had been settlements of Jews in England until they were expelled from the country by King Edward I in 1290. From then until Cromwell's time they were not allowed to settle in England, but in 1655 the Protector allowed them to return and a number came over, particularly during Charles II's reign, when Dr Fernando Mendes, a Portuguese Jew, was appointed physician in ordinary to Queen Catherine of Braganza.

The Jews who came to England during the late seventeenth

century were of two kinds, the Iberian or Sephardim, and the Eastern European or Ashkenazim. The former, whose numbers in London in 1680 are said to have been about 2,000, descended from the refugees of Spanish oppression in the fifteenth century who had fled to Portugal and while there were forced by Manuel I to take the Christian faith and be baptized. But not unnaturally they always secretly maintained their faith and came to England when the opportunity occurred, to escape further oppression. Some of them came here via other parts of the Continent, particularly the Low Countries. Among those that came from Holland was a Henriques, ancestor of the late Sir Basil Henriques, who did so much for the Jews in the East End of London and founded the Bernard Baron St George's Jewish Settlement in the street which is now named after him, and whose work is being carried on so ably today by Lady Henriques, his widow.

These Sephardic Jews had earlier intermarried with the Spanish, many with the aristocracy and had been on the whole wealthy, mainly merchants or bankers, and they were a helpful influence in England's commercial life. Although they were at first, and are even today, a closely-knit community, intermarrying within their own religion, some gradually infiltrated into other spheres through marriage with Christians or through becoming Christians. Many people therefore in investigating their ancestry may discover, perhaps to their surprise, that they have Jewish forbears.

The Sephardic Jews are fairly easy to trace, for they have distinctive surnames and tended because of their interest in commerce, to be centred in London. Their synagogue was the great synagogue in Bevis Marks, and their marriages, published in 1949, are particularly useful in giving the parentage of both bride and bridegroom. The birth and burial registers of this community can also be seen.

Some of these Jews kept their names and the coats of arms to which many of them were entitled. Mr W. S. Samuel, in an interesting lecture to the Society of Genealogists, delivered in March 1932 and published in the *Genealogists' Magazine* that year, gives the example of Dr Fernando Mendes, who was a court physician, and Senhor Alvaro da Costa, who, when they came to London after the Restoration, kept their names and coats-of-arms, making no outward show of their religion 'although subsequently the synagogue records refer to these two Portuguese gentlemen as Moses Mendes and Jacob da Costa'.

More often it was thought prudent to discard the ancestral name and take a Jewish name for the purposes of the faith but adopt a commercial pseudonym. Thus Abraham Israel de Sequeira of Bury Street traded there under the name of Gomez Rodriguez and his son, Isaac Israel de Sequeira, as Alphonso Rodriguez. Other sons of this Abraham took other surnames. They included Symon Henriques (who was sometimes called also Symon Rodriguez) and Pantaleon Rodriguez Mogadouro. Isaac Haim Pereira was known outside Jewish circles as Manuel Lopes Pereira and also, for trade purposes, as Manuel de Velasquez and also again as Jacques Vandepeere. One of the difficulties in tracing back these Jewish families is the fluidity of their surnames. However, once these Portuguese Jews were settled in England they retained the same surnames, though they might use another name for trade purposes, a custom which persists today just as much among non-Jewish as among Jewish people. In the course of time some of these Sephardim surnames became anglicized, Martinez becoming Martins, Rodriguez becoming Rogers, Benhamo, Benham, and Londo, Lindon.

The Sephardic Jews were regarded as the aristocracy of the Jewish word. The Ashkenazim were often poor refugees from oppression in Russia, Poland and Rumania. They came later than the Sephardim. A number came over during the eighteenth and early nineteenth century, but from 1880 onwards they came in increasing numbers, fleeing from the pogroms of inhospitable countries. Many arrived over here penniless and many settled in the East End of London, because the Anglo-Jewish community there went out of their way to welcome them, setting up in Whitechapel a board of guardians to look after their welfare, and also because there already existed in Stepney some synagogues and also opportunities for keeping the Jewish dietary laws. This accounts for the large Jewish population which Stepney possesses even today. Many of these Jews were tailors, cabinet makers, cigar makers, old clothes dealers or pedlars, but at the same time some were learned rabbis who had to earn their living by working at some trade.

These Jews, at any rate during their early days in England, tended to keep Jewish customs and retain their form of name, being known as son (Ben) of their father. This was rather like the custom in England before surnames were adopted, such surnames from personal names, as Johnson, deriving from 'John's son', and Robertson, from 'Robert's son'. Thus Isaac, a son of Israel, would be called Isaac ben Israel. Alternatively they were often known by the name of their birthplace. Samuel gives an example of this in Mordecai, the son of Moses, who came to London from Hamburg at the end of the seventeenth century and was known as Mordecai Hamburger, though among gentiles he was known as Marcus Moses, and his eldest son, among Jews, was known as Moses ben Mordecai, but in general circles as Moses Marcus, the name Marcus being a variant of the Biblical Mordecai. These Ashkenazic Jews who settled in England tended to alter their names, which in due course became the surnames of their descendants. Thus Jews called Zevi, which in Hebrew means 'a stag', became by Teutonic translation 'Hirsch', or 'Hirschel', which sometimes became anglicized into 'Hart' and even developed into 'Harris'. 'Ben Uri' became 'Phillips' and 'Ben David', 'Davis'. Another example of name-change is found in the well-known Jewish family of Lopez. Sir Massey Lopes, created a baronet in 1805, from whose sister the present Lord Roborough, Lord Lieutenant of Devon, descends, was originally called Menasseh Lopez.

Jewish records of birth, marriage and burial exist in the various synagogues throughout England and there have been publications of some of these by the Jewish Historical Society in their Transactions. Some notice of them is made in 'Jewish Ancestors and where to find them', an article by Edgar R. Samuel, a son of W. S. Samuel, in the *Genealogists' Magazine*,

XI, 412 (December 1953). The works of Cecil Roth and of A. M. Hyamson should also be consulted. There are also great collections of Anglo-Jewish genealogies, like that of the late Sir Thomas Colyer-Fergusson, which he bequeathed to the Jewish Historical Society of England and which are now housed in the Jewish Museum at Woburn House, London W.C.1.

There is a valuable alphabetical index by Arthur Arnold of all the ascertainable wills and administrations of Jews proved in the P.C.C. This is contained in *Anglo-Jewish Notabilities*, published by the Jewish Historical Society of England in 1949, and this same volume also contains a brief biographical dictionary and a list of Anglo-Jewish coats of arms.

In general the amount of matter available relating to Jewish families is quite considerable and because they were a closely knit community their ancestry sometimes, for that very reason, is more easily revealed than that of the main English population. This applies equally to the next great community to be considered.

The Huguenots

The main wave of Huguenot refugees came to this country during the latter part of the seventeenth century following the revocation of the Edict of Nantes in 1685. These French protestants, fleeing from religious persecution, set up their own churches in this country and for several generations continued to use their native tongue, though they soon learnt English.

Many Huguenots settled in London, mainly in the area around Spitalfields and here there are still a few of their houses to be seen with their long extra-wide top floor windows which were designed to allow maximum light for their silk-weaving looms. There are still street names which bring them to memory, streets such as Fleur-de-Lys Street and Fournier Street. Other Huguenots settled further outside at Wandsworth, or in provincial towns like Norwich, Southampton, Bristol, Exeter and Plymouth.

Gradually they became absorbed in the life of this country, though still looking with lingering nostalgia back to their homeland. Today nearly all the French churches have disappeared and the Huguenots worship in English churches, and in many cases their names have been anglicized, so that people are often unaware of their Huguenot origins. The Huguenot Society has published a number of their records and several of their genealogies are well documented. This society was founded in 1885 for the purpose, among other matters, of publishing Huguenot archives and literature. Among these have been many of the Huguenot church registers and the Returns of Aliens and Certificates of Denization (or naturalization). In England there are three libraries devoted to Huguenot archives and records. These are the libraries of the Dutch church of Austin Friars and L'Eglise de Londres, better known as the Threadneedle Street church, and the joint library of the French Hospital and the Huguenot Society. The manuscripts of the Dutch church have recently been deposited on permanent loan in the Guildhall Library. Some of their records have been published, edited by J. H. Hessels.

The Threadneedle Street Church Library, which is next to the French Protestant church in Soho Square, has records not only of its own church but also of several other London churches, and its collection has been described in the *Proceedings of the Huguenot Society* XIV and XVIII. The same proceedings, XIII, give an account of the third library, the combined one of the French Hospital and of the Huguenot Society itself. This library is now housed at University College, Gower Street, London. In addition a number of other libraries have collections of Huguenot archives, among them the two university libraries at Oxford and Cambridge, the Guildhall Library, Dr Williams Library and that at Lambeth Palace.

Huguenot records are on the whole well kept and many of their church registers date from the late seventeenth century, or from the time these Huguenot churches were first established in these islands. Some thirty volumes of these registers have been published. A number of original registers are at the Public Record Office. Among other records churches often have lists of congregations at various periods.

Among the most valuable publications of the Huguenot Society are those concerning denization, naturalization and returns of aliens. They cover the period from 1523 to 1800 and cover other races beside the Huguenots themselves, such as the Jews.

There are also many purely genealogical records held by the Society. C. E. Lart's valuable MS collection was given to the Hospital Library by his daughter after his death. This is a very large collection by a specialist in Huguenot genealogy and also in French *noblesse*. They include seventeenth and eighteenth century French armorials. Then there is the Wagner collection of pedigrees, which are listed in Volume XIII of the *Proceedings* and for which there is also a card index at the Hospital Library, which includes some additions to the collection. There are also abstracts by the same compiler of Huguenot wills at Somerset House.

While some Huguenot surnames, like Bosanquet and Minet, continue in their French form, others, as mentioned, have been severely anglicized, which is rather sad and unfortunate. For instance 'Chapuis' has become 'Shoppee', some Beaumonts are now Beemans and Batteleurs have lost their French identity in 'Butler'. These have at least some semblance of their former structure. Much more difficult to connect are those which have been translated into their English equivalent. 'Le Blanc' has become 'White', 'De la Rue' been transformed into 'Street'. These are, unfortunately, often difficult to trace, because no record may have been made of the change.

Not all Huguenots came direct to this country. Some may have emigrated first to Switzerland, Holland or one of the German states, and then later emigrated to England. The whole history of these people is a fascinating one and many of us in our pursuit of ancestors, in discovering Huguenots among them, may thus be introduced to another intriguing facet of our history.

Other Immigrants

As a country with a reputation for giving sanctuary to people escaping oppression, England has naturally in the course of its history attracted many such people. Among them were those who came here to escape from the terrors of the French Revolution in 1789. Some of these were aristocrats, many of whom eked out an existence by teaching dancing in places like Cheltenham and Bath. The majority of them returned to France when the restoration came, but a few married English wives or husbands and settled down in this country. Many of these French immigrants were in distressed circumstances. Some account of them can sometimes be traced in the grants in aid of the 'French Emigrés in England', which are recorded in the Bouillon Papers in the P.R.O., the Prince de Bouillon having been appointed the administrator of the help given to these refugees by the British Government. A good general account of them is given in *The French Exiles* by Margery Weiner, published in 1960.

There were lesser influxes after the second and third French revolutions, but there were some refugees from European countries following the year of revolution, 1848. Then there have been the immigrants from the Russian Revolution after the First World War and those from Poland after the Second World War. Many of the latter have changed their names, some unfortunately to prevent retaliatory action being taken against their relatives in their home country. It is particularly important and desirable that their ancestry should be recorded, even if this is kept from publication, so that their links with their former country may not be lost and that their descendants may know their true origin.

[17]

SCOTTISH RECORDS I

The Scottish people have always been interested in their forbears and, being an exact and legally-minded race, have kept careful records. So that, apart from some haphazard destruction during their troubled times, such as the destruction of the Brechin Burgess records during the '45, their records are rich in genealogical material, far richer in most ways than those of England.

Civil registration of births, marriages and deaths began later in Scotland. It was not until 1855 that Scottish law required such registration. But when it did start it was greatly superior to that of England or Ireland, in fact the first year of that registration may be called the *annus mirabilis* for genealogical searchers in Scotland, for the amount of detail in all the certificates is quite astonishing. Unfortunately they attempted something a little too thorough and found the difficulties in obtaining such full details too great to keep up. Therefore a modified certificate came out in 1856 and this was again slightly modified and improved upon in 1861 and the marriage certificate only was again a little altered in 1922.

This year 1855, this *annus mirabilis*, gives the following details.

Birth Certificate
The name and baptismal name if different; sex; year, date of month and hour of birth; place of birth (if in lodgings, so stated); father's name, rank, profession or occupation, his age and birthplace, when and where he was married and his other

issue, both living and deceased; the mother's name and maiden name, her age and birthplace; the signature of the father or mother or other informant, and residence if out of the house in which the birth occurs; when and where registered and the signature of the Registrar.

The 1855 *Marriage Certificate* gives for bride and bridegroom:

The date and place of the marriage and in what form the marriage took place; the present and the usual residence; age, rank or profession and, if related, the relationship of the parties; status (widow or widower and if so whether second or third marriage and the number of children by each former marriage, living and dead); birthplace, and when and where registered; the names with the rank, profession or occupation of both the parents in each case; if a regular marriage, the signature of the officiating minister and of the witnesses, or if irregular, the date of the extract, sentence of conviction or decree of declarator and in what court pronounced; the date and place of registration and signature of the Registrar.

The 1855 *Death Certificate* gives the following information:

Name, rank, profession or occupation; sex and age; place of birth and length of time in the district; names, rank, profession or occupation of both parents; if married, wife's name; issue in order of birth, their names and ages; year, date of month and hour of death; place of death; cause and how long the disease continued, medical attendant certifying, and when he last saw the deceased; burial place and name of undertaker certifying it; signature of informant (usually mentioning relationship if related); date and place of registration and signature of the Registrar.

You will notice the valuable additional information over the English certificates; for instance, in the birth certificate the mention of the parents' age and place of birth and the place and date of their marriage; in the marriage certificates the details of any former marriages, with issue if any, and the birthplace of the parties; in the death certificate the place of birth of the deceased, the names of the deceased's parents and the details of any marriage and any issue of it. This is infinitely superior to any corresponding certificate in England and Wales or in Ireland and is probably not excelled by any of the certificates in the dominions, many of which are very full.

But even the curtailed form of certificates gives more valuable information than the corresponding certificates in England and probably in most other places. In the birth certificates 1856–60, the age and birthplace of the parents is omitted and also details of their marriage and of any other issue; but in the certificates from 1861 onwards the date and place of parents' marriage is restored.

In the marriage certificates 1856–60 the heading 'Residence' is substituted for 'Residence, Present, Usual', and details of any former marriage and issue and the birthplace of the parties are omitted: from 1861 onwards the information is substantially the same, the heading 'Residence' being altered to the more useful 'Usual Residence'. In the 1922 certificates the information is also similar, except that the names of the parties, in addition to their signatures, are given in full, the only information being omitted is the relationship, if any, of the bride and bridegroom.

The Death Certificates from 1856 to 1860 omit the deceased's place of birth and details of any marriage and its issue. From 1861 onwards the information is in effect the same, except that the burial place and the undertaker's certification are not included.

It will be seen there that even in these curtailed certificates the value of the information is greatly superior to that given in the English certificates. These advantages may be summarized as follows: In the *Birth Certificate* (except for 1856–60) the date and place of parents' marriage; in the *Marriage Certificate* the name and maiden surname of the mother of each party, and, in the *Death Certificate*, the deceased's condition (married, single, widower, widow), his parents' names and the rank, profession or occupation of his father. There are of course occasions when columns will be marked 'unknown' or left blank, particularly in the death certificate when, for instance, the deceased died in lodgings and the lodging-house keeper did not know the names of his parents. On the whole, however, they have been completed fully, the Scottish being a conscientious race regarding ancestry.

All these records are held in the New Register House, Princes Street, Edinburgh 2. If you want only to see a single entry, then for your 1s. 6d. fee you are allowed, unlike England, to see the original entry and to take notes in pencil of it. Only if you want an official certificate is it necessary to pay a further fee which is 3s. 9d. This is a great advantage to the genealogist, who seldom wants an official document, but usually only the information from it. If you want a certificate by post the fee is, as in England, 6s. 3d. for the search and 3s. 9d. for the certificate.

The general search fee is a pound and here again you have a far more liberal grant of time than in England. For this fee you can search any registers you like over a period of two working days. It is hoped that one day the English authorities will take a lesson from the Scottish in generosity and allow the records to be seen without having to get an official certificate. There are, in fact, good grounds for opening the records of over a hundred years ago free to bona fide searchers in the same way that the probate records are.

Parish Registers

The old parish registers in Scotland were often badly kept and probably far more of them have been lost than in England. Sometimes all that survives seems to be a rough note-book of the parish clerk, which may have been used to copy the entries into the actual register, which has subsequently been lost. Few of the registers, except in the larger towns, start before the early eighteenth century, some far later, for example, those of Stornoway in the Isle of Lewis in the Outer Hebrides, which did not start any register until 1780.

While the Scottish registers may not compare favourably with the English ones regarding regularity and commencement, they are usually in some respects better and possibly very much better. Scottish registers in fact are far more variable than the English ones and they seem to have depended more on the whim of the parish clerk. Sometimes he was conscientious and gave a great deal of information: at other times he was careless and gave little or none.

Another disadvantage is that there were virtually no records of burials. In some parishes there are accounts for the hire of the mortcloth at funerals which gives you an approximate date of death. Some of the larger burial grounds too have records of their burials but these are not normally of an early date. There has been some progress in recent years in the copying of monumental inscriptions in church graveyards, but so often there was no stone or the old stones were used again on the other side for new inscriptions. In the latter case you can of course sometimes make out the old inscription.

These are the principal disadvantages, but now let us turn to the advantages which on the whole more than compensate.

One of the great advantages in Scotland is the mention of the mother's maiden name. This was in accord with Scottish practice, when a woman was not regarded as losing her maiden name altogether on marriage. In all legal documents even today a woman will be referred to by both her maiden and married name, as, for instance, 'Mrs Mary Mackenzie or Gordon' for a Miss Mackenzie who had married a Mr Gordon. Thus the usual form for a baptism in a Scottish register is like this:

> Robert Johnston Son Lawful to Mr Daniel Johnston Surgeon in Cumnock and Mary McKie his Spouse was Baptized the 4th of Jany. 1754 years.
>
> (From the *Old Cumnock Parish Register*)

It will thus be appreciated that you discover the maiden name of the mother on finding the baptism of any of the children. Apart from the direct information it greatly aids identification, because in England with a common surname, such as 'Smith', you cannot be certain that a 'Jane, daughter of John and Mary Smith' was a sister of 'John, son of John and Mary Smith' even when in the same parish, but a daughter of a 'John Smith and Mary Robertson, his spouse' in Scotland could be identified as a sister of a 'John Smith' of similarly described parentage in the same parish.

Another help in baptisms is the not-infrequent recording of witnesses, for these were naturally often relations. Sometimes the relationship is even mentioned and occasionally the information is extensive. This is an example from Ayr parish register, but it must be emphasized that this amount of information is rare.

> 1739. John Hamilton son lawl. to John Hamilton merch. at present in Jamaica and Mrs Margarit Montgomery his spouse was born on Wednesday the 24th of Octr. 1739 bapt: thursday the 25 of the sd month by Mr Hugh Hamilton Mintr. of the Gospell at Garvine uncle to the Child. Presented by Alexander Montgomery of Coylsfield uncle to the child in absence of the Parent. Witnesses Thomas Garvan prit. Provost of Ayr uncle in law to the Child, Mr Patrick Woodrow mintr. of the Gospell at Tarbolton.

The recording of a child of good social position, as the above, tends to be fuller than those of people in the lower social scale. But this is not always so. Here, for instance, from the same parish, is one of the sons of a coalheaver which has very valuable information.

> 1734. Mathew Hall son lawl. to Mathew Hall Coalheaver in Newton & Helen Hunter his spouse was born friday the 8th of Feby. 1734 bapt. at Supra [i.e. Ayr] witness James Hall grandfather to ye child & John Hall uncle to the child.

Sometimes in fact the information can be diminished through the higher social position of the parents. For instance a baptism from Maybole Parish in Ayrshire merely records:

> Margaret Hall procreate betwixt Mr and Mrs Hall spouses in Auchindrain was born the 12th of July 1774 and baptized said day at her father's house by the Ordinary Minister.

The father in this case was a small landowner and the fact that he is described as 'Mr' indicates that he was of some local standing, but as a result we lose the christian names of both parents, the maiden name of the mother and, probably because the baptism was carried out privately in the home, the names of the witnesses also.

While the English tended to name sons after earlier generations, the Scottish were even more conventional in this matter and this is a help to the genealogist. The eldest son of an eldest son is nearly always named after the father's father, and the eldest daughter of an eldest daughter after the mother's mother. The second son is usually named after the father and the second daughter often after the mother. This applies also to a great extent in the families of the younger sons. Second christian names are seldom found until the nineteenth century,

A FINE OF 1193: The Latin original, with many words contracted, reads in extended form:– Haec est Finalis Concordia facta in Curia Domini Regis apud Westmonasterium a die Pasche in tres septimanas anno Regnon. Ricardi Regis Angliae et Franciae quarto...' 'This is the final agreement made in the Court of our Lord the King at Westminster in the third week from the day of Easter in the fourth year of the reign of Richard King of England and France'.

The fine, after recounting the names of the persons before whom the proceedings took place, show that John Waleys, clerk, William Snapedon and Nicholas Fortescue were the plaintiffs and John Boold and Margaret his wife the deforciants in a suit concerning five messuages and the quarter part of an acre of land in Sutton Prior and Sutton Vautor, near Plymouth, Devon. In the outcome the former paid John Boold and his wife ten silver marks.

These fines were in three parts, each being separated by cutting the parchment with a wavy line, as can be seen in the illustrations. The end part, known as the foot of fine, was registered and kept in Chancery and from the seventh year of King Richard I until this form of land transfer ceased during King William IV's reign the series is almost perfect. They are now kept in the Public Record Office.

If there was any dispute about the matter later the two parties had to bring their respective parts of the deed together and show that the wavy lines fitted. This was an ingenious and simple way of warding against fraud. Genealogically these fines help in tracing the descent of land and often establish relationships at an early period.

FROM THE AUTHOR'S MS COLLECTION.

but from about 1800 we get second names creeping in and these were sometimes surnames from the mother's family.

Often the witnesses, if not relations, were influential friends and this may prove useful information. In the larger towns the list may be both long and impressive. Here is one from the Canongate parish of Edinburgh:

> January 1701. John Hamilton of Bardonoch, Baillie of the Abbey of Hallyroodhouse and Catherine Arbuthnot alias Arbuckles his lady had a sone born upon monday ye 30 Oct 1700 and baptized upon fryday ye 10 of January 1701 Named Gerard after ye Surname of Elizabeth Dutchess of Hamiltoun: witnesses – Sir Archibald Cockburn of Lantourne, Sir John Johnstoun of Westerhall, John Cuninghame of Ba'ndalloch, Mr Gavin Johnstoun brother to Westerhall and several others.

The father was only remotely related to the Duke of Hamilton, but the latter was hereditary Keeper of the Palace of Holyroodhouse, and John Hamilton of Bardannoch was his deputy. The duchess referred to is the wife of the famous James Douglas, fourth Duke of Hamilton, who was killed in 1712 in the duel in Hyde Park with Charles, Lord Mohun (the 'Lord Murdered' of Thackeray's *Henry Esmond*). He had married, as his second wife, Elizabeth, daughter and heiress of Digby, Lord Gerard.

It will be noticed here, in accord with Scottish practice, the Laird of Westerhall is referred to by his estate instead of his surname.

This same John Hamilton of Bardannoch's own baptism

THE DIOCESES AND ARCHDEACONRIES OF ENGLAND IN 1797: This map, published by John Andrews on 18th November that year shows the diocesan boundaries and the general localities of the archdeaconries. It is therefore useful in indicating not only where a person's will is likely to have been proved, but also, for people married by licence, under whose authority that licence is likely to have been granted. The table at the side shows that the total number of churches in England and Wales at that time was 9083, and that there were 26 deaneries and 60 archdeaconries.

BODLEIAN LIBRARY, OXFORD.

in the Edinburgh 'High Kirk' parish register in 1642 gives an idea of the information in a register of that period. It is usually, as previously mentioned, only in the larger towns that you find a register going back as far as that.

> Baptism 25 Januarii 1642 Johnne Hamiltoun of Murehouse [and] Anna Elphingstoun a S.[on] N.[amed] Johnne. Witn: Johnne Mr of Balmironoch, Mr Johnne Cokburne, Mr Johnn Elvis Advocat.

It is interesting to note in the above entry that the abbreviation for the Scottish title of 'Master' is the same as the ordinary 'Mr', which indicates that they were still at that period both pronounced 'Master'.

In Scotland the registers give only the proclamation of marriage, which is somewhat like the banns in England, and therefore it is not an absolute proof that the marriage took place, though it normally did, of course. Sometimes the register will also state that it did so. Proclamations are usually recorded in both bride and bridegroom's parish and the information in one may be fuller than that in the other. As the record is of proclamation you do not get witnesses' names normally and this is a disadvantage compared with England after 1753. On the other hand, particularly in the larger parishes, the father of the bride is sometimes mentioned, though seldom the father of the bridegroom.

The following is an example from Edinburgh:

> *Marriage Proclamation.* 12 Decemr. 1794.
> Daniel Morison, Mercht. High Church parish and Margaret Montgomerie Hall, Tron kirk parish, Daughter of John Hall, Farmer at Ayr.

The following is an example from a small country town, Inch in Wigtownshire, and the corresponding entry in Ayr:

> *Inch Parish* Marriage Proclamations.
> August 19th 1797. Alexr. Kelly in this Parish and Catherine Hall in the Parish of Ayr gave in their Names in Order for Proclamation of marriage

Ayr Parish Marriage Proclamations
Ayr. 26th August 1797. Quo Die Alexander Kelly in the parish of Inch and Katharine Hall in Ayr parish gave in their Names to be proclaimed in Order for marriage and After proclamation were married accordingly.

It will be noticed that the entry in Ayr, where the marriage was performed, states that they were married.

In certain circumstances a marriage might be authorized by the Elders without proclamation. This corresponds roughly to the English licence, but it was not used so frequently and in fact is rare and there was no loss of social status in being married by proclamation.

Such an event would appear in the register usually in the form below, from the registers of Kilbride, Isle of Bute.

Under 'Marriage Proclamations'. 1729 July 30th Gerard Hamilton and Margaret Stewart were married without proclamation by appointment of Elders for certain honourable causes.

It will be noticed that the information in the marriage recordings is more uniform and regular than that of the baptisms. Its principal advantage over the English entry is that it often gives the name of the bride's father. On the other hand there are far more gaps in registers than in the English ones. Sometimes, though the register is not missing, there is a gap of twenty to thirty years in it, probably through the carelessness of the parish clerk in not bothering to make the entries.

The old registers are today well kept and carefully bound, but it is unfortunate that so few have been copied. The efforts of the Scottish Record Society have produced in print some half dozen or so, and these are about all that exist. It is to be hoped that some attempt will be made to have them either photostated or microfilmed, or a typed copy or duplicated copies of the registers made and indexed, thus saving wear and tear on the originals. Scotland, being a comparatively sparsely populated country has only some nine hundred old parishes and their registers are certainly among the most valuable records of that historic and romantic country. Here lies an opportunity for some philanthropist to give a sum to carry out a really worth-while piece of work.

$\lceil 18 \rfloor$

SCOTTISH RECORDS II

People tracing their ancestry in Scotland have several advantages over those doing so in England and Wales. One of these is the existence of the voluminous *Sasines Registers*. In Scotland the ceremony of taking possession of property in land, which took place in a traditional way on the ground itself, when the new owner took 'actual and corporal possession' receiving certain symbols, such as earth and stone, was carefully recorded in the appropriate registers. Something similar took place in England and Wales also, but unfortunately this transference of land was not recorded in any central register.

In Scotland, therefore, you can trace the ownership of a parcel of land, even if it is only a small cottage or croft, from at any rate the early seventeenth century. These records thus preserve the titles for the whole of the land in the kingdom.

The registers are in three parts, namely:

(i) The *Old General Register of Sasines*, 1617–1868 contained in 3,779 volumes. There are also minute books, which are kind of digests or abstracts and which are much the best way of searching the portions which are unindexed.

(ii) The *Particular Registers of Sasines* for the various counties, running parallel with the above General Register. For a brief period, 1599–1609, there is also what is known as the *Secretary's Register*.

(iii) The *New General Register*, which is kept in county divisions. This modern register had by 1928 reached 36,000 volumes and is increasing at the rate of about 500 folio volumes a year.

The Scottish Record Office is gradually indexing both the General Register and the various county particular registers. The county registers were being indexed alphabetically and have so far covered for varying periods as far as Forfarshire. If your ancestor lived in one of these counties you are lucky. The General Register has been indexed for the period 1700–1720.

From 1781 there are abridgements to the sasines, both general and particular and there are excellent indexes for both persons and places for these. The abridgements, though greatly reduced in length from the original documents, give most, if not all, of the information a genealogist is likely to want, so that it is often quite unnecessary to consult the original document, though it is always advisable to do so in the case of important members of the family, as there is sometimes hidden away in the original some significant item. For instance a person may be described in the abridgement as of such and such a place, whereas in the original he may be described as 'merchant' of such and such a place, this additional piece of information being perhaps vital.

It will be seen therefore that the ownership of land from 1781 is easily traced. The MS indexes are of course in the Historical Section of the Register House. If you are not able to pay a personal visit (but I think if you discover you have Scottish ancestry you will sometime want to visit the capital) then it will be necessary to get the services of a record searcher. There are several good ones with whom the Record Office will put you in touch.

Another valuable record is the *Retours of Service of Heirs*, usually referred to just as *Service of Heirs*. In Scotland when a landowner died his lands did not pass to his heir until the latter's claim had been established. This was done by a procedure under a Brief of Succession issued by Chancery. A jury, empanelled by the Sheriff of the County, had to decide that it was the true heir on the examination of proofs submitted to them. When the heir had proved his succession he had still to take sasine of the property. The relationship of the heir is always specified, and sometimes you may get a string of generations revealed, if a distant relative succeeds to some property.

These services exist from 1544. The early services have been published in three folio volumes, well indexed. These cover the period from the earliest recorded services to 1699. From 1700 onwards there are decennial indexes, which give the relationships and often all the information required by the pedigree seeker. The Special Services relate to land and the General Services to other property. The latter are particularly valuable in that there is no sasine record to supplement it.

One of the most valuable records is the *Register of Deeds*. This contains all deeds which had a clause consenting to their registration for preservation and execution. Almost anything may be recorded in this great register and often it can contain information of the highest value to the genealogist. At the moment a great portion of it is unindexed, though the indexing is progressing steadily. The searching of the unindexed portion is a somewhat laborious and tedious process, but may nevertheless be well worth while.

Like the Sasine Register, there are three series. The first, in 621 volumes, covers from 1554–1657. The second series is subdivided into three which run parallel with each other chronologically. They are divided between the three offices of the three principal clerks, i.e.,

(i) 313 volumes in Dalrymple's office
(ii) 350 volumes in Durie's office
(iii) 296 volumes in Mackenzie's office

and these cover the period from 1661 to 1811.

The third series is the more modern series and consequently of less interest to the genealogist, though the early period of it is valuable to him. It runs from 1812 to the present day and by 1928 had already reached 5,259 volumes and is increasing at the rate of about 80 volumes a year.

This third series is numbered consecutively and is indexed in MS. There are also printed indexes of the earlier periods published by the Scottish Record Office, down to 1692 (1966). The gap of the unindexed portion is therefore from then until 1811, but it is a gap which is gradually closing.

These are the principal public registers which are most likely to help the genealogist in Scotland. There are a number of other registers which may be helpful in particular cases. These are principally as under.

The *Registers of Acts and Decreets* contain the decisions of the Court of Session from 1542 to the present time. There is unfortunately no adequate index.

The *Register of Hornings, Inhibitions and Adjudications*. The *Horning* has a quaint and curious origin. It was a legal process by which a creditor could get redress against a debtor. The latter, on refusing to obey an order of the court, i.e. to pay his just debts, was denounced as a rebel against the King by a messenger-of-arms blowing three blasts on a horn. After this the debtor's goods were held escheat to the Crown against the creditor's claim, and the debtor was liable to imprisonment. This process is still current, though seldom today resorted to by creditors. The register consists of 1,284 volumes, covering the period 1610–1902. As there is no index its consultation is a matter of time and patience, but there is a minute book from 1661, which is the quickest method of tracking down information.

Letters of Inhibition prevented a debtor from alienating or burdening his hereditable property to the disadvantage of the creditors. The *Bond of Interdiction* was a voluntary method of obtaining the same result. There are two series of these registers and a minute book covering the period 1652 to 1868.

Scotland being a small country, the *Register of the Privy Council* often contains information about lesser people. Before the institution of the Court of Session in 1532 it had jurisdiction in civil and criminal cases. After that its functions were more limited, but covered appeals and seditious offences against the peace. The Register is printed in abbreviated form from 1545 to 1686 in eight volumes and is well indexed, so that it is easy to consult and therefore worth doing, even though the genealogical content may not be great.

The *Accounts of the Lord High Treasurer* have been published in eleven volumes from 1473 to 1566 and are equally well indexed and therefore as easily consulted.

The *Registrum Secreto Sigilli*, or Register of the Privy Seal, has been published from 1488 to 1542 in two volumes. It covers such matters as pensions, tacks of Crown lands, commissions to minor officers of state or of court, presentations to benefices and so forth.

The *Registrum Magni Sigilli*, or Register of the Great Seal, includes all the grants of land by the Crown to subjects, the confirmation of charters by these subjects to their vassals, patents of nobility, commissions to the great officers of state, letters of pardon and remission, of legitimation, charters of incorporation and a few birth-briefs, or certificates of descent.

A volume edited by Dr Maitland Thomson includes all the early surviving charters and also William Robertson's *Index of Missing Charters* (published in 1798) with a number of additions. This covers charters from 1306 to 1424. From that date onwards the registers have been printed in 10 volumes continuing the series down to 1668 and the work is still continuing. The charters are in condensed form and are in Latin to 1652, afterwards in English. There is hardly a family of any note in Scotland which does not appear somewhere in this register.

Notaries' Protocol Books contain sasines of lands, contracts of marriage, bonds and obligations and other legal transactions of a varied character. They often contain deeds not found elsewhere. These are the books which were presented to a notary on admission to office in which he was bound to record all his official acts. They had, on his death, to be returned to the Lord Clerk Register, but unfortunately this did not always happen and many have turned up in private hands. As a notary was a local officer the names found in his protocol book are often those of people living in the district in which he practised. The Scottish Record Society has published a number of these books. Others are to be found in the Old Register House, where there is an index to them.

The *Lyon Office Records* are the official records of the Lyon King of Arms, Edinburgh, whose offices are in the front of the Old Register House, on the first floor.

The principal registers are the *Register of Genealogies* which begins in 1727 and continues to the present day, with a gap between 1796 and 1823. This register has not been used greatly, owing to the high fees for registering genealogies in it. Far more valuable is the other great register, the *Register of All Arms and Bearings in Scotland* which extends from 1672, the year of the Act requiring all persons claiming arms in Scotland to register them, until the present day. Because the cost of registering genealogies in the Register of Genealogies was expensive, people used often to include a great portion of their genealogy in their matriculation of arms and therefore, particularly in recent times, the Register of Arms is often most valuable. In Scotland it was necessary for younger sons to prove their right and to have their arms registered, or matriculated, with a difference to show that they were a cadet of the family. Although this was often not done, those conscientious members of the family who did so brought the information about the family up to date in these matriculations. There are also in the Lyon Office nine volumes of birth briefs, funeral entries and funeral escutcheons and these have been indexed and published by the Scottish Record Society.

Apart from the official records in the Lyon Office there is an extensive library there which contains much valuable material and the Lyon Office officials are very co-operative in allowing you to consult it. Here there are many printed and MS family histories and indexes. If there is any likelihood that the family you seek were armigerous a knowledge of Scottish heraldry is useful. A good book is *Scots Heraldry* (2nd ed. 1956) by the present Lyon King of Arms, Sir Thomas Innes of Learney, but the tracing of the existence of arms prior to 1903 can be done through Sir James Balfour Paul's *An Ordinary of Scottish Arms in the Lyon Register* published that year. *The Scots Peerage*, edited by the same person, is often valuable, as it is very full and traces collaterals to a considerable extent. It is in nine volumes and has an excellent index.

The *Scots Magazine* (1739–1826) is roughly the equivalent north of the border to the *Gentleman's Magazine* in England. This magazine contains many notices of birth, marriage and death, and there is a MS index to it in the Lyon Office. A background of Scottish history is certainly a great asset. A short history, interestingly written, is *The Story of Scotland* by Janet Glover (1960) and a rather fuller one, in six volumes, is Agnes Muir Mackenzie's *History of Scotland.*

The Edinburgh City Library has a good reference library for Scottish material and also has its Edinburgh Room, where there is a great deal of material, including runs of Scottish newspapers, such as the *Edinburgh Courant* and the *Edinburgh Evening News*, covering the late eighteenth century and the nineteenth century. The National Library of Scotland, near St Giles', is the equivalent in Scotland to the British Museum Library.

There is also the Scottish Genealogy Society, at present at 21 Howard Place, Edinburgh, which publishes *The Scottish Genealogist*, a quarterly publication, and holds meetings in Edinburgh, usually monthly.

The Scots Ancestry Research Council is another organization which might be consulted. Its headquarters is at 20 York Place, Edinburgh 1.

For ministers of the Church of Scotland and their families, there is the excellent *Fasti Ecclesiae Scoticanae* in seven volumes, with two supplement volumes. These contain many thousands of notices of all the ministers of the Presbyterian Church of Scotland and much information about their families. Further information about them and of ordinary church-goers, may be obtained from the *Kirk Session Records*, which are either in the Scottish Record Office or still in the hands of the minister or session clerk. These may contain information on the arrival of a new member of the congregation, with a note as to the parish from which he or she came.

[19]

IRISH RECORDS

It is no use beating about the bush and trying to play down the appalling loss to Irish Genealogists in the destruction in 1922 of the Four Courts in Dublin. This act of vandalism caused immense havoc and much of the history of Ireland was lost in the destruction of irreplacable documents. All but a handful of the wills, both originals and bound copies, of the Prerogative Court of Armagh and of the other diocesan courts were destroyed and all those Protestant church registers of baptism, marriage and burial which had been deposited there, numbering about 1,000. Such a blow to the Irish genealogist was staggering and many genealogists will not in consequence undertake genealogical research of families in Ireland. In general it needs to be said that, unless the parish registers of the locality happen to be among those surviving, because they were never sent to the Four Courts, or unless the family concerned owned property, it is not usually possible to trace Irish families.

This may sound depressing, but it is as well to realize the position before setting out, so that you are not disappointed later on. Having said this one can now turn more optimistically to examine what survives.

Possibly the very destruction of these valuable records has pricked the Irish conscience and determined them to collect and edit what is left, for a great deal has been done to collect what is called substitute material and the Irish Record Office in Dublin and the Northern Irish Record Office in Belfast have done valiant work in the last few decades in this direction. Then there already existed a great deal of material in print, for the Irish, like the Scots, took interest in their forbears.

It is useful, as always, to have a background knowledge of the history of the country, to remember that Ireland is made up of composite elements, divided between Protestant and Catholic. There have been many waves of invaders and settlers even since Norman times, who incidentally took with them a number of Welsh people. The settlement of Englishmen during Elizabeth I's reign, the 'Undertakers', is well known. They were granted large tracts of land on condition that they settled them with Protestant settlers. Then there came the settlement in Cromwell's time and after the Restoration the main Scottish Presbyterian settlement in Ulster. Among William III's forces which landed in Ireland and defeated James II's army at the Boyne, were some French Protestants, a number of whom remained in the country. Huguenots have settled in Ireland and so have Quakers, and of course there have been many minor waves of settlers throughout Ireland's history, although in the nineteenth century one thinks of it as a country from which its people emigrated, mostly to Canada and the United States, rather than one to which people immigrated.

Returning to the surviving records, fortunately the civil registration of births, marriages and deaths was not destroyed, these records being in a building on the Quays, the Old Custom House. Unfortunately civil registration in Ireland did not start until 1864, which is later than both England and Wales, and Scotland, and it did not have the advantage that the later start in Scotland had of being far better than its predecessor when it did begin. The Irish civil registration gives only the same details which the English one gives and cannot emulate the Scottish registration. There was, however, a registration of Protestant marriages from 1845.

The registration is on a county basis, which is rather more convenient than the registration districts in England. However, like most civil registrations, it would have been far more useful had it been started earlier. Most family researches even today are concerned with a period further back than the civil registration, even from the information they cull from family sources. However, sometimes a marriage taking place just after the commencement of the registration may be useful, especially a Protestant one, which may have taken place shortly after 1845 and will give you the father of the two parties.

In Ireland there were only two kinds of probates, that in the Diocesan Court and that in the Prerogative Court. In general, if all the property was in one diocese, it would be proved in the diocesan court. There were no archdeaconry courts, as in England and no peculiar courts, which made it much easier. You may be thinking this information is rather tantalizing as the wills do not exist, but it is useful to bear this information in mind, for, as mentioned above, there is a certain amount of substitute material available.

The most valuable of this material are the Betham extracts of wills, which are extracts from almost all the wills proved in the Prerogative Court of Armagh from 1536 to 1800. They consist of the genealogical information in the wills taken down by a former Ulster King of Arms. These are at the Public Record Office in Dublin and there is another set at the Genealogical Office, Dublin Castle, done out in pedigree form, with many annotations, sometimes inaccurate. There are also some abstracts of wills of a later period, covering wills throughout the whole island proved between 1829 and 1839, taken on behalf of the Tax Commissioners. There have been several lists of wills known to exist, published in the Reports of the P.R.O. in Dublin and in 1930 Father Clare produced a list of copies of wills known to exist and their whereabouts. The Reading Room at the Record Office in Dublin has also a card index of all wills or abstracts in their possession. The indexes of the probates and administrations since 1857, when, as in England, their registration was centralized, still exist and can be seen at the P.R.O. and though the wills themselves are absent, the indexes give useful information, such as the date of death, the address and names of the executors. An index of Prerogative wills from 1536 to 1810 was published by Sir Arthur Vicars and there have also been published indexes of a number of the diocesan wills.

There are also MS indexes to marriage licence bonds for some dozen dioceses, indexed under both the man's and the woman's name. Some of these have been printed, namely Cork, Ross, Cloyne, Dublin, Ferns and Kildare, but the printed indexes only go up to 1800, whereas the MS ones cover that often valuable period up to 1857.

At Dublin Castle, in which is the former office of the Ulster King of Arms, now the office of the Chief Herald of Ireland, there are, beside the Betham extracts, which are fully indexed, the Prerogative Marriage Licences from 1630 to 1858 and the Ossory Consistory Licences from 1734 to 1808. There are also here the heraldic records of the former kingdom, the Funeral Certificates, 1588 to 1729, which show the parentage of all those whose funerals were attended by the King of Arms or his representative, their arms, their wife's name and the names of their children and the date and place of burial. This collection has never been indexed, but extracts from it have been published. Here also are the official Grant Books, containing the Grants of Arms to people in Ireland or of Irish extraction up to 1958. The amount of material here is very great and Mr Basil O'Connell has been indexing the documents for several years. The material is not normally available to the public, but a comprehensive report of a family will be prepared for a reasonable fee.

The Friends' Meeting House in Eustace Street contains all their carefully kept records for all parts of Ireland, dating back to the mid-seventeenth century. These records are all well indexed and in clear beautiful writing. There are also some hundreds of MS pedigrees of Quakers in Ireland. A volume of Quaker wills has been published, edited by Miss Eustace and a book on Quaker records is being compiled by Miss Goodbody.

The Church of Ireland Representative Body in St Stephen's Green, Dublin, has a list of the Protestant Church of Ireland registers surviving and in local custody. This list, made after 1922, is arranged by dioceses. There are some 600 of these registers. Searchers are, however, advised to make detailed enquiries as to their exact whereabouts, because, with the diminishing Protestant population and the continual amalgamation of the churches, it is often found that the registers are now in some neighbouring church to that in which they are shown to be in this list. Often the editor of Crockfords is a good person to consult as to the up-to-date information regarding these registers.

The Church of Ireland Representative Body also has some other useful MSS in its library. These include collections of Canon Leslie, who published the succession lists of many of the Irish dioceses and the MS collection of the Rev. H. B. Swanzy, which contains, among other matters, some hundreds of pedigrees of families in various parts of the country, but particularly from the North of Ireland.

The principal salvation for the Irish genealogists is the existence of the Register of Deeds. This is in Henrietta Street and contains transactions relating to the transference of ownership or tenure of all land in Ireland since 1708. There is nothing corresponding to it in England and it can be compared with that of the Register of Sasines in Scotland, though that registration goes back much further.

This Irish register is a vast one. Even up to 1832 there were some 800,000 deeds and since then they have swollen enormously. All the deeds have been transcribed into registers so that the original need not be referred to unless there is doubt as to accuracy in copying or you want to see an actual signature. These deeds often contain copies, complete or extracts, of wills when these relate to some land transference.

There are two great indexes to these deeds, one of names and the other of places. The indexes are completely alphabetical, unlike the calendars for the P.C.C. wills at Somerset House, except for a period from about 1790 to 1800, when they are only alphabetical as far as the initial letter and you have then the tedious work of looking through all names beginning with that letter.

Unfortunately the name index only includes the grantor, or person transferring the land, whether by sale or gift, and not the grantee (or new proprietor). However the topographical index will show you the succession of owners of any given property and you can thus trace when the ownership first came into a family. These indexes themselves are vast and occupy a whole wall of shelves in the building. There are probably some thousand volumes of the indexes alone.

These deeds are valuable in revealing, not only the ownership of land with all the relationships recorded, but also such documents as marriage settlements, articles of partnership, bonds, mortgages and so forth when they concerned land.

There is no charge made, either in the Public Record Office or in the Register of Deeds, for people working on their own family history. A useful recent publication is the three volumes of abstracts of complete wills for the period 1708–85 which have been found among the deeds in this register edited by Miss P. B. Eustace.

There are a number of other libraries and institutes which have considerable genealogical material. The National Library, is particularly wealthy in local newspapers and also files of sales notices of properties which went through the Incumbered Estates Court. These give the right by which former owners held land and its descent through the family.

The Trinity College Library has much valuable material, such as the lists of Chester Refugees. The Royal Irish Academy has a number of seventeenth century inquisitions giving details of land transactions.

Since the establishment of the Republic, Belfast has had its own Record Office. There have been some steps taken to avoid overlapping, but inevitably there is material in Belfast referring to the Republic and vice versa. The Belfast office has an excellent card index covering the whole of one wall, mainly to typed parish registers, early lists of freeholders and tenants, tithe payments, extracts from deeds and law suits, hearth tax, musters and subsidy rolls. It is also compiling a series in photostat of copies of Ulster parish registers and there are also there some original registers from Northern Ireland.

The Presbyterian Historical Society in Belfast has a fine collection of typed and indexed parish registers and other material on the Presbyterian elders and their families. The Linenhall Library in Belfast has the best collection of Irish directories, parish and family histories and printed works on Ulster history. There is also here a most valuable genealogical item, namely the MS transcript of all the births, marriages and deaths published in the. *Belfast Evening Post* from 1738 onwards.

Irish newspapers in general can be of great use in view of the destruction of so many parish registers and other records. Dublin and a number of counties, Cork, Waterford, Limerick and Kilkenny, have newspapers which began their existence in the eighteenth century and which give space to notices of birth, marriage and death. When they mention a marriage they usually mention also where it took place, so that often a good local paper will give the information which the lost register would have done.

You do not need to go to Ireland or employ a record searcher in Ireland to see many Irish newspapers. There is a good collection of them at the British Museum Newspaper Library at Colindale. In general, however, they do not begin before 1826, in which year an order was made that a copy of every Irish newspaper should be sent to the English government. A particularly useful paper was the *Hibernian Chronicle* and the Irish Genealogical Society in Great Britain has a card index of all births, marriages and deaths for long runs of it.

No searcher of Irish records should neglect the valuable abstracts made by W. H. Welply, from documents since destroyed. There are some twenty volumes in typescript of his work at the Society of Genealogists, one of three existing sets and the only one this side of the Irish Sea. One volume of the wills has been indexed by Mr Michael Leader, who is also the author of two excellent articles on Irish records in the *Genealogists' Magazine* for September and December, 1958.

The number of printed works of interest to Irish genealogists is considerable. The edition of *Burke's Landed Gentry of Ireland*, published in 1958, brings many Irish families up-to-date, though one is sorry to see many others have dis-appeared from its pages. On the other hand there are valuable pedigrees of families which have not previously appeared. The series of volumes called *Memorials of the Dead in Ireland*, published by the Irish Memorials Association, contain many thousands of inscriptions from gravestones and other memorials. Many of them are indexed in the great slip index of the Society of Genealogists. It will therefore be seen that though searching in Irish records may be a disappointing and heartbreaking affair, yet there is more material available than may be first realized after appreciating the great losses of records which they have suffered.

$\begin{bmatrix} 20 \end{bmatrix}$

WELSH RECORDS

In general modern Welsh genealogy follows the pattern of English genealogy. The civil registration since 1837 is for England and Wales and the probates of Welsh wills since 1858 are recorded in the calendars at Somerset House. In earlier times, too, the Church of Wales recorded the baptisms, marriages and burials in its parish registers, though it must be remembered that nonconformity was strong in that principality. Earlier wills, too, were proved in the ecclesiastical courts, as in England. The four bishoprics of St Asaph, Bangor, Llandaff and St David's had their consistory and archdeaconry courts and there were a number of peculiars, mainly in Herefordshire and a certain amount of overlap in jurisdictions in the diocese of Chester and in Shropshire. These jurisdictions are explained and listed in A. J. Camp's *Wills and their Whereabouts*, referred to earlier, in the section on Wales. It should be noted that a large number of wills of Welsh people were proved in the Consistory Court of Chester, and these are now held with the other Welsh wills, all of which have now been moved to the National Library of Wales at Aberystwyth. Here they are being well cared for and indexes gradually compiled for those sections not adequately covered by existing ones. If unable to visit the library a letter to the librarian there will receive every attention.

Very few of the Welsh parish registers have been published and some of them have been lost or have been kept badly. But there are a certain number of MS copies, some held by the Society of Genealogists, and the Bishops' Transcripts are held at the National Library.

It is particularly valuable in dealing with Welsh pedigrees to have some knowledge of the Principality's customs and history. As with other Celtic races living in a mountainous country, racial feeling was strong and the habits of centuries not easily discarded. The Welsh, like the Scots, were noted for having a great love of heraldry and genealogy, and 'as long as a Welsh pedigree' is a well-known old proverb. Unfortunately, as in Scotland, many of the old pedigrees, stretching far back, were recorded from memory and are not often able to be substantiated by documentary proof. Nevertheless a great many Welsh pedigrees have been recorded and it is interesting to note that up to 1804 as many as 7,773 of them had been registered at the College of Arms.

The Welsh people earlier on did not use surnames but used the Welsh 'ap', meaning 'son', like the Celtic 'Mac' or the Norman French 'Fitz'. This absence of surnames, together with a limited number of christian names in a family, makes tracing of lines somewhat difficult.

Another difficulty is that in these Welsh pedigrees dates are seldom mentioned and the family home not always given. Some of these pedigrees recorded descents of fantastic length and Guttun Owain in one case traces an Elizabethan landlord to 'Adam, son of God'!

One of the best known books on Welsh pedigrees is Lewis Dwnn's *Heraldic Visitation of Wales*, published in 1846, but there are a number of publications of value such as Richard Fenton's *A Tour in quest of genealogy*, 1807, and his *Historical Tour through Pembrokeshire*, 1811 (new edition 1903), and Sir Samuel Rush Meyrick's edited *Heraldic Visitation of Wales* mentioned above and his *History and antiquities of the county of Cardigan*, 1810.

The Welsh records in the Public Record Office are in the process of being transferred to the National Library of Wales. They are listed in the 1963 *Guide to the Public Record Office*, Volume I.

The earliest Welsh records date from 1277, after the subjection of the rising of Llewelyn ap Griffith. At this period the MS known as the Welsh Rolls begins and it is continued until the time when the Principality was incorporated with England. They contain a vast amount of personal detail. There are extracts from them in the B. M. Harleian MS 320 and also calendars of Welsh Rolls were printed by Sir Joseph Ayloffe in 1774.

The Welsh language continued in use until comparatively recent times and is still used in the more rural parts. A knowledge of the language, if you are doing any extensive search in Welsh genealogy is naturally useful and it may be necessary for you to enlist the services of some Welsh genealogist who is familiar not only with the language but also with the customs of the nation.

The use of surnames became stabilized in Wales far later than in England, and not until about the turn of the sixteenth century. Thus in 1650 a man might be described as David Jones, and in 1550 his ancestor may have been designated 'David ap John ap Rhys'. While the earlier designation tells us that he was David the son of John, who was in turn the son of Rhys, there is no surname to link him to any family. On the other hand the man of 1650 is no easier to identify, for Jones was the Smith of Wales, the most common surname there. Next in order of prevalence come Williams, Davies, Thomas and Evans. You will notice that Smith does not even appear among the five most common names in Wales, as it does in England and Scotland and even in Ireland.

It is interesting how far back a name recorded in the Welsh language can take you. John Jones of Gelli Lyfdy, who was writing about 1604–08, mentions his 'Uncle Harri Wynn ap Tomas ap Rrys ap Howel ap Ifan Vychan ap Ifan ap Adda', thus recording in one short statement seven generations or some 250 years in space of time. Such record is certainly valuable, but it tells us nothing about the individuals, and does not help us much to identify them, for instance, as husbands. This in combination with a surname would have been far more valuable. The Russian system of names comes near to this, for in that, while each person has a surname, his second christian name indicates the name of his father. Thus Nicolas

Borissovitch Youssoupoff we know at once was of the family
of Youssoupoff and that his father was Boris Youssoupoff.
His father would be called Boris Gregorovitch Youssoupoff,
because he was the son of Gregory Youssoupoff and so on,
each generation indicating the previous generation.

The publications of *Archaeologia Cambrensis* and of the
Transactions of the Honourable Society of Cymmrodorion
have contributed much to the study of Welsh Genealogy.
For those interested particularly in earlier Welsh genealogy,
there is an article by Major Francis Jones, Wales Herald
Extraordinary, in the latter publication, being an address to
the 1948 Session and published in the Transactions in 1949,
entitled 'An Approach to Welsh Genealogy'.

[21]

THE DOMINIONS, THE U.S.A.
AND OTHER COUNTRIES

Possibly because the people in the dominions, formerly British colonies, were anxious to preserve their links with their mother country, the civil registration in general in them is much fuller than that of England and Wales and can be compared favourably with that of Scotland. A death certificate of Tasmania of the period following 1897 gives, for instance, the date and place of death, usual residence and length of residence in the Commonwealth; the name, surname and birthplace, sex, age, rank or profession, age at marriage and re-marriage, issue, living and dead, males and females, cause of death and name of medical attendant, name of the informant, with his or her signature, description and residence, where registered and the signature of the registrar. A marriage in Tasmania in 1843, on the other hand, gives only the date and place of marriage, names and surnames of bride and bridegroom, ages, rank, their signatures, the name of the clergyman, etc. performing the marriage, when registered and the signature of the registrar or officiating minister, and below, the names of the witnesses and the statement as to the rites and ceremonies under which the marriage was performed. A New Zealand certificate of death of the late nineteenth century gives, in the description of the deceased, the date and place of death, christian name, surname, rank, profession or occupation, sex, age, cause of death, duration of last illness, medical attendant certifying and when he last saw the deceased. Under the heading 'Parents' it gives the name and surname of both father and mother, the maiden surname of the mother and the rank or profession of the father. Under the heading 'If burial registered' the date and place of burial, name of minister officiating, or names of witnesses, and the religion of minister. Under 'Where born' it gives the place of birth and how long the deceased had been in New Zealand. If deceased was married the questions to which answers are required are: Where married, at what age married, to whom married, age of widow, if living. If issue living, then the ages of each sex. The final requirement is the signature of the informant, his or her description, residence and if entry a correction of a former entry, signatures of witnesses attesting the same. This is followed by the signature of the registrar and the date of registration.

Probably few if any dominion registrations equal or excel this New Zealand registration for detail, but those of Canada and South Africa are good.

Details of the information which is given in such registration can be ascertained from a useful government publication of the General Register Office, called *Abstracts of arrangements respecting registration of births, marriages and deaths in the United Kingdom and other countries of the British Commonwealth ... and in the Irish Republic*, published in 1952. It includes lists of registers and records kept at Somerset House and elsewhere in England and Wales.

Many dominions have census returns of an earlier date than those surviving in England. The Australian Genealogical Society, with its headquarters at Lanark House, 148 Phillip Street, Sydney, has done much work in indexing early registration and census returns. This society publishes a journal and there is also the *Quarterly Journal of the Genealogical Society of Victoria*, which publishes articles particularly connected with that state. A series of such, called 'Tracing Ancestors and Constructing Family Trees' by C. E. S. Davies, beginning in the issue for December 1962, gives a good account of how to trace information in the state.

Wills in the dominions and colonies naturally vary in their completeness. As in England in earlier times, they were at first under the church authorities and the civil registration of wills started approximately at the same time as it did in England and Wales, varying with each dominion and state. As early immigrants often still had some property in England, their wills may also be proved in the P.C.C. or, if in Scotland, in the appropriate commissariot.

The libraries in the headquarters of the High Commissioners in London of many of the dominions have much information about early immigrants. That for Australia, for instance, has microfilms of some census returns. The staff of the library may be able to help you and are usually co-operative.

American Ancestry

The number of people who emigrated to the United States particularly in the late eighteenth and nineteenth centuries, is far greater than most people imagine. On the other hand, if all those families who claimed to have gone over in the *Mayflower* had really done so, they would have required, not the accommodation of a small vessel of a few hundred tons, but the combined resources of the *Queen Mary* and the *Queen Elizabeth*. But great numbers of people came over in later times and it is estimated that between 1770 and 1890 eleven million people crossed the Atlantic to the States from Great Britain alone. This is the estimate in *The Great Migration* by Edwin C. Guillet, published by the University of Toronto Press in 1963.

The ancestry of people who emigrated from the British Isles to the United States can vary greatly in the ease or difficulty with which it can be traced. One of the main difficulties is in discovering where in this country the immigrant came from. If that can be discovered then his ancestry in this country may be traced for a number of generations.

Had the Custom House in London not been burnt down in 1814 it might have been comparatively easy to trace an emigrant's home in England, for it was the responsibility of the local customs houses from where emigrants sailed to record certain details about them, which included their age, place of residence and trade. Unfortunately these local records were called in to London for deposit in the Custom House there in the early nineteenth century and thus were destroyed in this disastrous fire in 1814. However, it is no good crying over spilt milk and one must just make use of surviving records as much as one can.

The first task is to find out all you can about the emigrant on the United States side of the world. There are many good books on genealogy in the United States and it is not proposed to go fully into that matter in this work. But among records in the United States there may be mention of the home in Great Britain from which the migrant came and this clue can then be followed up. It is the cases where no such clue can be found that are the difficult ones. Even then, if the surname is an uncommon one it may not be so difficult. Such a book as Guppy's *Homes of Family Names* may provide the clue. Then, when the name is uncommon, it is worth while searching the P.C.C. wills for the period before and after the ancestor emigrated, as someone of the name may have proved his will in the P.C.C. and may in it mention relations in the United States. His will in any case should give his description and will no doubt reveal where he came from, or at any rate, the county. Then Boyd's Marriage Index at the Society of Genealogists and the Index of Apprenticeships there will probably reveal people of the name and indicate the locality from which they came. It depends of course on the date when the emigrant left the British Isles. Naturally it is easier to trace more recent emigrants. Those who migrated in Stuart times are already on the fringe of the time before which it is seldom possible to trace any but the more exceptional families.

It is necessary to be thinking about the historical background all the time. There is no doubt that many of those who in the time of Charles I refused to pay the forced loans emigrated to America in search of a freer life. Information about some of these may be gleaned from the Domestic State Papers in the P.R.O.

From early times until the fifth year of the reign of Charles I, the King in his own name granted licences to people to 'pass beyond the seas'. After that year the power to grant such licences was delegated to officials. Unfortunately very few of the records listing these licences have survived. Of them, those of emigrants to America have been published in Hotten's *Original List of Emigrants*. Some of these licences have also been published in *The Genealogist*.

In the case of a common name where no clue can be discovered as to the place of origin in this country, the only thing to do is to make abstracts of all wills, both in the P.C.C. and in local courts, of people of the name for some ten or so years before and after the time when the person emigrated; in the hope that some mention may be made of the relation in the United States. It is useful to remember that during the Commonwealth period in England all the wills were registered centrally, the local courts being abolished; so that the wills of this period are an indication of the county from which people of a particular name came.

Where the surname is common, an unusual christian name may prove very valuable. This has been mentioned generally in the first chapter. The christian name pattern should be carefully examined for the generations which are known on the American side of the Atlantic, for it is likely that immigrants may have been even more anxious to perpetuate christian names of ancestors in Great Britain than those were who remained in their mother country. That same tendency is also noticed in those who emigrated to the British Dominions and in both these cases an unusual christian name can sometimes be as useful as a rare surname.

Other Foreign Ancestry

People sometimes come across an ancestor who is a foreigner and, regarding it as a dead end, do not pursue the matter further. There is no need for them to feel that way and it may be quite possible, and will certainly be interesting, to trace the ancestor for some generations in his own country. It will of course vary according to the country concerned, for some countries have much better records than others. But on the whole, where the records still survive, they are usually better and fuller, at any rate as far as European countries are concerned, than those of England and Wales.

If the ancestor is a fairly recent one, say of the nineteenth or late eighteenth century, the best way is to write to the Consul General of the country concerned in London (his address can be found in *Whitaker's Almanack*), giving him the details and asking him to tell you to whom you should write. He will then give you further information on the matter. There have been a number of articles on sources for genealogy in various countries in the *Genealogists' Magazine* in recent years. These are listed in the Bibliography at the end of this work. A number of countries also have genealogical societies and these may be able to help you.

The three extracts given below, one a baptism of 1841 from the then newly formed country of Belgium, the others, a marriage and a burial certificate from the Grand Duchy of Brunswick in 1829 and 1857 respectively, will give some idea of the amount of information which can be expected in some European states.

Eglise Evangélique. Consistoriale Française et Allemande de Liège. Baptême.

[translation] On the 29th August 1841, at the time when the English service is celebrated in the temple, was baptized by Dr Etough, English priest, ANNA ELIZA legitimate daughter of Freelove HAMMOND, Barrister, and of Lucy *Tyeth*, his wife, living at the Château de Bomal near Marche (Luxembourg Belge), where the child was born the 5th April 1840.

The Godfather and Godmother were: William Hammond Esq. Doctor of Medicine, living at Whitstone in Middlesex, (England) and Anna Eliza Green, living in London.

The other translated extracts are from a church register of Brunswick at a time when it was an independent state under the rule of the Grand Duke of Brunswick.

EXTRACT from the REGISTER of PROCLAMATIONS and MARRIAGES, of SAINT CATHARINE in BRUNSWICK.

On the 4th October 1829, here in the HOUSE of SAINT CATHERINE, were married, Mr *Michael Charles Edwards*, 2nd Lieutenant in Great Britain and Lieutenant in the Service of the Grand Duke of Brunswick, son of Mr John Edwards formerly landowner in the county of Hampshire in England, and of his wife, Mrs Massey Maria, née Hawkins, their lawful son, and *Johanne Dorothea Henriette Heineking*, spinster, daughter of the late burger and master tailor, Johann Heinrich Christian Heineking and of his surviving widow Dorothea Christiane Elizabeth, née Krämer, their lawful daughter.

EXTRACT from the REGISTER of Those Buried in SAINT CATHARINE in Brunswick.

In the year 1857, on the evening of the 26th June at 5 o'clock, Lieutenant *Michael Charles Edwards*, formerly in the Service of the Grand Duke of Brunswick, born the 30th September 1795, died of a stroke and was buried on the 30th June.

The Germans, with their love of detail, tended to be full and informative in their records of birth, marriage and burial, and the Dutch records are very good also. But the civil registration in Spain must surely be the fullest in Europe or of any country in the world.

This civil registration unfortunately was only established in 1870. Before that time people were dependent on the church registration, which was, however, very good.

The details given in the civil registration include the following information.

Birth Certificates: Christian name, surname, age, place of birth, residence and profession of the person who presents the child to the Registrar and his or her relationship to the child.

Hour, date and month and year and place of birth of the child. Sex. Christian name of the child.

Christian names, surnames, places of birth, residence and profession of the parents and maternal and paternal grandparents if known and nationality if they were foreign.

Legitimacy or illegitimacy of the child if known. In the latter case the type of illegitimacy is shown except in the case of children known as 'naturales', which is a legal term for children born of unmarried parents where the paternity is admitted.

Marriage Certificates: Details of the registers in which the births of both parties were recorded and the date of the entries.

Christian names and surnames, places of birth, marital state, profession and residence of the parents and of the paternal and maternal grand-parents if they are known.

Legitimacy or illegitimacy of both bride and bridegroom in the latter case mentioning the type of illegitimacy unless they are 'naturales' or abandoned children.

In cases where one of the parties cannot be present and the marriage is by proxy, details of the document by which the absent party gives authority to the proxy and the christian name, surname, age, place of birth, residence and profession of the proxy.

Dates of the publication of banns or specification of marriage in *articulo mortis* or dispensation of banns with mention of the authority concerning the same.

Statement that there is no impediment to the marriage.

Permission of parents if either party is under age.

Names of any 'natural' children who are made legitimate by the marriage.

Christian names and surnames of any previous husbands or wives of either party who are dead, with dates and places of death and registers in which the deaths were recorded.

Mention of the reading of the bride and bridegroom of the articles of the laws of marriage which they should know.

Declaration of mutual acceptance by both parties and declaration by the Church that they have been united.

Death Certificate: Day, hour and place of death.

Christian name and surname, age, place of birth, profession and residence of the dead person and of his wife or her husband if the deceased were married.

Christian names and surname, residence and profession

of the parents of the dead person, if known, and mention whether they are still living.

Cause of death.

Whether the deceased has left a will, and if so, the date and place and name of the lawyer who drew it up.

The cemetery in which the dead person is to be buried.

⌈22⌉

VARIOUS OTHER SOURCES

Not every apprentice had to sleep under the table and not all of them were unfairly beaten or starved. Many of them in fact were kindly treated by their masters and quite a number of them married a daughter of their master. This last fact is, of course, of particular importance to genealogists. There is the story of how John Osborne, apprenticed to Sir William Howitt, saved his master's daughter when she fell from a window of their house on London Bridge, and later married her and founded the line of wealthy merchants who later became politically important and dukes of Leeds. Not all apprentices saved their master's daughters in such dramatic circumstances and founded ducal houses. But apprenticeship affected the lives of these young boys in several ways. They often moved to a new locality and afterwards stayed there.

Apprenticeship is one of the earliest forms of learning a trade or skill. The young boys were bound by indentures signed by the parents and the master to whom they were apprenticed for a term of years, usually five or seven. Apprentices lived under strict discipline and the penalties for disobeying a master or for running away were severe. Indentures of the seventeenth century enacted that 'by and dureinge all which said terme the said John Smith his said Master will and faithfully shall serve, his secrets shall keep, his Lawful Commandments every where shall gladly doe. He shall not wast the goods of his said Master nor lend them unlawfully to any person. He shall not comitt fornicacon nor contract Matrimony within the saide terme. He shall not play at any unlawful games; Taverns nor Alehouses he shall not haunt neither shall he absent himselfe by day nor by night but as a true and faithfull Servant shall behave himselfe towards his said Master as well in wordes as in deeds dureinge the said Terme'. Altogether he had to be a pretty good and well-behaved young man and if his master came across him one night 'haunting' one of his favourite alehouses, there was trouble in the wind.

These indentures were held by the master and the parents and were not registered centrally, though the City Livery Companies of London and some provincial cities and boroughs, such as Nottingham, have surviving registers of apprentices going back a long way, as also have a number of parishes of the apprentices bound by the parish. But in 1710 a tax was put on apprenticeship indentures, and this, fortunately for the genealogist, meant a central registration of all apprentices. The original registers are now in the P.R.O. and one of the most valuable collections at the Society of Genealogists is the Apprentices Index, which is a typescript index of information from the registers, covering all England and Wales between the years 1710 and 1774. For each entry is given the name of the apprentice, followed by the name of his father (or mother, if she was a widow), the name of the master, the trade to which he was apprenticed and the amount paid. Often the place of residence of the father and of the master is mentioned. The information in the years after 1760 is not so full and unfortunately often leaves out the parent's name. However, this is an extremely valuable index, as the number of boys apprenticed during that period is great and it is covering one of the difficult periods in genealogical research. Among its other uses, it often indicates the movement of a family from one locality to another.

There are, however, two classes of apprentices which are not found in this index, because they were exempt from the stamp duty. One is the parish apprentice, the poor boy or girl, perhaps an orphan, who was apprenticed by the overseers of the parish to learn a trade. The other is the apprentice paying less than a shilling fee for his indenture, in other words merely a nominal amount. These were often boys apprenticed to a relation, who took the boy on for a nominal amount out of kindness. It is unfortunate genealogically that this particular category should be missing.

The City of London is unique in many ways. One of these was the system of livery companies. Until the end of the eighteenth century you could not practise a trade within the city boundaries unless you were a freeman of the city. There were three ways in which you could get such freedom, namely, by patrimony, by servitude or by redemption. To become a freeman by patrimony you had to be the son of a freeman who was such at the time of your birth. Obtaining your freedom by servitude meant serving an apprenticeship in one of the livery companies. On completion of such apprenticeship you were admitted a freeman of the company and this qualified you for the freedom of the city. After some years of service in your trade you might be admitted to the livery of the company to which you belonged and you were then known as a 'liveryman'. Obtaining your freedom by redemption meant being admitted by paying a sum of money for the privilege, but in this case you were not a member of a livery company and had none of the privileges attached to it.

Members of the livery companies were described as 'citizen and grocer', or 'citizen and draper' and so forth, according to the company to which they belonged. In earliest times this meant that they were actually occupied in the trade indicated, but even in Jacobean times it was becoming customary for people to enter some livery company merely for the honour and privilege and these people might be earning their living in quite a different way. Thus you might find a member of the Glovers Company earning his living as a butcher or as an attorney. Early on, of course, fathers put their sons' names forward for apprenticeship in their own company, just to keep the family link and there are several families which can show a long period of unbroken family connection with a particular livery company. Today sometimes sons are apprenticed to members of the company, their father's friends, a mere nominal apprenticeship, though the indentures must still be signed and properly executed. One of the conditions of such, as we have already seen, is that the apprentice shall not marry during his apprenticeship and if he should do so the young man, perhaps a recent graduate from one of the universities, must write seeking his master's forgiveness for doing so. This is, of course, readily given and usually a dinner party is thrown in to celebrate the occasion.

If it is known that an ancestor was a member of a particular city livery company, then the records of that company may give valuable information about his parentage and other details of his career. You should write to the clerk of the company concerned, whose address can be found in *Whitaker's Almanack*. But if you do not know that he belonged to any company but know that he was a freeman of the city (and he probably was if he was practising a trade there), then you should apply to the City Chamberlain, in whose office are kept the registers of freemen. For a small fee he will have them searched for you for a period of five years and then, if an entry is found, further details will be supplied for a small additional fee. The City Chamberlain's office is in Gresham Street, near the Guildhall.

The matriculation registers of the universities have already been mentioned. Another large and growing class of record is that of the registers of public and other schools. Some of these go back a long way and are well produced. An example of an excellent school register is that of Westminster. Eton, strange to say, has a poor one. The best of these registers give useful information about parentage and also about the subsequent career of the pupil. This source is not confined to public schools. There are many lesser-known schools, such as Bury St Edmunds Grammar School, which have had excellent registers published. Apart from published registers, if it is known that a boy went to a certain school, enquiry there may produce much information from MS sources there and if the school is contemplating publishing a register sometime it may be glad of any additional information you can give them of individuals who were there.

Sometimes in a will a reference may be found to some insurance company policy, or an old policy may be found among family papers. This can lead to useful information. In early times when someone wanted to take out a life insurance policy, the companies did not have medical examinations, but relied on information about other members of the family. Thus old proposal forms often contained replies to questions as to the names of parents, brothers and sisters, their ages if still living or if dead, their age at death. This might have to be supported by documentary evidence or may have been checked against such evidence. Unfortunately many of the old insurance companies have destroyed their earlier records or sent them for pulping during the drive for paper in the last war. Some, however, have kept them, or at any rate their early registers. The latter, though not nearly so valuable as the proposal forms, will tell you the date at which a policy was taken out and will give the address of the person then and possibly other information.

Other possible sources of information about people are the records of banks. Many private banks, which flourished particularly in the eighteenth and early nineteenth centuries, have now disappeared, but this is usually through being taken over by one of the bigger banks and it is not too difficult to trace what has happened to a particular bank. Their records may be carefully preserved, and these may give valuable clues as to their clients, their movements and perhaps their financial position. Sons frequently went to the same bank as their fathers, often being introduced when twenty-one, with a present of five pounds to start them off. Present-day information from banking accounts is, of course, confidential, but banks would probably be willing to reveal information in their books of, perhaps, a hundred and fifty years ago.

Another interesting and little realized source of information is contained in the tontine ledgers and papers at the P.R.O. A tontine is a form of annuity in which each subscriber invests money and the interest from it is shared by the subscribers during their lifetime, or by the subscriber's nominee during his or her lifetime. As the nominees die the share drawn by the surviving nominees increases, until eventually one nominee is drawing the total interest. The British government organized three main series of life annuities and tontines on this basis during the eighteenth century. The first series were the three life annuities of 1745, 1746 and 1757. The second series were the three further life annuities of 1766, 1778 and 1779 and the tontine of 1789. The third series were the three Irish tontines of 1774, 1775 and 1777. These records belong to the National Debt Office records and are designated NDO 1, NDO 2 and NDO 3 respectively. The information in the annuity records is not as useful genealogically as that in the tontine. The latter give, among other details, the following information: Name of the subscriber, his address, name of the nominee (usually a young child), the names of his parents, the age of the Nominee, the date when the nominee died or was buried, the names of the executors, administrators and assigns, and the volume and folio where the will or assignment may be found, the names of attorneys and the reference for the powers of attorney. When it is remembered that the number of subscribers, mainly middle class, for the English tontine of 1789 was 8,349, the extent of this source can be estimated. There is an interesting letter on this source written by Francis Leeson, giving fuller information of the details revealed, in the *Genealogists' Magazine XIV, 10* (June 1964).

You will notice in Appendix A, one of the questions in the suggested questionnaire for sending to members of the family inquiries about any old receipt books which may survive in the family. This inquiry may sound more culinary than genealogical, but the information old receipt books can reveal is sometimes quite surprising. In the days before cooking had achieved its commercial glorification, receipts were handed down as valued knowledge in families, and the special receipts were frequently named after their exponents, who were often members of the family, or else close friends. An old receipt book of the early nineteenth century which I am fortunate enough to have, reveals, for instance, the wholesome ingredients of 'Mrs Tyeth's plain cake', 'An Excellent

Pudding' in accordance with Mrs Lloyd's receipt, 'Mrs Thomas of Dickett's receipt for furniture paste', Mrs Coster's plain Cake'. Mrs Coster was my great-grandmother, and Mrs Tyeth her mother, while Mrs Lloyd was the former's elder sister. Mrs Thomas of Dickett's was a friend, in fact nearly all the people who had conferred their name on some priceless receipt were relations or friends. It will be thus appreciated that among all these culinary plums there were many genealogical clues.

[23]

PLACES OF SEARCH

I. The Society of Genealogists

The library at the Society of Genealogists at 37 Harrington Gardens, London, S.W.7, near Gloucester Road Underground Station, is unique in having the best collection of printed books and MSS on genealogy in the British Isles. As far as the printed books are concerned, it is probably true that most of them are in such national libraries as the British Museum Library, the Bodleian Library and Cambridge University Library, but in all these libraries it is necessary to apply for each book and then wait for its delivery, which can take as long as half an hour or more. At the Society you have the inestimable advantage of finding these books all on open access shelves. So often in genealogy you only want to look at a book for a matter of seconds, to glimpse in the index or at the chapter headings to see if it is at all likely to have information you want.

The library has arrangements for allowing occasional searchers to use it on payment of a half-day or full day fee, but if you are likely to use it more than a few times it more than pays you to join the Society, for in addition to being able to use the library whenever you want to, you have other advantages, such as being able to get the magazine at the members' rate and being kept in touch with developments in genealogy by attending the annual general meeting and lectures. You are also allowed to borrow certain books from the library, where there are duplicates for loan.

The library is arranged in a series of rooms, named after former presidents of the society, and some indication as to the contents of these may be the best way of giving you an idea of the material available.

The Farrer Room, on the ground floor, facing you as you come into the hall, contains the card indexes, the index of family histories, of which the society has probably the best collection in England, including many privately printed which are not in the national libraries and many in pamphlet form. Then there is the index of parish register transcripts, and other material relating to, and arranged under, counties. At the east end of this room are shelves containing books on professions, the law, medicine, the church, etc., and also a number of runs of genealogical magazines, such as *Miscellanea Genealogica et Heraldica, the Ancestor*, and the *Genealogist*. There is naturally also here a complete set of the Society's own periodical, *The Genealogists' Magazine*, which, with its indexes, is invaluable for searching out a wealth of information which has been contributed to it over the years. There are also the various genealogists' guides, such as the invaluable *Genealogists' Guide* by G. W. Marshall, with the sequel to it by J. B. Whitmore, and the more recent American publication by Smith and Gardner in three volumes *Genealogical Research in Great Britain*. Then there are the Society's own two publications, which are complementary to one another, *A Catalogue of Parish Register Copies in the Society of Genealogists* and the *National Index of Parish Register Copies* by H. K. Percy-Smith and K. Blomfield, which contains those registers of which copies are known to exist outside the Society of Genealogists. A new and far fuller edition of the latter is nearly completed and its publication should begin shortly.

Here also are a fine set of Army Lists, going back to the mid-eighteenth century, though unfortunately there are a number of gaps; and a good set of the Navy Lists covering the same periods; a collection of regimental histories; collective naval biographies, such as Marshall's *Royal Naval Biography* and O'Byrne's *Naval Biographical Dictionary*.

The remainder of the room is in general given over to books, arranged by counties, of county or parish histories and other topographical works. These exclude works on London, and Middlesex, Scotland and Ireland and places abroad, which are in other rooms. In these shelves, besides printed books there are MS copies of parish registers and of monumental inscriptions (referred to as M.I.'s). At the west end of this room are the MS indexes compiled by the late Percival Boyd, of London Citizens, and also Snell's collection referring to Berkshire. The larger county histories, such as the folio volumes of Bigland's *Gloucestershire*, which are too large to arrange with their counties, are at the east end of the room.

Upstairs on the first floor are two rooms, Raglan and Tweeddale. Raglan, the south room, contains books on London, including a good collection of directories going back to the mid-eighteenth century, on Scotland, Ireland, Wales and the United States. In this room also are two TS collections which are among the most valuable the Society possesses. One is Boyd's Marriage Index, which is a very large TS index of marriages from many parishes. Many are arranged by counties, though unfortunately many counties have not been covered. For those that have been the index is of great assistance, for it includes nearly all the printed and MS copies of registers. They are arranged in twenty-five-year groups, from the earliest times up to 1837. There are also a great many miscellaneous volumes, which contain various parishes and in some cases marriage licences and extracts from such publications as the *Gentleman's Magazine*.

The second great collection in this room is the *Apprentices Index*, to which reference has already been made in Chapter 22. It covers the period 1710 to 1774 and the preface to Volume 1 gives details of the abbreviations and the system followed.

In this room also are the published matriculations of Oxford and Cambridge and other universities, and the school registers, of which there are a good and growing collection. There are here also records of the City Livery Companies and of admissions to the Inns of Court.

The Tweeddale Room, opposite, is devoted to the MS collections. There is first of all the *Great Card Index*. This has been built up through the industry of members of the society over the years. Though not now added to, it contains several million slips of a miscellaneous kind, sorted under surnames and subdivided into christian names and possibly then by periods. In general it contains extracts from parish registers, indexes to collections like the Smith MS collection, to marriage licences, chancery proceedings and so forth. As it is easy to consult it is always worth while doing so, as it is surprising what clues it may unexpectedly produce.

Individual pedigrees and information on families are arranged in boxes in alphabetical order on the shelves on the north side. These may produce for you, if you are very lucky, a ready-made pedigree of the family you are seeking. There are also boxes containing information about localities and these too should be consulted, as background information about the places where your ancestors lived is often valuable.

There are a number of very useful smaller collections. There is, for instance, the slip index collection of the late J. R. M. Glencross, which is particularly rich in material on Devon and Cornwall. There is a slip index made by the late C. W. Winstanley of wills proved in the P.C.C. from 1720 to 1725, a most useful period. It is a pity more people have not followed Mr Winstanley's example, as the amount of time wasted in consulting the indexes at Somerset House for P.C.C. wills is enormous, as these calendars are only alphabetical as far as the first letter and thus entail searching through the whole of the letter of each year.

The *Macleod Collection* is a large collection of material from Scottish records, sasines, wills, service of heirs and so forth. It is roughly indexed.

The *Fawcett Index*, a card index, is much concerned with clergy and also with Durham and the North of England.

Before you leave this floor it may as well be noted that the stacks in the large landing contain mainly peerages, Burke, Debrett and Collins, and the various editions of *Burke's Landed Gentry*, *Walford's County Families*, *Kelly's Titled, Landed and Official Classes*, the *G.E.C. Complete Peerage*, Balfour Paul's *Scots Peerage* and other such publications. The south side of this large case has the society's books on heraldry, including an interesting collection of bookplates, some from the Crouch Collection and arranged by Professor Gale in a number of loose-leaf books. There are also printed and MS volumes of marriage licences and indexes of some wills, both printed and MS, but not including those published by the Index Society, British Records Society or Harleian Society, which are kept together in the Raglan room with other publications of those societies.

The basement contains the Stamp Room, which mainly houses the many family histories. Reference has already been made to Thomson's index of printed family histories. Most of these are here, together with many others, some mimeographed from typewriting or in MS. There is in the society an annotated copy of Thomson's index, which has additions of family histories published since the last edition of the work. In this room are also a number of important MS collections. In a cupboard on the east wall are the Williams MSS, which relate particularly to Welsh families, and the Smith MSS, containing extensions of many visitation pedigrees and also rich in families connected with the West Indies. The great slip index contains the index to this collection. There are also down here a number of *Royal Calendars* and similar publications, which, rather like an early form of *Whitaker's Almanack*, contain lists of officials and of officers in the Army, Navy and civilian life.

Outside in the passage are runs of the *Gentleman's Magazine*, the *London Magazine* and the *Scots Magazine* and in the small room at the end of this passage, which is at present unnamed, there is the splendid collection of material on India largely built up by Colonel H. K. Percy-Smith. Not only are there many printed works, such as excellent sets of the *East India Register*, Indian Army Lists and books like V. C. P. Hodson's *Officers of the Bengal Army*, but there is an MS card index of persons connected with India, whether in the Indian civil or military services or as early Europeans in India, free merchants and traders, in fact any British subject connected with India during the English occupation.

Also in this room are books and MSS of other parts of the British Commonwealth, Canada, Australia and South Africa, but more particularly of the West Indies. This section of the library is, however, a small one and there is probably more material to be found, for instance, in the library at Australia House and in similar Commonwealth libraries in London.

Apart from the more direct advantages of belonging to the society one must not overlook such facilities as the members' room, where there are copies of genealogical and allied subject periodicals from all over the world and where at four o'clock on most days you can get a cup of tea and cake or biscuit. There is nothing like such refreshment after an arduous and perhaps frustrating search, especially when one meets other enthusiasts who will sympathize with you, probably help you and surely stimulate you in your efforts. Here you may meet many members with years of experience whose combined wisdom and knowledge is quite extraordinary and who, like Private Willis in *Iolanthe*, 'think of things that would astonish you.'

[24]

PLACES OF SEARCH

II. The Public Record Office

The Public Record Office in Chancery Lane was established in 1851 to house all the national records of England and Wales, which before that were scattered in a number of repositories, such as the Tower of London, the Admiralty, War Office, Somerset House and so forth.

Many records of the utmost value to genealogists are here. In general, government departments hand over their records to this depository after a hundred years, but in some cases they do so earlier. Therefore records of a hundred years ago and backwards are available to searchers. It is, of course, necessary to obtain a permit to search here, but that is not a difficult matter if you can show you are engaged in original research, which genealogical work usually is.

It is only possible in this short chapter to indicate some of the vast amount of material which is here and which is of value to the genealogist. The *Guide to Contents of the Public Record Office*, published in 1963, a revision and extension to 1960 of the well-known Giuseppi's Guide, in its two volumes outlines fairly fully the main records. If you want a less lengthy and more general guide to them, Professor Galbraith's *Guide to the Public Records*, published in 1952, is a useful book. Then a succinct article 'Genealogy in the Public Records' by L. C. Hector appeared in the *Genealogists' Magazine* in June 1938. Many public libraries have the official lists of records of H.M. Stationery Office, giving the records in the various departments, such as the War Office, Admiralty, Home Office, Colonial Office and so forth. But one is inclined as a novice to be overwhelmed by the mass of detail thrust before your eyes and it is advisable to get guidance from one of the officials at the Record Office, who are very helpful. You cannot, of course, expect them to do more than indicate the useful sources, as they have their time taken up in many directions. The Record Office staff will, however, answer by post a small inquiry not entailing a great deal of research and this is useful for someone living at a distance from London. If the subject entails a longer search, they will send you a list of searchers who work there on such matters. Many of these are experts, but genealogy is such a specialized study that it is often better to find out the name of one who has had experience particularly in genealogical work, or to employ someone you know otherwise to be a reputable genealogist.

Among the great sources here for genealogists are the census returns of 1841, 1851 and 1861. These are in the Long Room and can be obtained in about half an hour from the time of applying for them. Some of the towns are indexed by streets so that you can find in which volume the person you seek will be. With villages and smaller towns there is usually no index, which entails searching through the whole population, but this is not such an overwhelming task as it sounds. The details you will get out of these census returns have already been explained in Chapter 4. The beginning of each enumerator's book indicates the area covered and this will often mention the particular street or square for which you are searching. It is always advisable to consult a good map of the area to see where the different parts of the town or village lie. The Admiralty and War Office records are in the Round Room. On the shelves there will be found the lists of such records. There are some useful MS lists, such as the lists of returns of officers' services for 1828 and 1829. There is also a most useful calendar of extracted information of parentage from the baptismal certificates in the Lieutenants' Passing Certificates for the Royal Navy. This has been more fully mentioned in the chapter on naval ancestry.

Chancery proceedings can reveal considerable information about families. Some further information about them will be found in Chapter 28.

Home Office records may reveal details of naturalization and, for people who have served in that office, there may be records of service, which give useful information about the individual.

The Army records themselves are usually supplied in the room above the Long Room. This room has an almost complete set of Army Lists and is about the most convenient place in London to consult them. There is also a very useful card index to officers' marriages. The officials in this room are mostly specialists in military records and can be very helpful to you with their suggestions. It was through one of them that I was first introduced to the Commander-in-Chief's Memoranda papers, which proved so valuable a source to me about officers' first commissions and promotion.

$\lceil 25 \rceil$

PLACES OF SEARCH

III. The British Museum and other Libraries

The Library of the British Museum is one of the most fascinating places in the world. The number and variety of characters who use and have used it is so great and so interesting that it is a study in itself. One sees every nationality under the sun, young men carrying their books in carpenters' bags, affecting the *ouvrier* style, men in skull caps who appear to spend much time sleeping, tall gaunt impressive statesman-like men and small insignificant quiet scared creatures who may be among the most brilliant of the population. Apart from one's purpose in going there it is an experience in itself.

Here again it is necessary to satisfy the authorities that you are engaged in research which cannot be carried out easily elsewhere and you will then be provided with a ticket which you must show to get past the guard at the doorway.

You will quickly find that a large section of the round room is devoted to genealogical works, because a large number of people who use the library are engaged in such work. Until you begin to work in this field you do not realize how many other people are interested in it.

On the shelves in the Reading Room you will find such sets as the *Gentleman's Magazine, Scots Magazine, London Magazine* and so forth, and this is one of the best places to consult them, as even the Society of Genealogists has not, for instance, a complete set of the *Gentleman's Magazine* and in the museum library they are well bound and easily get-at-able. You will find also on the shelves volumes of the *Victoria County Histories* and other county histories, such series as the *Rolls Series*, and the publications of the various learned societies. In the centre is the catalogue, which, as already mentioned, should be consulted to see if any family history or pedigree of the family exists already. Also it may reveal details of any member of the family who may have written a book or pamphlet at some time or other. Around these centre shelves also will be found the decennial indexes to the Scottish Service of Heirs, mentioned in the chapters on Scottish records.

Other books must be applied for, and take from half an hour to an hour to come to your seat. The library has also good collections of early newspapers, such as the *Burney Collection* (see Chapter 10), which are in this building, as also is a complete set of *The Times*. But other newspapers are out at the Museum's Newspaper Library at Colindale.

The MS Department of the British Museum is also in this building and is very large. It is necessary to get a separate ticket to use it, but this can be done quite easily. Apart from many heraldic and family papers, diaries and so forth, there are such original MSS as the returns made for O'Byrne's *Naval Biographical Dictionary*, which as mentioned in Chapter 13 often contain far more information than the dictionary itself.

The map room here is another asset. Here you can track down the map of your district nearest to the date you want and apart from the enormous collection of maps made by individuals throughout history, there are the complete sets of the earliest Ordnance Survey maps, the six inch and the twenty-five inch to the mile scales being especially valuable. There are also tithe redemption maps, which gave much detail of an earlier period.

The Department of Prints and Drawings may also have useful genealogical material. There is, for instance, the Franks Collection of Bookplates. Of these there are indexes published which you can see in most large reference libraries. Similarly the index to engraved portraits may sometimes be useful if you have an ancestor sufficiently prominent to have been painted by some well-known portrait painter, which may also have been engraved.

Probably the library of next greatest importance to the genealogist in London is that of the Corporation of London, or the Guildhall Library. This great and efficiently run library has probably most of the books a genealogist will normally require and it has one great advantage over the British Museum and that is that any book you apply for will be brought to you within a matter of minutes, so that it cuts out those half-hours of waiting at the British Museum Library. On the other hand, a disadvantage is that there are far fewer books on open access here. The resources of the library are, however, freely available to the public without any formality such as obtaining a ticket and persons to recommend you. It is not, of course, a lending library.

The library was established to provide material to illustrate the development and history of London and naturally it is very rich in London material, and because London is the capital of England and the centre of its trade, all the main source books of English history are also here. There is an extensive commercial library and other fields are also covered selectively, so that here you have all the material of a general kind you would expect to find in a large reference library, besides the particular and extensive special fields. There are, however, some fields excluded, such as modern fiction, poetry and drama, but this is not likely to perturb the genealogist.

The London collection, the most extensive anywhere, comprises printed books, manuscripts, prints, drawings and maps. Although the emphasis is on the city itself, the county area is also covered to a considerable extent, and to a lesser extent the suburbs outside the GLC boundaries.

The manuscript collection includes many of the original parish registers of the city churches, which have been deposited here and are therefore easily consulted. The Harleian Society have published a great many of these city parish registers, but there are many more here which are so far unpublished and of which no MS copies exist. There are also here the wills and administrations of the Archdeaconry of London and of the Bishop of London's Commissary Court up to 1858. There are many deposited MSS of the city guilds and of the wards. Among these records of great use to genealogists are the registers of the Society of Apothecaries. As has been explained in the chapter on the records of doctors, many medical men got their qualification by becoming a Licentiate of the Society of Apothecaries.

It should be noted that the City of London's municipal archives, that is the record of their day-to-day activities, are not kept here, but in the Corporation's Record Office nearby.

The Guildhall Library has the best collection of London directories anywhere and it also has a very fine collection of directories of other towns and counties.

The library of the University of London, which is housed in the tower of the Senate House in Bloomsbury, has a large section specializing in bibliography. It also has one of the best biographical libraries, including all the corrections and additions to the *Dictionary of National Biography* which have been contributed to the *Bulletin of the Institute of Historical Research* in the special section of it devoted to such corrections and additions. These are kept in alphabetical order and can therefore easily be consulted. There are here a good collection of collective biographies, such as Boase's *Modern English Biography* which is less often come across in reference libraries.

The public libraries of the various London boroughs combine to cover the publication of all books, each library being allotted a section of the Dewey Classification and undertaking to purchase all books published in that section. In this way it is made certain that some public library in London has a copy of any book published.

The library which covers the section of the Dewey Classification dealing with genealogy and heraldry, namely Class 929, is the Kensington Borough Library. It had already specialized to a great extent in this field and in the new large reference library in its building off Kensington High Street you will find a very comprehensive collection of books on the subject. There are, for instance, on the open shelves all the editions of *Burke's Landed Gentry*, including the 1847-52 second edition, with the useful index of names. There are also good runs of *Burke's Peerage* and of genealogical publications of the past and present.

The library of the College of Arms, with its extensive collection of genealogical and heraldic books and MSS will be dealt with in the chapter on *Genealogy and Heraldry*. The library is not, however, open to the public.

Various libraries specializing in particular aspects of genealogy, such as the Minet Library with its Huguenot collection, have been mentioned under the chapter dealing with such records.

While the majority of specialized libraries tend to be in London, there are some in the provinces which have good genealogical collections. Manchester Public Library specializes in published family histories and its published catalogue of this section is well worth consulting. Queen's College, Oxford, has a fine collection of genealogical MSS given to the college by Sir Joseph Williamson, but the collection relates almost entirely to seventeenth and earlier centuries. Gonville and Caius College, Cambridge, has also a good genealogical collection of MSS. A number of depositories and other places where genealogical MSS may be found are mentioned in Richard Sims' *Manual for the Genealogist, Topographer, Antiquary and Legal Professor*, but, as this useful book was published in 1856 much of the information in it is out-of-date. The very great deal of detailed information in it is, however, valuable as a guide to what exists, even though the place of its existence may have changed.

The setting up of county record offices throughout the country has greatly assisted in preserving many genealogical records. The earliest county to have a record office was Bedfordshire, where one was opened in Bedford in 1914. Since then, and particularly since the war, many have been established so that today most counties have record offices and many boroughs today have their archives department which is recognized by the Master of the Rolls as an official depository for records. This not only makes the public far more record-conscious and willing to deposit records which they may have, but also, in the case particularly of the county record offices, has resulted in many parish registers being deposited in them on varying terms, very often with completely free access for consultation. Many of the county records offices have an additional role as Diocesan Record Office, which means they hold the records formerly kept in the Diocesan Registry and such records as the bishop's transcripts. They are also becoming more and more the depository for the wills prior to 1858 of the consistory, commissary and archdeaconry courts. This is, of course, an advantageous position, for all these records are now being well looked after and in the hands of trained archivists who appreciate the value and have an interest in the records. It has in fact lead to a considerable opening-up of these records and eventually, it is hoped, will lead to a far better indexing and calendaring of them.

You can easily find out the existence and address of the county record office or of any local depositories by enquiring at your local public library.

Another body which has done valuable work since it was set up in 1945 and which is closely linked with these county record offices, is the National Register of Archives, which has its headquarters at Quality House in Chancery Lane, not far from the Public Record Office with which it works in close collaboration. Most districts have local committees of the National Register of Archives. The main object of the register is to list the existence and whereabouts of all archives which may be of value nationally. This includes private collections of deeds belonging to great or small estates, records of charitable institutions, public bodies such as boroughs, local treasury, educational, police and fire services, in fact the records of any body or individual which may be of interest and value. These include diaries, journals, family photographs, especially if they are identified, marriage settlements and so forth. One of the great services which these bodies have performed is in the saving from destruction of so many of these records, which individuals may have thought to be just so much old junk and had no idea interested anyone.

[26]

GENEALOGY AND HERALDRY

In theory heraldry should be the greatest assistance to genealogy but in practice, owing to its abuse, the assistance it can give is limited and may often be misleading.

The law of the right to the use of armorial bearings is quite clear in the British Isles. In England and Wales the granting and registration of armorial bearings is under the jurisdiction of the Earl Marshal, assisted by the College of Arms, acting on behalf of the Sovereign under charter granted to him and them.

Unlike a British peerage, which descends ordinarily only to one representative, usually the eldest male descendant of the original person to whom the peerage was granted, arms are different in that they descend to all sons and to their sons in perpetuity, and to daughters who may also, if they are heiresses or coheiresses in heraldry, transmit the right to quarter those arms to their children, provided the husband is entitled to bear arms. But to have a right to arms in England and Wales you must be able to prove you are descended in the male line from someone to whom arms have been granted or to whom the right to bear arms has been recognized at one of the visitations made by the kings of arms or heralds during the sixteenth and seventeenth centuries, or have obtained a grant of arms yourself.

In theory only the eldest son and his eldest son in perpetuity bear the undifferenced arms. Younger sons should bear difference marks, such as a crescent for the second son, a fleur-de-lys for the sixth and a cross moline for the eighth son.

These should be carried on, so that a sixth son of a second son would bear a fleur-de-lys upon a crescent. But you can see how impractical such a scheme becomes when it has gone, say, four generations, when the difference marks have become far too small to recognize. Had these difference marks been placed next to each other instead of on top of each other, rather like a row of medals along the top of the shield, then it would have been easy to see that someone was a fourth son of a second son of an eldest son of an eighth son and so forth. This would have been of the greatest value genealogically. But no such simple plan was adopted. The heralds said the cadency marks must be on top of each other. Consequently cadency marks are seldom used and are today regarded as optional by the College of Arms. Another reason why they may not have been used is that it would have required a very exact knowledge of your descent and many people could not be bothered to find that out. Heraldry came to be abused even in the eighteenth century, people adopting arms to which they had no right because they did not want to admit they were not entitled to any arms at all. This snobbery reached its height during Victorian times. Stationers used to advertise that they would let people know the arms to which they were entitled if they would send them their name and county. Some people may even have thought they really were entitled to the arms conferred upon them by these unworthy stationers. Others were quite content to salve their consciences by not enquiring too deeply into the matter. Thus, if you find your grandfather used a certain crest (which is an integral part of armorial bearings and not something which can exist alone), this should enable you to identify him with the family to which he belonged, but if it was used spuriously, then it will only mislead and disappoint you. It is always worth while investigating any crest or shield of arms you may come across which is reputed to be your family arms, but refer the matter to the College of Arms, who will not charge much merely to indicate to whom this crest or these arms belong. But be prepared to find you have no connection with the family in question and you will not be disappointed. If, on the other hand, the arms are genuinely borne, then you will be led to much information about the family straight away and it will have been well worth your while investigating the matter. Remember, however, that the number of people genuinely armigerous is very few in relation to the population. Fox-Davies' *Armorial Families* is a useful work, as the editor tried to include only persons genuinely armigerous. The few exceptions are shown in italics, to indicate that their right to the arms shown had not been produced. The first edition of the work was published in 1895 and the last in 1929.

In Scotland the law of arms is somewhat different from that in England and Wales. The authority which acts on behalf of the crown is the Lyon King of Arms. He has the advantage over his English colleagues in being himself a judge and the enforcement of the proper use of arms in consequence is far stronger in Scotland. In general the same right exists to arms, namely that you descend from someone to whom arms have been granted, but there were no visitations in Scotland. In 1672 an Act was passed requiring all persons entitled to arms to register them in the Register of All Arms and Bearings in Scotland and even today, if you can prove that your ancestors in the male line used arms, it is possible to register that right to yourself without getting a grant. This is done by what is called 'matriculation' which merely means registering, in the same way as you register, or 'matriculate' in a university. In Scotland, as in England, only the eldest son is entitled to use the undifferenced arms. A younger son has the right to matriculate his arms, that is, to register them, when the Lord Lyon will give him some difference to signify that he is a cadet and not the eldest son. This requirement has kept the use of arms much purer in Scotland. Unfortunately few younger sons today trouble to register or matriculate their arms. Nevertheless even those who do so help to keep the system regularized and today the registers of matriculations are not only wonderful examples of heraldic art but contain a great deal of genealogical information. For in matriculating your arms the Lyon Court encourages you to record as much of your genealogy as you can, so that there will be on record, not only your male line but your female lines also, as far as you know them and can substantiate the descents with reasonable proofs.

The situation in Ireland differs also, owing to the destruction of so many of their records. Before the establishment of the Republic of Ireland the armorial authority in Ireland was the Ulster King of Arms. He had the right to issue to you a Confirmation of Arms if you could reasonably show that certain arms had been used by your family for three or more generations. This sounds a loose arrangement and it was so, compared with the requirements of other parts of the Kingdom. But it was felt that Irishmen should not be debarred from their inheritance of arms through the destruction of their records. Today Northern Ireland is still controlled by Ulster King of Arms, whose office is now amalgamated with Norroy, so that he is known as Norroy and Ulster King of Arms.

The Republic of Ireland has taken over the records at Dublin Castle and has established a Chief Herald of Ireland, who is responsible for all matters of heraldry in the Republic. He and his office are very helpful and will send you extracts from his records for reasonable fees.

Heraldry is a large subject and it is not possible in this short chapter to deal more than very briefly with it. A number of books on the subject are mentioned in the bibliography for those who may be interested in further reading.

In Scotland, as mentioned in the chapter on Scottish Records, the Lyon Office library is open to people for consultation on application and payment of a small fee. No such facility exists in England. The College of Arms collection belongs to the College and is normally only consulted through an officer of arms. One can understand the college being careful of its unique collection and not wishing it to be handled by the general public, who are not always too careful in handling precious records. But it does seem a pity that it is not more accessible to suitable people, perhaps on similar lines to documents in the Public Record Office. Some steps towards the opening up of these records has developed in recent years. One is the founding of the Friends of the College of Arms. Another is the publication of Sir Anthony Wagner's *Records and Collections of the College of Arms*, which gives a good idea of the records which exist there. The recent volume of the *Survey of London* covering the college, deals very fully with it and its collection.

In Ireland also a number of recent publications have given some indication of the contents of the records at Dublin Castle under the Chief Herald of Ireland.

[27]

GENEALOGY AND BIOGRAPHY

The biographer's dream no doubt is to discover new and unpublished information about some great person which can be revealed to the world amidst much excitement and great publicity. Perhaps he might discover in some old lumber room an old faded bunch of letters written by Dryden or Pope, or some further diary by Samuel Pepys! But such hopes must in general remain just dreams, though the amount of material of great historic or literary value still surviving quite unknown must still be considerable.

In the usual way, however, the biographer is led to write about someone because he has great interest in some great figure and because he feels he can write of him from some new angle, or else he starts to work on some lesser figure to whom his interest has been drawn, perhaps just because he has found some interesting letters or papers about him which he thinks can make an interesting book.

Many figures who in the past were not of particular interest may, through the mellowing influences of time and because interesting letters and diaries have survived giving a vivid picture of their lives and times, have become of sufficient interest to justify a book about them. This is where the genealogist may be of great help to the biographer, for the genealogist, in his searching amidst the minutiae of unimportant people, may come across something which reflects on some greater person, or something which throws light on some great historical event, showing it up in a quite different way to that generally accepted. The genealogist is searching for little items of information about a great number of people. The biographer is seeking many items about one person. It will be seen therefore that there is a point at which their paths cross.

Biographers in general know little of genealogical methods and it is hoped this book may assist them. Occasionally the 'sly shade' of a biographer may be seen in the literary room at Somerset House, searching for a will in the P.C.C. of his subject or some relative of his subject. But it is doubtful if many biographers do even this and fewer still pursue the search for a will to the minor courts, the bishops and arch-deacon's courts, or have any idea where to search for them. In the same way they may know about parish registers, but be unaware, if these are missing, that there is always hope that the bishop's transcripts may survive.

There are many printed by-roads which biographers are not aware of and along which a genealogist can conduct them with surprise and excitement. In all these ways it is well worth while a biographer getting the assistance of a genealogist. Some do so, particularly those American scholars who are increasingly writing British biographies. I have noticed some biographers using the Society of Genealogists collections, usually on a day-search basis. It would probably pay them to join the Society and have continued access to its valuable collection, which can be of great assistance to them. It would also pay the Society of Genealogists to develop their bio-graphical side somewhat more and make more point of draw-ing attention to it. For instance, a complete run of the obituary notices of *The Times*, kept pasted on cards in alphabetical order, would be most valuable to both genea-logists and biographers. I know that you can get the volumes of *The Times* out in various libraries and that there are annual or quarterly indexes covering these obituaries, but think of the convenience of being able to turn one up immediately. But there is in any case an enormous amount of material available at the society for the biographer. The chapter on its contents will have indicated that. It is up to him to use it. One great advantage in doing so is that all these books are on the shelves and available for immediate consultation. There is none of the waiting necessary at the British Museum Library or in the Public Record Office. This is particularly valuable when you may only want to glance at a book for a minute or two, or just look in the index of it.

But it is in the MS collection of the society that he may make his most useful find. Here there may be real new unpublished information for him. It is unfortunate that there is no comprehensive catalogue of the contents of the MS collection at the society. That is something that still awaits doing. The task is a large one and, as in so many matters, would require finances which are not at present available. Nevertheless the rough arrangement under families in boxes in alphabetical order is helpful, as is the similar arrangement of topographical information.

Probably one of the best libraries of biography in London next to the Society of Genealogists Library is that of London University. As mentioned in Chapter 25, the library specializes in biography. Here are the corrections to the *Dictionary of National Biography* which have appeared in the Institute of Historical Research bulletin for some years. Here, too, is the best collection of collective biographies I have discovered in any library outside the British Museum and depository libraries, and it is much more accessible.

County Record Offices can of course often help a biographer with information about some person belonging to the county. Apart from their collection of MS archives, they often have attached to them a useful collection of printed books covering the county and it is handy to have such a collection all together and easily consulted.

[28]

FURTHER BACK

It has already been emphasized that the chances of getting your pedigree back further than the seventeenth century are remote. If you are fortunate and the parish registers of the parish in which your ancestors lived go back to the time of their institution in 1538, then you may reach back to that date. You may even get back further if the wills of your ancestors survive, the earliest of which in the P.C.C. is 1383.

Another possible but even more fugitive source is the manor court roll. These rolls are to a great extent still in private hands and, apart from the difficulty in tracing who owns them, the chances of their surviving at all are not great. Nevertheless many such manor court rolls do survive and those known to do so are registered with the Historical MSS Commission, Manorial Documents Register, Quality House, Quality Court, Chancery Lane, London, W.C.2. There is legislation today guarding against their destruction or sale overseas.

Should such rolls survive, then you may learn much of your earlier ancestors and may succeed in tracing them, even though they were only humble people, for perhaps two hundred years prior to the start of the parish registers, that is, back into the fourteenth century. In the manor court rolls were recorded all copyholders' deeds, such as marriage settlements or mortgages of an estate. Furthermore, the jury which assembled at the death of a tenant of the Lord of the Manor recorded after their investigations of what estate the tenant died possessed, the name and relationship of his heir and what fine and heriot was due to the Lord. Such 'presentments', as they were called, often included extracts from the deceased's will and other deeds.

Apart from these possibilities, one is only able to trace further back than the mid-sixteenth century people of distinction and rank, or those who owned land.

There are a great many records which may have bearing on the pedigrees of such landowners. Many of these are fully described in Richard Sims' *Manual for the genealogist, topographer, antiquary and legal professor*, but it must be remembered that this volume was published in 1856, before the opening of the P.R.O. and therefore much of the information regarding the locality of deeds and records is out-of-date. Moreover, since Sim's day, a great deal has been done to open up records to the public, many deeds and calendars have been issued and much work indexed and copied. Sims is very valuable in giving you an idea of the contents of various records and the two volumes of the recently published *Guide to the Public Record Office* will indicate which of them are now there and give recent information about them.

In this work I can only indicate briefly some of the more important genealogical sources among these early records.

Chancery proceedings are of high importance in this respect. It is often said that few land-owning families have gone through history without some dispute resulting in a Chancery case. Such a case, if discovered, may reveal a host of information about relationships, and the papers of the case may include chart pedigrees (among the Master's papers), certificates of baptism, abstracts of deeds and wills and other documents from the family muniment room.

The proceedings in Chancery are by bill of complaint, which is in the form of a petition to the Lord Chancellor, Lord Keeper or to the Lords Commissioners of the Great Seal. The bill is followed by the answer and the evidence is given by means of affidavits, depositions and other proceedings. Thus the whole story is told on paper and you can read today all the evidence which was considered at the time by the court.

One of the difficulties in making use of Chancery proceedings is the discovery of their existence. Apart from some very early proceedings, there are no printed calendars and the MS calendars in the P.R.O. are divided between the six clerks in Chancery (or 'Prothonotaries' as they were called), whose calendars run concurrently. It is thus necessary to search each year in six different places. Apart from this it is very difficult to identify a particular case, for the calendar or index merely says 'Smith *v.* Jones', or whatever the names are. This may not be so bad if you are searching a rare name, where you would be interested in any case concerning someone of the name. But where the name is common, as Smith or Jones, as mentioned above, then the process of searching can be one of length and weariness. Such a search could only be undertaken where a very great deal depended on the result. But, if fortunate, you may discover the existence of a chancery suit through other sources. Sometimes there is mention of a chancery suit in a will and when you know there was definitely a suit and have some idea of the date, then it is not too long a task to track it down even though dealing with a common name and you have to search through a number of 'wrong numbers'. Another possible clue is the mention on the back of a deed that it was produced in some Chancery suit. Solicitors had the habit of making such notes and sometimes gave the actual reference of the case.

Early transfer of land can sometimes be traced by the discovery of a deed of Bargain and Sale, which is by indenture, enrolled in one of the courts of Westminster, or else in the county where the lands were. It is unfortunate that the provision of the statute enacting such procedure was evaded through the use of the 'Lease and Release' method devised by lawyers for conveying land, for if the method of 'Bargain and Sale' had been continued there would have been an almost universal record of the conveyance of freehold land throughout our history, rather like the Sasines Registers in Scotland.

The records of Bargain and Sale belong mostly to early periods, though the procedure was not abolished officially until the nineteenth century. They are enrolled on the Close Rolls and the grantors are indexed in books called 'Indentures', while the grantees are covered by the Close Roll index. These records are, of course, at the P.R.O. Some early conveyances were also by charter.

Many of the deeds relating to Lease and Release, which were not, unfortunately, registered centrally, but merely held by the two parties, are finding their way into the various county record offices and gradually some record of land holding is being built up by these offices.

'Feet of Fines' are another valuable record of land transfer and genealogically are of first class importance, because the vendor joined with his wife and children or other heirs in order to avoid or overcome entail or dower. The foot of the fine was enrolled in the court, the other two pieces being held by the two parties. The records of these feet of fines are almost perfect from the time of King Richard I until 1834 and they form a rich record of a proportion of the land ownership in the country.

The Court of the Exchequer had also an equity side, the pleadings in which can be of value, particularly the depositions of the court, which may often reveal relationships. The calendar of these is in the 38th and following reports of the Deputy Keeper.

Lay Subsidy Rolls and Hearth Tax Returns are also useful as indicating the existence, locality and to a certain extent the status of people. Inquisitions Post Mortem, which were held on the tenants-in-chief, are found only for the larger landowners, but in those cases are most valuable. They reveal the heir of the property concerned and his relationship to the previous owner. Indexes for them have been published for a number of years and some counties have printed or typescript abstracts of them. They end with the close of Charles I's reign.

The Recusant Rolls are useful in giving the names and residence of people who were found guilty of non-conformity, either as Roman Catholics or Protestant dissenters. These are in the P.R.O., but there is a useful return of all recusants who were convicted, giving their quality and place of abode, in August 1677, in the British Museum MSS Department (Add MS. 20,739). The Protestation Oath Rolls of 1641–2 are kept in the Record Office of the House of Lords. These are lists of people holding office who affirmed their loyalty to the crown, and another similar roll is the Association Oath Roll signed in 1696 when William III was on the throne. The latter are in the P.R.O.

As location is such an important feature in genealogy it is often useful to note in cases where an ancestor was a tenant of some landowner, as perhaps revealed by manor court rolls, whether the same landowner had property in other parts of the country. Sometimes tenants, who were often also employees, moved to some other estate of their employer and landlord, because he was able to offer them employment there of a better nature or interest. You may therefore find, when a line seems to disappear, that it continues back on some other estate of the same landlord.

[29]

SEARCHING IN THE UNITED STATES

If your forbears have been for several generations in the United States, the considerations mentioned in the first chapter of this book apply equally. Do all you can to discover from relatives, particularly the older ones, what is already known about the family. Once again you must be persistent. Question your Great-Aunt Mary and your elderly Cousin Agatha over and over again about the family and note down carefully what they tell you. There will be links with historical events in the United States, just as there were in England.

Your grandfather may remember that his grandfather or great-uncle fought in the Confederate Army in the Civil War. Try to find out from him what regiment the ancestor served in, and whether he survived. This may all lead to topographical clues as to the movement of the families, and you may also be able to learn from military records something of his career and family. You may even discover by questioning members of the family that there is a link with an ancestor who fought during the Revolutionary War. Here again the pension records in the National Archives at Washington may give information as to where he lived and whom he married.

The nineteenth century in the United States was a great period of migration, especially after the Civil War. You must consider the Homestead Act and the effect it may have had on your family through encouraging them to migrate to the Great Plains. Events stand out in the older relatives' minds more than actual dates. It would be more easily remembered, for instance, that a forbear fought at Gettysburg than the actual date when he lived, but this will give you something firm as a date for his adult existence.

All that has been said earlier in this book about family Bibles applies equally to families on the American side of the Atlantic. You will be fortunate if you discover one, but you should certainly make all enquiries you can as to its possible existence.

At the same time that you are questioning relatives you should be checking that there are no MS or printed accounts or pedigrees of your family already in existence. For printed family histories, just as in England you turn to the British Museum Library catalogue, so in the United States you turn to the catalogue of the Library of Congress in Washington. A list from this library entitled *American and English Genealogies in the Library of Congress*, 2nd edition, was published in 1919, and the 'subjects' catalogues under the heading 'Genealogy' will direct you to any publications after that date. You will be fortunate if you find a ready-made history of the family, but there is a greater possibility that there is some brief account of it at some period in one of many printed sources.

These genealogies, often referred to as 'buried genealogies', can be discovered through a number of indexes of genealogies which correspond roughly to Marshall's and Whitmore's guides in Great Britain, but are more extensive. The most prominent of these are the *American Genealogical Index*, edited by Fremont J. Rider, in 48 volumes, which was published between 1942 and 1952, indexing individual names from several hundred family histories and also the names in the census of 1790 In addition there is the *American Genealogical Biographical Index*, by the same editor, which is a continuation and expansion of the previously mentioned work. It includes a further selection of family histories, and all the names published in the *Boston Evening Transcript* in its genealogical section from 1906 to 1941; it also includes names from sixty-three volumes of lists of Revolutionary War soldiers. This publication began in 1952 and when completed will be a vast work. There are also the Durrie series of indexes and Munsell's indexes.

In addition to the Library of Congress itself there are a number of libraries in the United States which have special collections of genealogical works. Among the most important of these is the Newberry Library in Chicago. This library has an index of family sketches in all the local histories acquired up to about 1909. This index has been reproduced by photo offset and is therefore available in several other larger libraries.

From your enquiries among relatives you will probably get a reasonable idea as to where the earlier members of the family lived. A local history of the town or county in which they lived may give some information – if not directly about them, then at any rate about the kinds of occupations and lives the people were leading in that area. There may also be collections particularly referring to that district in local libraries. An example is the *Catalogue of American Genealogies*, in the Library of the Long Island Historical Society, published in New York in 1935; it lists over 8,000 books connected with genealogy.

In the United States there are far more periodicals devoted to genealogy than in Great Britain. Many of these are related to particular states or districts. Among the more important of them is the *New York Genealogical and Biographical Record*, *The American Genealogist* (formerly the *New Haven Genealogical Magazine*), which deals particularly with New England records prior to 1800, the *Virginia Magazine of Biography and History*, the *William and Mary Quarterly*, *Tyler's Genealogical Quarterly* (these last three being particularly concerned with Virginian genealogy), the *Pennsylvanian Magazine* and *The Old Northwest Genealogical Quarterly*. There are also periodicals concerned with particular societies, for example, the *Daughters of the American Revolution Magazine*, which has been published since 1892, and the *Minute Man*, the bulletin of the National Society of Sons of the Revolution, first published in 1915. A useful index of these and other books on American genealogy will be found in Gilbert H. Doane's book *Searching for your Ancestors*, (3rd edition 1960). Jacobus's *Index to Genealogical Periodicals* indexes the articles in a number of these publications.

The Town Records

Great Britain is geographically a compact unit. To search for births, marriages or deaths since the civil registration was established you only need to look in three places: the registration of England and Wales, of Scotland, and of Ireland. The United States is a far greater area and there the basis of the civil organization is the state and within the state the county. The earliest dates for civil registrations of births, marriages and deaths, or vital records, as they are called, vary considerably from state to state. In general, they date back to the middle of the nineteenth century, when certain federal laws requiring such records to be kept were passed, but in some of the older eastern states there are records going back considerably earlier. These are usually found in the office of the town clerk of the town or township in which the family lived. Their condition varies considerably. Sometimes, though not frequently, they are indexed, but sometimes the index is a poor one. Only occasionally do you find them really well kept. In addition, many of these records, as in England, have unfortunately been destroyed by fire or other causes. Before 1850, there were practically no general laws which governed the registering of births, marriages or deaths, and even in states where there were such laws they were often observed very carelessly or even ignored completely. However, the details required for registration were fuller than those required in England and Wales. For instance, the parentage of the deceased was entered on the death certificate during the latter part of the nineteenth century.

Church Registers

The records discussed above were civil records. The registers of the churches amplify these and, as in Britain, extend further back. Those of the eastern states often date back to the earliest colonial days. Curiously enough, in these early colonial times marriage was considered as a civil contract and not a religious ceremony. Thus even from the time of the Pilgrim Fathers marriages were performed before a magistrate, and so only baptisms and burials were recorded in the church registers in early times; however, the publication of banns which preceded the civil ceremony was recorded in the church registers.

Unfortunately, in the United States church records are often difficult to locate. The registers were usually kept by the minister himself, probably in his own home, and sometimes when he moved he, in error, took them with him. Later they were sometimes returned to the church to which they belonged, but often they were forgotten. Sometimes church records were destroyed by fire or other calamities, or they were mislaid. Occasionally they were deposited in some place for safe keeping.

The whereabouts of registers, particularly of churches which have now ceased to exist, are difficult to discover. Occasionally the state historical societies have been given the custody of these church records, and sometimes the state library has them. Many of the records belonging to the Baptist Church in North America are held by the American Baptists Historical Library at Colgate-Rochester Divinity School, in Rochester, New York. Similarly many Methodists Church records are held by the Drew Theological Seminary in Madison, New Jersey. Information about Roman Catholic records can be found in Cora C. Curry's *Records of the Roman Catholic Church in the United States*, published in 1935. Episcopal Church records are mainly held in the parishes, but those of churches which have ceased to exist, or of earlier missions, are kept in the diocesan offices. Two bodies which have large collections of Jewish records are The American Jewish Archives, Cincinnati, Ohio, and The American Jewish Historical Society, New York, The records of the Mormon Church at Salt Lake City, Utah, have already been mentioned in Chapter 10. They are naturally as important for tracing ancestry in the United

States as elsewhere. Their great card file containing over 5,000,000 names is an index to an enormous number of sheets of family records. The Society of Friends in the United States have published the records of their Quaker meetings in the *Encyclopedia of American Quaker Genealogy*.

Monumental Inscriptions

As in England memorials to prominent or more wealthy citizens are found on the walls of many churches and on stones in some of the early graveyards around the churches, but there were at an early period many private cemeteries, and in the era of expansion and movement into new territories people might often be buried in a private plot of ground on the border of their own land. Such memorial stones are, of course, often difficult to locate. Nevertheless efforts should be made to try to ascertain where earlier members of the family were buried, as the information on a gravestone is usually far fuller than that given in a burial register or on a civil death certificate.

Having discovered from earlier members of the family where their forbears have been buried, or may have been buried, it is a good idea if possible to persuade some one of the older generation, perhaps your grandfather or great uncle, to accompany you to the burial place, as when you have located the stone of one or more members of the family he may remember that other members were buried nearby. In addition, unknown to you persons of other surnames and related by marriage may be pointed out as being buried nearby, as was the custom. In any case you should take notes of nearby graves in case they later turn out to be graves of relations.

A little study of styles in tombstones will soon enable you to allocate roughly a stone to its period. A useful book on this subject is Harriette Merrifield Forbes's *Gravestones of Early New England and the men who made them, 1653–1800*, which was published in 1927.

Unfortunately, as in England, some stones have weathered badly and are illegible. However, often a stone which at first seems indecipherable, may with patience be read, sometimes by observation from different angles. Even before 1850, these stones usually gave the age of the deceased as well as the date of death. It is of course always possible that individual members of the family may have been buried away from the family graveyard, and it is advisable to search for them in cemeteries in neighbouring areas.

Census Returns

The United States has the advantage over Great Britain in having earlier census returns which list names. Their first census was in 1790. This lists the heads of families throughout the country by name, and the whole of the surviving part of this census was published in 12 volumes by the Bureau of the Census in 1909. Unfortunately the censuses of certain states are missing, having been destroyed when the British burnt the Capital at Washington in the War of 1812. These missing censuses are for the states of Delaware, Georgia, Kentucky, Tennessee, New Jersey and Virginia, but partial returns from the last mentioned state have been built up from the state's own tax lists from 1782-1785. It has been estimated that from these the names of the heads of families for nearly half the state have been recovered. These lists form the Virginia volume in the census publication of 1909.

Census records were made after 1790 every ten years. These are held among the national archives at Washington and a number of larger libraries hold microfilms or microcard copies of them.

Probate Records

Searching for a will or administration in the United States is a much simpler operation than it is in England. You do not have the complications of the different courts before 1858, the archdeacon's, the bishop's, the archbishop's, nor those elusive depositories, the peculiars. Wills in the United States were proved normally in the District Probate Office which was often in the county town. The probate district is not necessarily identical with the county boundaries but is usually so. Occasionally the probate office may be situated in a town other than the county seat.

The probate laws vary from state to state and some study of the laws affecting the area in which your forbears lived is helpful in your searching. There were two types of will, the nuncupative, or spoken will, given before witnesses, and the written will, which is signed and witnessed as in England. The latter are by far the more prevalent. The nuncupative wills mostly belong to the early colonial days.

You should try to visit the probate office personally and make abstracts of any wills which concern your family in the way suggested in Chapter 7, pages 61–2.

A useful probate office record which has no exact equivalent in England is the Distribution List. This gives the distribution of the estate, showing what property went to each of the beneficiaries and it usually names the relationship. As in England, if a person died intestate his estate was distributed according to certain laws. In some states a guardian had to be appointed for children who were minors. The record of such appointments would indicate the relationship. Sometimes considerable details of the family life and conditions are revealed by it.

These offices are normally called probate offices or probate courts, but in New York the term 'Surrogate's Court' is used.

Descent From Revolutionary Times

Naturally United States citizens have always been anxious and proud to establish descent from the heroes of the Revolution. These include, of course, those who signed the Declaration of Independence, those who took part in the Boston Tea Party and the many who served in the Revolutionary War. Similarly those who came over with the early Pilgrims or who took part in the Civil War are of interest to their descendants. Organizations like the Daughters of the Pilgrims, the Sons of Confederate Veterans, The Society of Cincinnati and the Holland Society in New York have built up their own archives which reveal the genealogical descent of many present-day Americans from those early patriots. The

Daughters of the American Revolution in particular have collected vast archives and have more than 200,000 names recorded and filed in them at their Memorial Continental Hall in Washington. They have also published a number of lineage books. In the National Archives in Washington there are records of pensions granted to soldiers who fought in the Revolutionary War. These will often reveal details of their families.

$\left[30 \right]$

WRITING IT UP

Do not put off for too long writing up or at least producing a pedigree of the results of your labour. Some people postpone doing this until, as they say, they have collected all the material. The result often is that they never do put their results on paper, because there never will be a time when you have collected *all* the material. It may be difficult to decide at which particular point you should write up what you have collected. Certainly when you have, for instance, got back to the eighteenth century you might consider putting your results into some form which will record your work and make it available to others who may be interested, particularly, of course, future generations. How often genealogists sigh and say 'If only grandad had put down even on a small piece of paper some of what he knew about the family!' Make sure future generations do not say that of you!

Another advantage in getting out an account of the family fairly soon is that you will stimulate interest in other members of it and may get some of them sending in corrections, uncles writing indignant epistles declaring 'Great-uncle Joe was never in the 43rd – it was the 57th of course' or that 'Jeremiah never had a son called Geoffrey – he was actually christened "George", though always known as "Smug".'

In Chapter 2 I have made some suggestions on the best way of recording pedigrees in chart form and the methods by which it can best be reproduced. This chart pedigree is one of the simplest ways of recording information about the family and even if you decide, as I hope you will, to write up your family in some narrative form, you will need a chart pedigree or perhaps several chart pedigrees to illustrate it. There is no doubt the chart pedigree shows the family ancestry in a clear and simple way, but you are limited in the amount of information you can get on it for each member. Often pedigrees in historical works or biographies, perhaps produced by people far from expert in such matters, are deplorably lacking in detail and sometimes in clarity. On the other hand, if they are overburdened with detail the thread of the line is lost. An example of chart pedigrees with a great deal of detail but still not overburdened are Crisp's *Visitations*, which are a kind of modern nineteenth century equivalent of the Herald's visitations of earlier times.

Turning to narrative pedigree, perhaps the simplest kind is that which forms notes to a chart pedigree. This can be quite effective and is merely done by having note marks, either numbers or letters, preferably in brackets to show they are nothing to do with the information, against the person; and against these note marks, on as many separate sheets as they may require, you can give as full details as you like on the person in question. This keeps the chart pedigree from becoming unwieldy and at the same time gives fuller information on individuals for those who want them. By this method you can often keep a chart pedigree of twelve or more generations on a single sheet, for it is only necessary to give brief details, enough to identify the person.

A clear and concise method of narrative pedigree is that used in such publications as *Burke's Peerage* and *Burke's Landed Gentry*. If you study the way in which the generations are recorded in these publications it will guide you for your own, should you decide to use this method. Such a form of pedigree can easily be duplicated from typewriting, in fact the Supplement to the 1952 edition of *Burke's Landed Gentry* is reproduced from a form of typewriting probably by one of the litho processes. This used no doubt a form of Varityper, which is a glorified typewriter in which you can get italic as well as roman type and other variations.

You will notice that in this kind of recorded pedigree it is necessary to continue the pedigree down one line, which is done by using the words 'of whom presently' against the person through whom you have decided to continue the line. This is often the eldest line, but need not necessarily be so. In the past with the landed families it was usually through the eldest son that the lands descended, and in the case of a peerage this also descended through the eldest son. But through whatever line you decide to take your pedigree, you must exhaust all the descendants of the other members of the family as you come to them. In the case of a pedigree which starts far back, this sometimes means continuing on for many generations, each one indented further and further into the page until you are approaching or even exceeding the half-way division. For this reason you cannot give too much detail for each person, or otherwise it may go on for several pages and get confusing. Some of the pedigrees of older families in the *Peerage* or *Landed Gentry* are very extensive and yet still keep their clarity. An example of an old peerage with many younger branches is that of the Earl of Huntingdon and a family in the *Landed Gentry* well extended is that of Giffard. A study of these and other such pedigrees will soon instruct you on how the matter is handled.

An important concern in this type of recording is the numerical notation beside each member of the family, which helps to show to which generation he or she belongs. Some people use a mixture of roman and arabic figures, both upper and lower case, in perhaps this order: I, 1, (1), (i). One slight disadvantage of the roman figures is that they take up varying space, i.e. I, II, III, IV and so on. But this need not be of great consequence, so long as the indentation is kept even, regardless of the number of spaces which the roman figures take up. Other people prefer to use arabic figures throughout, which, under 10, remain single-spaced. In either case after the first runs of generations are exhausted, they have to be continued with additional symbols and these are best in the form 1a, 2a, 3a, and then the children of those so marked will be 1b, 2b, 3b and so on, the figure always indicating the position in the family, with separate runs for sons and daughters. Thus a male 1b will be the eldest son of perhaps 1a or perhaps 2a. This may sound somewhat complicated, but an examination of pedigrees in this form will soon make the method clear. An example of such a pedigree is given in Appendix B.

But possibly you may want to try something a little more ambitious in the way of a family history. Various methods of doing this are outlined in Sir James Balfour Paul's introduction to Margaret Stuart's *Scottish Family History*. It is a great mistake to imagine that only the histories of famous families make interesting reading. All family histories are to a certain extent the history of the times through which they lived and the history of a family which never rose to prominence or held high position can make nevertheless an interesting contribution to social history. Unfortunately this is not true of many of those produced, but this is because of the way in which they are written rather than because the subject matter is uninteresting. Some are merely a schedule of dry facts which, although valuable to the immediate family, could be so much more attractively presented. Others, which try to relieve the monotony of such dull recitation, often tend towards the facetious, possibly impelled with a desire for modesty which is really a false modesty. This is irritating to the reader and worse than a mere factual account.

One of the interests in a family saga is in the recording of the reasons which enticed people to take up their occupations. This was often because their father or uncle was in that trade or job, but at other times it was a reflection of some national event. For instance, the movement of working class people from the country into the towns during the Industrial Revolution period affected a very large number of families. There was also the magnet of London and many families had adventurous members who moved into the capital during the period from about 1775 to 1825, some considerably raising their financial and social status in doing so.

If you decide to write up your family history in the more ambitious narrative style, then do try to infuse into its pages some of the atmosphere of the times through which it passed.

Let us take the following account of an imaginary family as an example.

John Smith, cloth-worker of Trowbridge, Wiltshire, married on the 15th July 1776 at Bradford-on-Avon, Wiltshire, Mary Roberts, daughter of William Roberts, woolworker there.
They had an only son, James Smith, baptized at Trowbridge 20th May 1778 and married at Bideford, Devon, on 17th June 1797 Anne Hodge. He served in the Peninsular War as a corporal in the 29th Foot and was present at the battles of Rolica and Vimiero in August 1808 and at Albuera on the 11th May 1811. He died at Bideford, aged seventy-three in September 1851 and was buried in the parish church there on the 16th of that month. His wife Mary died there in May 1820.
They had issue four children, namely ... etc.

This is a factual account which has value, but this sort of style can get very monotonous when carried on for many pages. Let us take these same facts and re-write them to include some historical background.

John Smith was a cloth-worker in Trowbridge, working in an industry for which that Wiltshire town was famous in the eighteenth century. In 1776, on the 15th July, only eleven days after the historic Declaration of Independence by the American colonists, the news of which when it reached this country was to cause a shudder of presentiment to pass through the minds of thinking Englishmen, this young cloth-worker married in the picturesque fourteenth century church of nearby Bradford-on-Avon Mary Roberts, whose father William was employed in the wool trade for which that town had long been renowned.
James, their only son, was baptized at Trowbridge on the 20th May 1778. He grew up during the French wars and as a young man of eighteen enlisted in the 29th Foot or Worcestershire Regiment. Promoted to corporal he found himself stationed with his regiment in the pleasant North

Devon market town and seaport of Bideford. It is not surprising therefore that he found a bride among the Bideford
girls and this nineteen-year-old, fair-haired, blue-eyed
Corporal of Foot on the 17th June 1797 was married in
the parish church of that town on the hillside of the
Torridge river to Ann Hodge of the same parish.

However he was not long able to enjoy married life at
home, for, a rebellion having broken out in Ireland, his
regiment within nine months of his marriage was sent over
there, embarking from the little port of Appledore at the
mouth of the Torridge.

From Ireland the regiment was later sent to Spain and there
Corporal Smith saw fighting in August 1808 at the battles
of Rolica and Vimiero, at the former of which his colonel,
Lt-Colonel the Honble. G. A. F. Lake, was killed and
the regiment suffered considerable casualties. At Vimiero
they were more fortunate, only losing a corporal and two
privates.

Later, in 1811, he was in action again at Albuera, and there
the regiment suffered severely, there being five officers, a
sergeant, a corporal and a drummer and seventy-four
privates killed, and the sergeant-major, three sergeants, two
corporals and forty-seven privates later died of their
wounds.

But John Smith survived to return to Bideford and lived
long enough to receive in 1849 the much delayed Peninsular
General Service Medal with clasps for the three battles in
which he had participated. Anne, his wife, predeceased
him by some thirty-one years, dying in May 1820. John
himself was buried in the grounds of Bideford parish church
on 16th September 1851, aged seventy-three.

They had four children ... etc.

This expanded account, expanded through adding some details of the background of the times, has, I think, infused some
colour into what Pooh Bah in *The Mikado* called 'an otherwise bald and unconvincing narrative'. It has required some
further research. A short history of Wiltshire gave the back-

ground to the towns of Trowbridge and Bradford-on-Avon and a history of the Worcestershire Regiment produced the information that the regiment was stationed in Bideford in 1797 and gave some account of its future history. The description books of the regiment at the P.R.O. would show Corporal Smith as having had blue eyes and fair hair on his enlistment. An historical chronicle, such as Steinberg's *Historical Tables* or Margaret A. Rolleston's *English History Note Book* will guide you to the contemporary events.

Whatever methods you decide upon by which to record your researches, when you have finally accomplished the task you will be able to sit back with the happy feelings of one who has, like Longfellow's village blacksmith, 'something attempted, something done' and like him 'earned a night's repose'. You may even experience some of the feelings of that great historian Edward Gibbon who, after years of toil and labour on his *Decline and Fall of the Roman Empire*, on at last completing it, felt that he was parting 'with an old and agreeable companion'. At any rate, in the tracing of your family you have met with many new companions who have, in the course of time, and as you have more and more unravelled the course of their lives, become in fact 'old and agreeable'.

APPENDIX A

Suggested Questionnaire for sending out to the family. The general queries may apply to most families, but the more detailed enquiries will, of course, vary greatly in different cases. Plenty of room should be left after each question for the replies.

General Questions
Do you know of the existence of any of the following, relating to earlier members of the family:

Family Bible, giving dates of baptism, marriage, burial etc. Family pedigree or written account or notes of the family. Any copies of wills, any diaries, note books, birthday books, old receipt books, account books, tontine or stock and share certificates, old deeds relating to property, estate maps, bank books, life assurance policies, apprenticeship indentures, family samplers, funeral cards or bookplates.

Baptism, marriage, death or burial certificates.

Deeds concerning the freehold, leasehold or receipts for up-keep of graves.

Letters of past members, particularly from those abroad.

The name of the family lawyer, and any marriage settlements.

Old family portraits, miniatures, or photographs.

Medals and decorations, certificates of service in the Army, Navy or East India Company. Any family traditions of service in these forces, any particular regiments with which they have been connected.

Any family traditions of any sort whatsoever, e.g. that they came from such and such a place or county, or from abroad, that they were engaged in a particular trade or occupation.

Specific Question
The earliest known member of the family is JOHN SMITH, who married at St Clement Danes, London, in August 1831, MARY ROBINSON. John Smith died 15 January 1876, aged 69, so was born about 1806–07. Have you any information as to where he was born, who his father and mother were and where they were married, or any other information?

APPENDIX B

Example of a Tabular Pedigree suitable for reproducing from typewriting and using only arabic figures.

STEVENS OF PLYMOUTH

ROBERT STEVENS, married at St Andrew's, Plymouth, 21 Feb. 1757, Mary, dau, of Nathaniel Smith, and had issue,

1. JOHN, of whom presently.
2. ROBERT, b. 18 June, bapt. St Andrew's 2 July 1765.
3. JAMES, bapt. St Andrew's 10 Nov. 1771.
1. JOAN, bapt. St Andrews 26 Aug. 1758.
2. MARY, b. 25 May, bapt. St Andrew's 4 July, 1760.
3. WINIFRED, b. 27 July, 1767.
4. JENNY, b. 3 Mar., bapt. St Andrew's 26 Mar. 1769.

The eldest son,

JOHN STEVENS, merchant and shipowner of Plymouth, b. 19 Sept., bapt. Charles Church, Plymouth, 27 Oct. 1762, d. at Plymouth 3 Feb. 1831, bur. at Plympton St Mary's, mar. at St Andrew's, Plymouth, 2 Aug. 1790, Sarah (d. in Plymouth 26 Feb. 1845, aged 75) dau. of John Lee of Modbury, Devon, and had issue,

1. JOHN, bapt. Charles Church, Plymouth, 20 Jan., d. 11 Nov. 1793, bur. at Plympton St Mary's.
2. ROBERT, bapt. Charles Church, Plymouth, 21 Sept. 1794, d. 11 Mar. 1795, bur. Plympton St Mary's.
3. JOHN LEE, of whom presently.
4. JAMES, shipping agent, bapt. Charles Church, Plymouth, 14 February 1798, d. unm. 13 June 1869.
5. THOMAS, shipowner and coal merchant, Mayor of Plymouth 1854–5, b. 23 Nov. 1799, bapt. Charles Church,

Plymouth, 3 Jan. 1800, d. Plymouth 8 Dec. 1869, mar. 20 Mar. 1821, Mary Maddick (b. 10 Feb. 1802, d. 28 Sep. 1876) dau. of George Sanders, of Brixham, Devon, and by her had issue,

(1) JOHN HOOPER JARMOND, b. 13 Jan. 1823, drowned at sea, 1843.

(2) THOMAS JONES, shipowner and coal merchant, b. 24 July, 1824, d. 19 Aug. 1901, mar. 20 Mar. 1846 his 1st cousin Mary Maddick Sanders (b. 23 Aug. 1823, d. 22 Mar. 1904) and by her had issue.

1a. JOHN, shipping agent of Plymouth, b. 21 June 1847, d. 21 Dec. 1885, mar. 17 Sep. 1877 Eliza Huxham (d, 29 June 1887) and by her had issue.

1b. GEORGE HERBERT.

2b. ARTHUR VIVIAN.

1b. KATE WINEFRED.

2a. THOMAS SAMUEL, master mariner, later in business in London, b. 10 Apr. 1849, d. 5 Sep. 1909, mar. 24 June 1874, Jessie Turner (d. 1924), 2nd dau. of Frederick Herron, of Plymouth, and by her had issue.

1b. FRANK HERRON, solicitor, b. 1875.

1b. BARBARA PEARL.

3a. MACKWOOD, clerk in Holy Orders, sometimes rector of Addington, nr. Winslow, Bucks, b. 3 Apr. 1853, d. 20 May 1920, mar. 1st, 19 June 1878, Alice Margaret Griffinhoofe (d. 9 Aug. 1881) and 2nd, 18 June 1895, Mary Christina Badcock (b. 17 Dec. 1853, d. 16 Nov. 1932), leaving no issue by either marriage.

4a. CHARLES, major in the Indian Staff Corps, b. 20 May 1857, mar. Mary Ann Englebach, and d.s.p. 13 Feb. 1932.

5a. PERCY, b. 19 Jan. 1859, d. unm. 1940.

1a. MARY, b. 13 Aug 1850, d. 7 Mar. 1852

2a. SALLY, b. 26 Aug 1851, living in Sep. 1901.

3a. IDA, b. 23 Aug. 1854, d. 2 Jan. 1925.

4a. ANGELINA, a member of the Clewer Sisterhood, Berks, b. 19 Jan. 1856, d. at Folkestone, Kent, 28 May 1901.

(3) SANDERS, shipowner and coal merchant, b. Plymouth 13 Jan. 1826, d. Teignmouth, 18 Mar. 1910, bur. Plymouth Cemetery, mar. Plymouth, 14 June 1851, Emma Ruth (b. in Plymouth 7 Jan. 1832, d. 17 Oct. 1889), dau, of James Marshall, builder, of Plymouth, and had issue.

1a. MARSHALL, a founder and first manager of the Manchester Ship Canal. M.P. for Eccles, Manchester, 1918–22, b. Plymouth 18 Apr. 1852, d. there 12 Aug. 1936, mar. 1873, Louisa Blamey (d. Torquay 8 Jan. 1932), dau. of Philip Blamey of Cusgarne and St Blazey, Cornwall, and by her had issue.

1b. DOUGLAS FAIRWEATHER, b. 1874, d. young.

2b. BLAMEY, M.Sc. Manch., mining engineer, b. Plymouth, 26 May 1875, d. Mexico, 1939, mar. in Brookline, Mass., U.S.A., 19 Feb. 1906, Phoebe Margaret (d. 5 Feb. 1948), dau. of Sameul Walter Reynolds, of Pinkneyville, Illinois, U.S.A., and had issue,

1c. REYNOLDS, b. Seattle, Washington, U.S.A., 19 June 1908, d. Manchester, 30 Oct. 1927.

2c. GORDON, b. Mexico City, 23 Oct. 1913, mar. Derby, 22 Mar. 1943, Edna, dau. of Leonard Roberts, and has issue.

1d. ROBERT BLAMEY, b. 1 May 1946.

2d. DAVID MICHAEL, b. 25 Sept. 1949.

1c. LOUISA ELIZABETH, B.Sc. Manch., b. Penticton, Canada, mar. 22 July 1948, Alejandro Manuel Raimúndez, B.B.C. European Service.

2c. VICTORIA, b. Brooklyn, New York, mar. Mexico City, 2 Nov. 1936, George Hinton, mining engineer, and has issue 1 s. and 2 daus.

BIBLIOGRAPHY

Bibliography of the principal books and articles mentioned in each chapter and a number of others. Place of publication is only mentioned when outside the United Kingdom.

Chapter 1. Discovering what is already known

ANDERSON, M., *Genealogy and Surnames: with some heraldic and biographical notices.* 1865

BERNAU, Charles Allan, *? County* [the first part of an index of surnames with the county of origin, compiled from the Chancery Depositions in the P.R.O.], 1932

GARDNER, David E. *and* SMITH, Frank, *Genealogical Research in England and Wales,* 3 vols [in progress] U.S.A., 1956–64.

GUPPY, Henry Brougham, *Homes of Family Names in Great Britain,* 1890.

GUMBLEY, Walter, *Unusual baptismal names,* 1956

HARCUP, Sara E. (compiler) *Historical, Archaeological and Kindred Societies in the British Isles,* 1965

HIGGS, Audrey H. *and* WRIGHT, Donald, *West Midland Genealogy: a survey of the local genealogical material available in the public libraries of Herefordshire, Shropshire, Staffordshire, Warwickshire and Worcestershire,* 1966.

HITCHING, K & K., *References to English Surnames in 1601: an index giving about 19,650 references to surnames contained in the printed registers of 778 English parishes,* 1910. [Similar work for 1602, (1911)]

HUGHES, James Pennethorne, *How you got your name: the origin and meaning of surnames,* rev. ed., 1961

HUGHES, James Pennethorne, *Is thy name Wart? the origin of some curious and other surnames,* 1965

JOHNSTON, G. D., 'Legal Terms and Phrases' *Amateur Historian* III, 249 (Winter 1957–8)

KAMINKOW, Marion J., *A New Bibliography of British Genealogy with notes,* U.S.A., 1965. [This valuable genealogical aid largely replaces H. G. Harrison's *Select Biblio-*

graphy of English Genealogy, 1937].

LEA, J. Henry, *Genealogical research in England, Scotland and Ireland*, 1906 [still useful for its succinct lists]

LOYD, Lewis Christopher, *The origins of some Anglo-Norman families;* ed. by Charles Travis Clay and David C. Douglas. 1951

MAIDBURY, Lawrence, 'Family History in Surnames', *Amateur Historian*, II, 114 (Feb-March 1955).

MANCHESTER PUBLIC LIBRARIES, *Reference Library – Subject Catalogue, Section 929 Genealogy*, 3 parts, 1956–8. [includes good collection of individual family histories].

MARSHALL, George, *The Genealogist's Guide*, 1903.

MULLINS, Edward Lindsay C., *Texts and Calendars: an analylitical guide to serial publications*, 1958 [Very useful in that it lists publications of official, national and local English and Welsh socities. Indexed]

PHILLIMORE's *Directory for Genealogists and Local Historians*, 1963 [gives addresses of county record offices and national and local organizations, for England only]

PHILLIMORE, William P. W. *and* FRY, Edward A., *Index to Changes of Name ... 1760–1901*, 1905.

PINE, Leslie Gilbert, *The Story of Surnames*, 1965

RYE, Walter, *Records and Record Searching; a guide to the genealogist and topographer*, 2nd ed., 1897.

STEEL, Donald John, 'The Descent of Christian Names', *Genealogists' Magazine*, XIV, 34 (June 1962)

THOMSON, Theodore Radford, *A Catalogue of British Family Histories*, 2nd ed., 1935

WALFORD, Albert John *and* PAYNE, L. M., *Guide to Reference Material*, 1959. Supplement, 1963, by Walford, Payne and C. A. Toase. [Sections on biography (920) and Genealogy and Heraldry (929) valuable].

WHITE, Geoffrey H., 'Companions of the Conqueror', *Genealogists' Magazine* IX, 417 (Sept, 1944)

WHITE, Geoffrey H., 'Notes on Anglo-Norman Genealogy', *Genealogists' Magazine* IX, 463 (March 1945).

WHITMORE, John Beach, *A Genealogical Guide: an index to British pedigrees in continuation of Marshall's Genealogist's Guide, 1903*, 1953.

WITHYCOMBE, Elizabeth Gidley, *The Oxford Dictionary of English Christian Names*, 2nd ed., 1950

Chapter 2. Keeping Your Records

GREENWOOD, Herbert William, *Document Photography*, 3rd ed., 1947

HARTLEY, W. C. Eyre, 'Document Copying', *Amateur Historian*, II, 311 (Feb-March 1956).

HOLMSTROM, John Edwin, *How to take, keep and use notes*, 1947

MINTO, C. S., 'Reflex Printing', *Library Association Record*, May and June, 1942.

Chapter 3. The Civil Registration

GENERAL REGISTER OFFICE, *Abstract of Arrangements respecting Registration of Births, Marriages and Deaths in the U.K. and other countries of the British Commonwealth ...and in the Irish Republic*, 1952 [includes lists and registers kept at Somerset House and elsewhere in England and Wales].

MAIDBURY, Lawrence, 'The General Register of Births, Deaths and Marriages', *Amateur Historian* III, 108 (Spring 1957).

SMITH, George Tulloch Bisset, *Vital Registration*, 2nd ed., 1907 [a manual of the law and practice concerning the registration of births, deaths and marriages... etc.]

Chapter 4. Census Returns

BERESFORD, Maurice, 'The Unprinted Census Returns of 1841, 1851, 1861, for England and Wales', *Amateur Historian*, V, 260 (Summer 1963).

HECTOR, Leonard Charles, 'The Census Returns of 1841 and 1851', *Amateur Historian*, I, 174 (June-July 1953).

Chapter 5. Parish Registers

BLOMFIELD, Kathleen and PERCY-SMITH, Hubert Kendall, *National Index of Parish Register Copies*, 1939 [Contains list of register copies not in the Society of Genealogists and is a companion to the Society's List. This index will shortly be superseded by the Society's new National Index of Parish Registers, which starts publication 1966, see below]

BRADBROOK, William, *The Parish Register,* 1910

CAMP, Anthony John, *A Key to Boyd's Marriage Index,* 2nd ed., rev. and enlarged, 1963.

CATALOGUE *of Parish Register Copies in the Possession of the Society of Genealogists.* Rev. enlarged ed., 1963

COX, John Charles, *The Parish Registers of England,* 1910

CRISP, Frederick A., (ed.), *List of Parish Registers and Other Genealogical Works edited by F. A. Crisp,* 1908. [Contains indexes to most of his publications].

GUILDHALL LIBRARY, *Parish Registers: a handlist, Pt. I. Registers of Church of England Parishes within the City of London,* 1963

GUILDHALL LIBRARY, *Parish Registers: a handlist. Pt. II.* containing 1. Registers of C. of E. Parishes outside the City of London 2. Non-parochial Registers and Registers of foreign denominations 3. Burial Ground Records, 1964.

LE HARDY, William, 'How to Read 16th and 17th Century Handwriting', *Amateur Historian,* I, 146 (Apr–May 1953).

LEWIS's *Topographical Dictionary of England.* [Various editions published 1831–49 – separate atlas with 1835 and 1842 editions].

Register of English Monumental Inscriptions, 2 vols, 1911–14

RIDGE, Alan D., 'All at Sea: observations on the Stepney Baptism Registers', *Archives,* VI, No. 32 (Oct. 1964)

STEEL, Donald John (ed.), assisted by Mrs Alice Elizabeth Frances Steel and Colin W. Field, *National Index of Parish Registers* [*in progress* Vol I. General prefatory material, and Vol V. S. Midlands & Welsh border, Herefordshire, Shropshire, Gloucestershire, Warwichshire, Worcestershire and Oxfordshire, are scheduled for publication in 1966. The whole work will be in 11 or 12 vols].

TUPLING, George Henry, 'Searching the Parish Records – the Parish Registers', *Amateur Historian,* I, 198 (Aug–Sept. 1953)

WRIGLEY, Edward Anthony, 'Parish Registers and Population History, I and II', *Amateur Historian,* VI, Nos 5 & 6 (Autumn 1964, Winter 1964–5).

Chapter 6. Non-Parochial Registers

BAKER, Frank, 'Methodist Archives', *Amateur Historian,* III, 143 (Summer 1957).

BESSE, Joseph, 'Collection of the Sufferings' [Quakers], MS at Friends House, London, 2 vols. 1753.

CATHOLIC RECORD SOCIETY, Publications Vol 1—, 1905—.

CONGREGATIONAL HISTORICAL SOCIETY, Transactions, 1901— [prints early records and bibliographies]

GREEN, Alan, 'The Archives of Congregationalism', *Amateur Historian*, III, 208 (Autumn 1957)

JONES, Robert Tudur, *Congregationalism in England, 1662–1962*, 1962.

MORTIMER, R. S., 'The Archives of the Society of Friends', *Amateur Historian*, III, 55 (Winter 1956–7).

NEWMAN, Josiah, *The Quaker Records*, 1908 [Vol II of *Some Special Studies in Genealogy*, ed. by Charles A. Bernau]

QUAKERS. *Journal of the Friends' Historical Society*, 1903 – date.

REGISTRAR GENERAL, *List of Non-Parochial Registers and Records in the custody of the Registrar General of Births, Deaths and Marriages*, 1841 [over 6,000 vols listed. Quaker records separately listed at back of vol. Does not include Roman Catholic nor Jewish Synagogues. Many records of Welsh Nonconformist chapels were not deposited. The records here listed have now been moved to the Public Record Office].

SHAW, Thomas, 'Genealogy in Methodist Repositories', *Genealogists' Magazine* XI, 179 (March 1952).

TURNER, Joseph Horsfall (ed.), *The Nonconformist Register of Baptisms, Marriages and Deaths, compiled by the Reverends O. Heywood and Dickenson, 1644–1702, 1702–1752*, 1881 [generally known as The Northowram or Coley Register]

WELCH, Charles Edwin, 'Nonconformist Registers' *Journal of the Society of Archivists* II, No. 9 (April 1964).

WELCH, Charles Edwin, 'Archives and Manuscripts in Nonconformist Libraries', *Archives*, VI, No. 32 (Oct. 1964)

Chapter 7. Wills and Administrations

BRINKWORTH, Edwin Robert, 'Records of the Church Courts' *Amateur Historian*, II, 50 (Oct.–Nov. 1954).

CAMP, Anthony John, *Wills and Their Whereabouts, a new ed. of B. G. Bouwens' work of the same title, but including information on Scottish testaments and other additional matter,* 1963.

COLE, E. J. J., 'Hereford Probate Records: abstracts of wills of Radnorshire testators 1540–1592' [to be continued], *Transactions of the Radnorshire Society,* XXIV–XXXIV, 1954–64

FRANCE, Reginald Sharpe, 'Short Guides to Records, 10, Wills'. *History,* L, 168 (Feb. 1965)

GARDINER, E. M. 'East Sussex Inventories', *Sussex Notes and Queries* XV, 124 (1939).

MARSHALL, George William, *A Handbook to the Ancient Courts of Probate and Depositories of Wills,* 1895

WALNE, Peter, *English Wills: probate records in England and Wales, with a brief note on Scottish and Irish wills,* U.S.A., 1964.

WHITELOCK, Dorothy, *Anglo-Saxon Wills, with translations and notes,* 1930

Chapter 8. Marriage Licences

Probably the best concentrated collection of printed and MS marriage licences is at the Society of Genealogists. Many marriage licences have been published by the Harleian and other societies (see Mullins, E. L. C. *Texts and Calendars*). Marriage licences will also be included in the Society of Genealogists' pending publication *A National Index of Parish Registers*

Chapter 9. Some Printed Sources

ADAMS, Charles Kingsley, 'Portraiture Problems and Genealogy', *Genealogists' Magazine,* XIV, 382 (Sept. 1964)

ADAMS, John, *Index Villaris, or an exact register of all the cities, market towns parishes, villages and private seats, etc. in England and Wales,* 3rd ed. 1700.

Angliae Notitia, or the present state of England, 1669–1755

ASLIB Directory: a guide to sources of information in Great Britain and Ireland, 2 vols, 1957.

BATEMAN, John, *The Great Landowners of Great Britain and Ireland* 4th ed. rev. *etc.* [Lists all owners of 3,000 acres and above] 1878.

BOASE, Frederick, *Modern English Biography*, 6 vols, 1892–1921, reprinted 1965.

BRAMWELL, B. S., 'Frequency of Cousin Marriages', *Genealogists' Magazine*, VIII, 305 (June 1939).

BRIDGER, Charles, *Index to Printed Pedigrees contained in County and Local Histories, the Heralds' Visitations, etc.*, 1867 [valuable as a bibliog. to the great county histories of the 18th and 19th centuries].

British National Bibliography, 1951 – date [gives published family histories for each year under the classification No. 929].

BURKE, *Sir* John Bernard, *The Book of the Orders of Knighthood . . . of all nations . . . with lists of knights and companions of each British order*, 1858

BURKE, John, *A Genealogical and Heraldic Dictionary of the Peerages of England, Ireland and Scotland, extinct, dormant and in abeyance . . .* [ed. by Sir J. B. Burke] . . . 3rd ed., 1846.

BURKE, *Sir* John Bernard, *A Genealogical History of the Dormant, Abeyant, Forfeited and Extinct Peerages of the British Empire*, 1883

BURKE, John *and* BURKE, *Sir* John Bernard, *A Genealogical and Heraldic History of the Extinct and Dormant Baronetcies of England*, 2nd ed., 1841.

BURKE, John *and* BURKE, *Sir* John Bernard, *The Knightage of Great Britain and Ireland*, 1841.

BURKE, John, *The Landed Gentry of Great Britain*, 1st ed. [as *History of the Commoners*] 4 vols, 1837–8: 17th ed. 1952. [The 2nd – 9th editions included Ireland, since then *The Landed Gentry of Ireland* has been published separately in 1899, 1904, 1912 and 1958. The 15th ed. (1937) had an Irish Supplement].

BURKE, John *and* BURKE, *Sir* John Bernard, *The Royal Families of England, Scotland and Wales, with their descendants, sovereigns and subjects*, 2 vols., 1847.

BURKE, *Sir* John Bernard, *Royal Descents and Pedigrees of Founders' Kin*, 2 pts., 1858

BURKE's *Genealogical and Heraldic History of the Peerage, Baronetage and Knightage*, 103rd ed., 1963 [1st ed. 1826; the early editions did not include the Knightage].

BURKETT, Jack (ed.), *Special Library and Information Services in the United Kingdom*, 1961.

BURTCHAELL, George Dames, *The Knights of England . . . incorporating a complete list of knights bachelor dubbed in Ireland*, 2 vols, 1906.

CHALLEN, William Harold, 'The Records of the City of London', *Genealogists' Magazine* VI, 503 (Sept. 1934).

COKAYNE, George Edward *and others* (editors), *The Complete Peerage*, 2nd ed. rev. and much enlarged, 15 vols. 1910–1964.

COLLINS, Arthur, *The Peerage of England*, 1812 ed. 9 vols, ed. by Sir Egerton Brydges, 1812.

'County Biographical Dictionaries, 1890–1937', *Bulletin of Inst. of Historical Research* XXXIV, 55, 1961 [a good list of local collected biographies].

Court Register, a monthly record of births, marriages and deaths associated with the aristocracy, etc, 21 Nos. 1861–5.

DEBRETT, John, *Debrett's Peerage of England, Scotland and Ireland*, 1803–1849 and 1864 to date [usually jointly with *Debrett's Baronetage*]

DEBRETT, John, *The Baronetage of England*, 1808–1840 [later editions from 1864 onwards usually jointly with *Debrett's Peerage*].

DELANY, John *and* TOBIN, James Edward, *Dictionary of Catholic Biography*, 1962

Dictionary of National Biography. [The main work in 22 vols to 1901, with supplements (3 vols), then Supplements to 1950. [Additions and corrections to this work have appeared in the *Bulletin of the Institute of Historical Research* and are included in the index to vols 1–25 (1954)]

DRYSDALE, Alexander Hutton, *History of the Presbyterians in England, their rise, decline and revival*, 1889

DUKES, G. R., 'Social Life in Worcestershire during the Eighteenth Century', *Transactions of the Worcestershire Archaeological Society*, N.S. XXX (1953)
English Local History Handlist, 2nd ed., 1952

FANE, A. G. C., *Complete Index to Family Names appearing in Burke's Royal Families*, priv. pr., 1932

FOSTER, Joseph, *The Royal Lineage of our Noble and Gentle Families together with their paternal ancestry*, 3 vols, 1887–91

GATFIELD, George, *Guide to Printed Books and MSS relating to English and Foreign Heraldry and Genealogy*, 1892. [Not yet completely superseded as it contains many references to MSS in the British Museum etc.]

GIBSON, Strickland, *Abstracts from the Wills... of Binders, Printers and Stationers of Oxford, 1493–1638*, 1907

GILSON, Julius P., *A Student's Guide to the MSS of the British Museum*, 1920 [*Helps for Students of History No. 31*].

GLASS, David Victor (ed.), *Social Mobility in Britain*, 1954

GODBER, Joyce, 'Bedfordshire County Records', *Genealogists' Magazine*, XI, 269, 304 (Dec. 1952, March 1953)

Government Publications Sectional List No. 24: Record Publications. [This pamphlet, revised every few years, lists all official publications of calendars, indexes etc. in the P.R.O. and Scottish Record Office]

HABAKKUK, Hrothgar John, 'The English Land Market in the Eighteenth Century' in *Britain and the Netherlands*, ed. J. S. Bromley and E. H. Kossmann, 1960.

HABAKKUK, Hrothgar John, 'English Landownership 1680–1740', *Economic History Review*, 2nd ser. X (1940)

HARRIS, Ronald Walter, *England in the Eighteenth Century, 1689–1793*, 1963.

HASKELL, Daniel Carl, *A Check List of Cumulative Indexes to Individual Periodicals in the New York Public Library*, 1942

HASSALL, William Owen, 'Local History Sources in the Bodleian Library', *Amateur Historian*, II, 130 (Apr. – May, 1955)

HOLLINGSWORTH, T. H., *The Demography of the British Peerage*, 1965 [Supplement to *Population Studies*, XVIII, No 2.]

HOWARD, Joseph Jackson, and CRISP, Frederick Arthur, *Visitation of England and Wales*, 21 vols + 14 vols notes, 1893–1921. [also *Visitation of Ireland*, 1897—]

HUGHES, Edward, *North Country Life in the 18th Century: the North-East, 1700–1750*, 1952

HUMPHREYS, Arthur Lee, *A Handbook to County Bibliography; being a bibliography of bibliographies relating to the counties and towns of Great Britain and Ireland*, 1917

HYAMSON, Albert Montefiore, *A Dictionary of Universal Biography*, 2nd ed., 1951

Index of Obituary Notices for the years 1880–1882, 3 pts, [An Index Society publication]

KELLAWAY, William, 'Record Publications of Societies', *Archives*, VII, 46 (1965).

Kelly's *Handbook of the Upper Ten Thousand* for 1878 (1879) 1879, 2 vols. [continued as *Kelly's Handbook to the Titled, Landed and Official Classes*, 1880 – date]

LASLETT, Peter, *The World we have Lost*, 1965 [useful sociological and statistical information on births, marriages and deaths in the past].

'Local County and Regional Historical etc. Societies in England', *Amateur Historian*, I, 213 (Aug,–Sept. 1953).

Men and Women of the Time, 15th ed., 1899.

Micro Methods Ltd, *Catalogue: Section D. Genealogy and Heraldry*

MOULE, Thomas, *The English Counties Delineated*, illus. by a complete set of county maps, 2 vols, 1837.

NATIONAL PORTRAIT GALLERY, *Catalogue, 1856–1947*, 1949, *Supplement 1948–53*, 1954

O'DONOGHUE, F. M., *and* HAKE, H. M., *Engraved British Portraits preserved in the Dept. of Prints and Drawings in the British Museum*, 6 vols., 1908–25.

ORMEROD, George, *Index to the Pedigree[s] in Burke's 'Commoners' . . . prepared . . . in 1840*, 1907.

POLL BOOKS
[The British Museum General Catalogue gives lists under each county].

PUGH, Ralph Bernard, *How to Write a Parish History*, 6th ed. (based on the work by J. C. Cox), 1954

Return of Owners of Land of one acre upwards . . . showing names of such owners arranged alphabetically, addresses, extents, etc, 1871 [arranged by counties].

RICHES (afterw. SUTTON) Phyllis M., *An Analytical Bibliography of Universal Collected Biography*, 1934

RIDGE, Cecil Harold, 'How Many Ancestors have we?', *Amateur Historian*, I, 18 (Aug.–Sept. 1952).

ROBERTS, Arthur Dennis, *Introduction to Reference Books*, 3rd ed., 1956.

ROUND, John Horace, *Family Origins and other studies*, 1930.

ROYAL COMMISSION ON HISTORICAL MSS, *Index to Persons in Publications issued from 1870 to 1911*, 2 vols., 1935.

ROYAL HISTORICAL SOCIETY, *Guide to Directories (excluding London) published before 1856*, 1950

ROYAL KALENDAR, *or Correct Annual Register for England, Scotland, Ireland*, 1767–1893 [The title varies – see *Bulletin of the Institute of Historical Research*, XV, 24, XVII, 130, XIX, 9]

RYE, Walter, *Norfolk Families* [with an index of names by Charles Nowell] 2 pts [1911–13].

RYLANDS, John Paul, *Disclaimers at the Heralds' Visitations*, 1888.

SHAW, William Arthur, *The Knights of England: a complete record from the earliest time to the present day etc*, 2 vols., 1906

SOMERVILLE, Robert, *Handlist of Record Publications*, 1951 [a classified and abbreviated list of publications of over sixty English publishing societies]

SQUIBB, George Drewry, *Visitation Pedigrees and the Genealogist*, 1964.

TATE, William Edward, *The Parish Chest: a study of the records of parochial administration in England*, 2nd ed., rev. and enlarged 1951.

THOMAS, Arthur Hermann, 'Genealogical Material in the Guildhall Records', *Genealogists' Magazine*, II, 45 (June 1926)

THOMPSON, Alexander Hamilton, *Parish History and Records*, 1926 [Historical Assoc. Pamphlet No. 66]

THOMPSON, Francis Michael Longstreth, *English Landed Society in the Nineteenth Century*, 1963

TURBERVILLE, Arthur Stanley, *English Men and Manners in the 18th Century: an illus. narrative*, 2nd ed., 1929.

WAGNER, *Sir* Anthony Richard, *Genealogy and the Common Man*, 1961 [Society of Genealogists Jubilee Lecture]

WALFORD, Edward, *etc., Walford's County Families of the United Kingdom,* 1860–1920 [From 1870 or 1871 onwards issued annually]

WARD, Thomas Humphrey (ed.), *Men of the Reign,* 1885 [mainly extracted but re-written from the 11 editions of *Men of the Time.* The 12th ed. (1887) ed. by T. H. Ward, cont. as *Men and Women of the time* 13th ed. (1891) to 15th ed. (1899)]

WARD, William Reginald, *The English Land Tax in the Eighteenth Century,* 1953 [Oxford Historical Series].

Who was Who, 5 vols, 1897–1959, (1920–63)

WOOD, W. R., *The Administration of the Window and Assessed Taxes, 1696–1798,* 1963 [Repr. from the *English Historical Review,* LXVII, No, 265 (Oct. 1952)].

WOODMAN, A. Vere, 'Buckinghamshire Records', *Buckinghamshire Record Society,* XI, 371 (Sept. 1953).

Chapter 10. Periodicals and Newspapers.

Amateur Historian, 1952 – date

Blackmansbury, a journal of notes and queries, ed. by M. Pinhorn, 1964 *etc.*

BRITISH RECORDS ASSOCIATION, *Handlist of Record Publications,* 1951.

BRITISH RECORD ASSOCIATION, *List of Record Repositories in Great Britain,* 1964.

British Union Catalogue of Periodicals, 4 vols, 1955–8 [a record of periodicals of the world from the 17th to present centuries in British libraries]
Supplement to 1960, 1962

CRANFIELD, Geoffrey Alan, *A Handlist of English Provincial Newspapers and Periodicals 1700–1760,* 1952 [Cambridge Bibliog. Soc. monograph 2].

European Magazine and London Review, 1782–1826

FARRAR, Robert Henry, *Index to the Biographical and Obituary Notices in the Gentleman's Magazine, 1731–1780,* 1891

FOSTER, Joseph, *Marriages* [*of the Nobility and Gentry*] *1650–1880* [The marriages from the *Historical Register* and *Gentleman's Magazine*, 1727–1867 (ed. by Miss Ada C. Gardner) and from other sources, including *The Times* 1865–80, but nothing was published beyond the name 'Alexander']

FRY, Edward Alexander, *An Index to the Marriages in the Gentleman's Magazine 1731–1768*, 1922 [Originally issued as a Supplement to *The Genealogist*, N.S. Vols 34–38]

Gentleman's Magazine, 1731–1868

Historical Register, 1716–1738 [like the *Gentleman's Magazine* contains lists of births, marriages and deaths].

INSTITUTE OF HERALDIC AND GENEALOGICAL STUDIES, *Family History*, ed. C. R. Humphrey-Smith, bi-monthly, 1962 etc.

London Magazine, or Gentleman's Monthly Intelligencer, 1732–1785.

MELLOR, George R., 'History from Newspapers', *Amateur Historian*, 11, 97 (Feb.–March 1955).

MILFORD, Robert Theodore *and* SUTHERLAND, Donald Martell, *A Catalogue of English Newspapers and Periodicals in the Bodleian Library 1622–1800*, 1936

Monthly Magazine and British Register, 1796–1843

MUSGRAVE, Sir William, Bart, *Obituary prior to 1800, as far as relates to England, Scotland and Ireland* ... ed. by Sir G. J. Armytage, 1899.

NICHOLSON, Cregoe Donaldson Percy, *The Genealogical Value of the Early English Newspapers*, 1934

READ, Donald, 'North of England Newspapers (c. 1700–c. 1900) and their Value to Historians', *Proceedings of the Leeds Philosophical Society*, VIII (1957)

TOWNSEND, James, *News of a County Town*, 1914 [Abingdon in Berkshire, drawn from *Jackson's Oxford Journal*, 1753–1835]

Chapter 11. Records of Clergymen

BAPTIST HISTORICAL SOCIETY, *Transactions*, 7 vols, 1908–20 [continued as *The Baptist Quarterly*]

BIRT, Henry Norbert, *Obit Book of the English Benedictines from 1600–1912*, rev., enlarged and cont. by Dom Henry Norbert Birt, 1913.

Clerical Guide, or Ecclesiastical Directory, containing a complete register of the prelates and other dignitaries of the Church; a list of all the benefices in England and Wales etc., 1817–1836.

CROCKFORD'S *Clerical Directory, a biographical and statistical Book of Reference for facts relating to the clergy and the Church,* 1858 – date.

DELANY, John Joseph *and* TOBIN, James Edward, *Dictionary of Catholic Biography,* 1962

FOSTER, Joseph (ed.), *Index Ecclesiasticus, or Alphabetical List of all Ecclesiastical Dignitaries in England and Wales since the Reformation,* 1890 [vol. for 1800–1840 only: no more published].

GILLOW, Joseph, *A Literary and Biographical History or Bibliographical Dictionary of English Catholics, from the breach with Rome in 1534 to the present time,* 5 vols, 1885–1902

GUMBLEY, Walter, *Obituary Notices of the English Dominicans from 1555 to 1952,* 1955

HART, Arthur Tindal, *The Eighteenth-Century Parson (ca. 1639–1830),* 1955

KIRK, John, *Biographies of English Catholics in the 18th Century,* ed. by J. H. Pollen and E. Burton, 1909 [needs to be used with caution].

MCLACHLAN, Herbert, *The Unitarian Movement in the Religious Life of England,* 1934

PAYNE, John O., *Records of the English Catholics of 1715 etc.* 1889 [consists of some 400 abstracts of wills].

WADDINGTON, John, *Congregational History, 1700–1800: in relation to contemporary events,* 1876

Chapter 12. Lawyers, Doctors and others

BEATSON, Robert, *A Chronological Register of both Houses of the British Parliament ... 1708 to ... 1807,* 3 vols, 1807

BOND, Maurice F., *The Records of Parliament: a guide for genealogists and local historians,* 1964.

BULLOCH, John Malcolm, 'Theatrical Families', *Genealogists' Magazine,* VI, 339 (Dec. 1933).

BURGESS, Frederick, 'County Masons', *Genealogists' Magazine,* XI, 274 (Dec. 1952).

COLVIN, Howard Montague, *A Biographical Dictionary of English Architects 1660–1840*, 1954

FOSTER, Joseph, *The Register of Admissions to Gray's Inn, 1521–1889, together with the register of marriages in Gray's Inn Chapel 1695–1754*, 1889

GIUSEPPI, J. A., 'Families of Long Service at the Bank of England', *Genealogists' Magazine*, X, 399 and 439 (Sept. and Dec. 1949)

GROVE, *Sir* George (ed.), *Dictionary of Music and Musicians*, 5th ed. edited by Eric Blom, 9 vols, 1954

GUNNIS, Rupert, *Dictionary of British Sculptors 1660–1851*, [1953].

INNER TEMPLE, *Students admitted to the Inner Temple, 1547–1660* [1877].

JACOBS, Phyllis M. (compiler), *Registers of the Universities, Colleges and Schools of Great Britain*, 1965.

JARIS, Rupert C., 'The Records of the Customs and Excise Services', *Genealogists' Magazine*, X, 219 (Sept. 1948)

JOHNSTON, William, *Roll of Commissioned Officers in the Medical Service of the British Army, who served on full pay within the period between the accession of George II and the formation of the Royal Army Medical Corps*, ed. by Lt-Col. Harry A. L. Howell, 1917

JOSLIN, David M., 'London Private Bankers, 1720–1785', *Economic History Review*, 2nd ser. VII (1954).

JUDD, Gerrit Parmele, *Members of Parliament, 1734–1832*, New Haven, U.S.A., 1955.

LINCOLN'S INN, *The Records of the Honorable Society of Lincoln's Inn*, 2 vols [Vol 1. Admissions 1420–1799, Vol II. Admissions 1800–1893], 1896.

NAMIER, *Sir* Lewis *and* BROOKE, John, *History of Parliament – The House of Commons, 1754–1790*, 3 vols, 1964 [Vols II and III consist of list of members for the period with biographical notes]

REDGRAVE, Samuel, *Dictionary of Artists of the English School*, new ed. rev. to the present date [by F. M. Redgrave], 1878.

ROBSON, Robert, *The Attorney in Eighteenth-Century England*, 1959.

SLONIMSKY, Nicolas (ed.), *Baker's Biographical Dictionary of Musicians*, 5th ed. New York, 1958

STURGESS, Herbert Arthur Charles, *Register of admissions to the ... Middle Temple. From the 15th century to ... 1944*, 3 vols, 1949.

Chapter 13. Naval Ancestors

Allen, Joseph, *The New Navy List and General Record of the Services of Officers of the R.N. and R. Marines, 1846–55*, 1846–55 [a continuation of *The New Navy List compiled by an Old Commander (C. Houltain) 1839–45*]

CALLENDER, Sir Geoffrey Arthur Romane, *Bibliography of Naval History*, Parts 1 and 2. [Historical Assoc. Leaflets 58, 61, 1924, 1925: a brief selected list].

CAMPBELL, John, *Lives of British Admirals*, 4 vols, 1779

CHARNOCK, John, *Biographia Navalis, or Memoirs of the Officers of the Navy from 1600*, 4 vols, 1794

CLOWES, Sir William Laird, *The Royal Navy: a history from the earliest times to the present*, 7 vols, 1897–1903.

Commissioned Sea Officers of the Royal Navy, 3 vols [1954] [pub. by the Nat. Maritime Museum, Greenwich].

FOTHERGILL, Gerald, *Records of Naval Men*, 1910 [*Genealogists Pocket Library*, Vol 8].

HAMILTON-EDWARDS, Gerald Kenneth Savery, 'Naval Ancestry', *Amateur Historian*, I, 325 (Apr.–May, 1954).

JAMES, G. F., 'Collected Naval Biography', *Bulletin of Inst. of Historical Research*, XV, 162, 1937–8

LEWIS, Michael Arthur, *England's Sea-Officers*, 1939

LEWIS, Michael Arthur, *The Navy in Transition, 1814–1864, a social history*, 1965

LEWIS, Michael Arthur, *The Navy of Britain*, 1948

LEWIS, Michael Arthur, *A Social History of the Navy, 1793–1815*, 1960.

LLOYD'S *Captains' Register, containing the names and services of certificated masters of the British Mercantile Marine now afloat, compiled from the records of the Registrar-General of Seamen*, 1869 [does not include those who during the five years prior to publication have not been afloat but gives full name of masters (incl. those so qualified but serving as mates) place and date of birth, port at which examined, date of examination, and details of ships served in since receiving master's certificate].

MAINWARING, George Ernest, *A Bibliography of British Naval History*, 1930 [primarily a guide on MS material and to periodical articles, with author and subject headings].

Mariner's Mirror, 1911 – date [the journal of the Society for Nautical Research]

MARSHALL, John, *Royal Naval Biography*, with supplements, 12 vols. [There is a TS index of this at the Society of Genealogists].

MERRIMAN, Reginald Dundas, 'Naval Records', *Genealogists' Magazine*, X. 95 (Dec. 1947).

Navy List, 1815–1870. [The official list, published quarterly from 1818, cont. in 2 pts 1870–1924, Active and Retired Officers (not published 1915).]

Navy Lists. The British Museum Printed General Catalogue gives printed lists of naval personnel etc. under 'England' (columns 2490–95).]

O'BYRNE, William Richard, *A Naval Biographical Dictionary, comprising the life and services of every living officer in Her Majesty's Navy from the rank of Admiral of the Fleet to that of Lieutenant* [serving in 1845], 1849.

O'BYRNE, William Richard, *Naval Biographical Dictionary*, new and enlarged ed., vol I and 4 pts of vol II 1861 [incomplete, to name 'H. S. G. Giles' only, but includes R. Marines, Pursers, Chaplains].

O'BYRNE, William Richard *and* O'BYRNE, Robert Henry, *The Sailor's Home Journal* [afterw. *The Naval Chronicle*] 1853–63

PERRIN, William Gordon, *Admiralty Library: Subject Catalogue of Printed Books, Part 1. Historical Section*, 1912. [Titles arranged under subject headings, but no general index].

RALFE, James, *The Naval Biography of Great Britain*, 4 vols, 1828 [a rare book].

STEEL, *List of the Royal Navy*, 1780–1816

Chapter 14. Army Records

APPLEBY, C. B., 'The National Army Museum and Genealogy,' *Genealogists' Magazine* XV, 14 (March 1965)

ARMY LISTS. See British Museum Printed Catalogue under 'ENGLAND' columns 1485–91. The official printed lists have been published annually since 1754.

DALTON, Charles, *English Army Lists and Commission Registers, 1661–1714*, 6 vols, 1892–1904

DALTON, Charles, *George I's Army 1714–1727*, 2 vols, 1910

HART, H. G., *The New Army List*, 1840–1916 [later New Annual Army List and cont. under varying titles]

FELLOWES, Edmund Horace, *The Military Knights of Windsor, 1352–1944* [1944]

FORTESCUE, *Sir* John William, *A History of the British Army*, 13 vols and 6 atlases, 1899-1930.

GODFREY, Michael, 'Documents in the Public Record Office: I. Personal Records of Officers of the British Army', *Amateur Historian*, VI, 192 (Winter 1965)

Journal of the Society for Army Historical Research, 1921–date

Chapter 15. The East India Company

Asiatic Annual Register, or a view of the history of Hindustan, 1800–12.

Asiatic Journal and Monthly Register for British India, Vols 1–25, 1816–28, vols 26–28, 1828, cont. under various titles to 1845 [45 vols].

BULLOCK, Humphrey, 'Anglo-Indian Family History', *Amateur Historian*, I, 117 (Feb.–March 1953).

CRAWFORD, Dirom Grey, *A History of the Indian Medical Service, 1600–1930*, 2 vols, 1914

CRAWFORD, Dirom Grey, *Roll of the Indian Medical Service, 1615–1930, compiled by ... D. G. Crawford*, 1930.

DANVERS, F. C. (ed.), *List of Marine Records of the late East India Company, preserved in the Record Department of the India Office*, 1895. [Useful information, including lists of ships' journals, logs and various miscellaneous papers].

DODWELL, Edward, *and* MILES, James Samuel, *East India Company's Bengal Civil Servants, 1780–1838*, 1839.

DODWELL, Edward, *and* MILES, James Samuel, *East India Company's Bombay Civil Servants, 1798–1839*, 1839.

DODWELL, Edward, *and* MILES, James Samuel, *East India Company's Madras Civil Servants, 1780–1839*, 1839.

DODWELL, Edward, *and* MILES, James Samuel, *Medical Officers of the Indian Army, 1764–1838*, 1839.

DODWELL, Edward, *and* MILES, James Samuel, *Officers of the Indian Army, 1760–Sept. 30, 1837*, 1838.

DODWELL, Henry Herbert, *Calendar of the Madras Despatches, 1744–1765*, 2 vols, Madras, 1920–30.

DODWELL, Henry Herbert, *A Calendar of the Madras Records, 1740–1744*, Madras, 1917.

East India Register and Directory [cont. under various titles] 1803–1895 [after which date the official *India Office List* and *Indian Army List* took its place]

FOSTER, *Sir* William, *Guide to the India Office Records, 1600–1858*, 1919

HARDY, Charles, *A Register of Ships employed in the Service of the ... East India Company from 1760 to 1810 ... rev. with considerable additions by H. C. Hardy*, 1811

HILL, Samuel Charles, *Bengal in 1756–1757: a selection of public and private papers dealing with the affairs of the British in Bengal during the reign of Siraj-Uddaula ed. with notes and an historical introduction by S.C.H.*, 3 vols, 1905 etc.

HILL, Samuel Charles, *Catalogue of the Home Miscellaneous Series of the India Office Records*, 1927

HILL, Samuel Charles, *List of Europeans and others in the English Factories in Bengal at the time of the Siege of Calcutta in the year 1756, with an appendix containing lists of European Sufferers*, Calcutta, 1902

HODSON, Vernon Charles Paget, 'India Office Records', *Genealogists' Magazine*, VI, 198 (March 1933).

HODSON, Vernon Charles Paget, *List of the Officers of the Bengal Army 1758–1834*, 4 pts, 1927–47.

HODSON, Vernon Charles Paget, 'Some Families with a long East India Connection', *Genealogists' Magazine*, VI, 18, 63, 103, 159, 247, 294, 355 (March 1932 – Dec. 1933).

HYDE, Henry Barry, *The Parish of Bengal 1678 to 1788*, Calcutta, 1899.

Hyde, Henry Barry, *Parochial Annals of Bengal: being a history of the Bengal Ecclesiastical Establishment of the Honourable East India Company in the 17th and 18th centuries, compiled from original sources*, Calcutta, priv. pr. 1901.

Ives, Edward, *A Voyage from England to India in the year 1754*, 1773 [mainly a description of the war].

Love, Henry Davison, *Vestiges of Old Madras 1640–1800*, 4 vols, 1913 [drawn from original records and well documented and indexed].

Low, Charles Rathbone, *History of the Indian Navy 1613–1863*, 2 vols, 1877.

Philips, Cyril Henry, *The East India Company 1784–1834*, 1940 [Univ. of Manchester Historical Series No 77].

Prinsep, Charles Campbell, *Record of Services of the Honourable East India Company's Civil Servants in the Madras Presidency, from 1741 to 1858 etc.*, 1885.

Sainsbury, Ethel Bruce (ed.), *A Calendar of the Court Minutes etc. of the East India Company. 1635–1639* [etc.] 1907 – [in progress].

Vibart, Henry Meredith, *The Military History of the Madras Engineers and Pioneers from 1743 to the present time*, 2 vols, 1881–3

Wilson, William John, *History of the Madras Army*, 3 vols, Madras, 1882–3.

Chapter 16. Jews, Huguenots and Other Immigrants

Jews

Anglo-Jewish Notabilities, their arms and testamentary dispositions, 1949. [Jewish Hist. Soc. of England publication].

Arnold, Arthur P., *A List of Jews and their Households in London, extracted from the census list of 1695.*

Bevis Marks Records, Part II. *Abstract of the Kutuboth or Marriage Contracts of the Congregation from earliest times until 1837*, with index, 1949.

Franklin, Arthur Ellis, 'Jewish Forenames', *Genealogists' Magazine*, VII, 244 (March 1936).

Hyamson, Albert Montefiore, 'The Jewish Obituaries in the Gentleman's Magazine [1731–1868]', *Miscellanies of the Jewish Historical Society of England*, Pt IV, 1942.

HYAMSON, Albert Montefiore, *Plan of a Dictionary of Anglo-Jewish Biography ... repr. from Anglo-Jewish Notabilities* [1949].

HYAMSON, Albert Montefiore, *The Sephardim of England: a History of the Spanish and Portuguese Jewish Community 1492–1951*, 1951

HORTON-SMITH, Lionel Graham Horton, 'Naturalisation and where to look', *Genealogists' Magazine*, X, 451 (Dec. 1949).

JACOBS, Joseph *and* WOLF, Lucien, *Bibliotheca Anglo-Judaica*, new ed. rev. and enlarged by Cecil Roth, 1937

JEWISH HISTORICAL SOCIETY OF ENGLAND, *Transactions*, 1895 – date

LIPMAN, Vivian David, *Social History of the Jews in England 1850–1950*, 1954

ROTH, Cecil, *Archives of the United Synagogue*, 1930

ROTH, Cecil, *A History of the Jews in England*, 1941

ROTH, Cecil, *Magna Bibliotheca Anglo Judaica: a bibliographical guide to Anglo-Jewish history*, new ed., 1937

RYE, Walter, *The Persecutions of the Jews in England ... a lecture ... repr. from the 'Anglo-Jewish Exhibition Papers'*, 1887

SAMUEL, Edgar R., 'Jewish Ancestors and where to find them', *Genealogists' Magazine*, XI, 412 (Dec. 1953).

SAMUEL, Wilfred S., 'Sources of Anglo-Jewish Genealogy', *Genealogists' Magazine*, VI, 146 (Dec. 1932).

WOLF, Lucien, 'Old Anglo-Jewish Families', in *Essays in Jewish History*, Jewish Hist. Soc., 1934

Huguenots and Other Immigrants

AGNEW, David Carnegie A., *Protestant Exiles from France in the Reign of Louis XIV; or, the Huguenot Refugees and their Descendants in Great Britain and Ireland*, priv. pr., 1866

HORTON-SMITH, L. G. H., 'Naturalisation and where to Look', *Genealogists' Magazine*, X, 451 (Dec. 1949)

LART, Charles Edmund, 'French Records', *Genealogists' Magazine*, VII, 1 (March 1935).

LART, Charles Edmund, 'French Nobless', *Genealogists' Magazine*, VII, 229 (March 1936).

LART, Charles Edmund, *Huguenot Pedigrees*, 1924—
LART, Charles Edmund, *The Huguenot Regiments*, 1911 [fr. *Proceedings of the Huguenot Soc.*, IX, 3 (1885)]
LART, Charles Edmund, 'The Huguenot Society and its work', *Genealogists' Magazine*, III, 50 (Sept. 1927).
MINET, Miss S., 'Huguenot Records', *Genealogists' Magazine*, XII, 149 and 185 (March and June 1956).
REAMAN, George Elmore, *The Trail of the Huguenots in Europe, the United States, South Africa and Canada*, 1964
WEINER, Margery, *The French Exiles*, 1960
WULCKO, Laurance M., 'Naturalisation and Where to Look (II)' *Genealogists' Magazine*, X, 496 (March 1950).

Chapter 17. Scottish Records I: Civil and Parish Records

BLACK, George Fraser, *The Surnames of Scotland: their origin, meaning and history*, New York, 1946
Book of the Old Edinburgh Club, 19 vols – [in progress] 1908 – date.
DONALDSON, Gordon, 'Scottish Registration', *The Scottish Genealogist*, July and October 1955.
HAMILTON-EDWARDS, Gerald Kenneth Savery, 'Civil and Parish Registration in Scotland', *Genealogists' Magazine*, XI, 1 (March 1951).
HOGAN, E. A., 'Scottish Registration', *The Scottish Genealogist*, April 1956.
JOHNSTON, W. *and* A. K., *and others*, *Gazetteer of Scotland* (incl. a glossary of the most common Gaelic names), 2nd ed., 1958.
STUART, Margaret, 'Genealogical Records in Scotland', *Genealogists' Magazine*, V, 277 (March 1931).
TURNBULL, William Barclay David Donald, *Scottish Parochial Registers: memoranda of the state of the parochial registers of Scotland*, 1849.

Chapter 18. Scottish Records 11: Sasines, Services, Testaments and other records

ANDERSON, A., 'The Scottish Record Office', *Genealogists' Magazine*, XV, 64 (June 1965)

BAIN, Robert, *The Clans and Tartans of Scotland*, 4th ed. enlarged and re-ed. by Margaret O. Macdougall, 1959.

DALTON, Charles, *The Scots Army, 1661–1688, with memoirs of the commanders-in-chief*, 2 pts, 1909

Epitaphs and Inscriptions from Burial Grounds and Old Buildings in the North East of Scotland, with historical, biographical, genealogical etc. notes, 2 vols, 1875–9.

Faculty of Advocates in Scotland, 1532–1943, 1944

FERGUSON, Joan Primrose S., *Scottish Family Histories held in Scottish Libraries*, 1960 [includes MSS and TS papers, pedigrees and genealogical charts].

FERGUSON, Joan Primrose S., *Scottish Newspapers held in Scottish Libraries*, 1956

FOSTER, Joseph, *Members of Parliament, Scotland, 1357-1882*, 2nd ed. rev. and corrected, 1882.

GENERAL REGISTER HOUSE, EDINBURGH, *Detailed List of the Old Parish Registers of Scotland*, 1872.

GIBSON, James, *Inscriptions on the Tombstones and Monuments in Memory of the Covenanters*, 1881

GRAHAM, Henry Grey, *The Social Life of Scotland in the 18th Century*, 4th ed., 2 vols, 1937

GRANT, Sir Francis James, *The County Families of the Zetland Islands*, 1893

GRANT, Sir Francis James, *Index to Genealogies, Birth-briefs and Funeral Escutcheons in the Lyon Office, Edinburgh*, 1908.

GRANT, Sir Francis James, 'Presbyterian Court Records 156–1935', in *Sources and Literature of Scots Law*, Stair Society Vol I (1935).

M'CONNELL, Ernest Whigham Jardine (ed.), *Marriages at Gretna Hall, 1829–1855*, 1949

Handlist of Scottish and Welsh Records Publications, Scottish Section by Peter Gouldesbrough and A. P. Kup; Welsh Section by Idwal Lewis, Br. Records Assoc. Publications Pamphlet No. 4, 1954.

INNES OF LEARNEY, Sir Thomas, 'Descent of the Chiefship and Chieftancy of Clans', *Genealogists' Magazine*, VIII, 191, 255 (Dec. 1938 and March 1939).

INNES OF LEARNEY, Sir Thomas, *The Tartans of the Clans and Families of Scotland*, 1964

JOHNSON, J. Bolam, *Scottish Records*, 1908 [*Genealogists'
Pocket Library* series, bound up with *Royal Descents*].

LART, Charles Edmund, *The Pedigrees and Papers of James
Terry, Athlone Herald at the Court of King James II in
France, 1690–1725*, 1938.

List of Owners of Property in Edinburgh 1634-6, in *The
Book of the Old Edinburgh Club*, 1924

LIVINGSTONE, Matthew, *A Guide to the Public Records of
Scotland deposited in H.M. General Register House,
Edinburgh*, 1905. [See also Supplements to this in the
Scottish Historical Review, vols 26 and 27 (1946–7)].

MacFARLANE, Walter, *Genealogical Collections concerning
Families in Scotland*, ed. by J. T. Clarke, 2 vols, 1887
[Scottish History Society].

MacKENZIE, Agnes Muir, *Scotland in Modern Times, 1720–
1939*, 1941.

MacLEOD, Walter (ed.), *A List of Persons concerned in the
Rebellion* [1745–6], 1890 [*Scot. Hist. Soc.*, Vol. VIII:
gives 2,590 names, mainly from East-Central Scotland].

*New Statistical Account of Scotland by the Ministers of the
Respective Parishes*, 15 vols, 1845 [under 'Scotland,
Appendix – Miscellaneous' in Br. Mus. printed Catalogue].

PATON, Henry (ed.), *The Lyon in Mourning; or, A collection
of speeches, letters, journals, etc., relative to the affairs of
Prince Charles Edward Stuart by the Rev. Robert Forbes
.... 1746–1775*, 3 vols, 1895–6.

PATON, Henry M., *The Scottish Records, their history and
value*, 1933 (Hist. Assoc. of Scotland pamphlets New Ser.
No. 7).

PAUL, *Sir* James Balfour, *The Scots Peerage*, 9 vols, 1904–14.
[Vol. 9 is an index].

RENNIE, James Alan, *The Scottish People; their clans, families
and origins*, 1960.

RIDDELL, 'MS Baronetage of Scotland', in Scottish National
Library.

ROGERS, Charles, *Monuments and Monumental Inscriptions
in Scotland*, 2 vols, 1871–2.

SANDISON, A. 'Shetland Surnames', *Genealogists' Magazine*,
XIII, 45 and 76 (June and Sept. 1959).

SCOTT, Hew, *Fasti Ecclesiae Scoticanae, the succession of ministers in the parish churches of Scotland from ... 1560*, New ed. rev. [ed. by W. S. Crockett and F. J. Grant] 7 vols, 1915–28

Scottish Family Histories: a list of books for consultation in the Edinburgh Reference Library 1958

SCOTTISH RECORD SOCIETY publications, 72 vols, 1898 – date. [Lists of commissariot records, burgesses and guild-brethren, and apprentices for various burghs and towns].

Sectional List No. 24 – *Record Publications*, H.M.S.O., 1965 [includes the indexes to Sasines and the Register of Deeds so far published].

SETON, *Sir* Bruce Gordon *and* ARNOT, Jean Gordon (editors), *The Prisoners of the '45*, 3 vols, 1928–9.

SINCLAIR, *Rt Hon. Sir* John, *Bart*, The Statistical Account of Scotland; drawn up from the communications of the ministers of the different parishes, 21 vols, 1791–9.

STUART, Margaret, *Scottish Family History*, 1930

TAYLER, Alistair *and* TAYLER, Henrietta, *Jacobites of Aberdeenshire and Banffshire in the Rising of 1715*, 1934.

TAYLER, Alistair *and* TAYLER, Henrietta, *Jacobites of Aberdeenshire and Banffshire in the Forty-Five*, 1928

THOMSON, John Maitland, *The Public Records of Scotland*, 1922.

TURNBULL, William Barclay David Donald, *Catalogue of the MSS relating to Genealogy and Heraldry preserved in the Library of the Faculty of Advocates*, 1852 [only 10 copies printed].

Chapter 19. Irish Records

AINSWORTH, John Francis, 'Research in Ireland', *Genealogists' Magazine*, VIII, 249 (March 1939).

BURKE, M. *and others*, *Walker's Hibernian Magazine: Index to Deaths in Walker's Hibernian Magazine, vols 1–35; compiled by M. Burke and others for the Fellowship of The Library Association of Ireland* [to be published].

BURTCHAELL, George Dames and SADLEIR, Thomas Ulick (editors), *Alumni Dublinenses; a register of the students, graduates, professors and provosts of Trinity College, in the University of Dublin*, new ed. [1593–1860], 1935.

CLARE, Wallace, 'Irish Records', *Genealogists' Magazine*, VI, 41 (June 1932).

Clerical Directory for Ireland; containing a list of the benefices, with their patrons; the names of the incumbents and curates etc., 1858.

CONNELL, Kenneth Hugh, *The Population of Ireland 1750–1845*, 1950.

CRONE, John Smyth, '*Bibliography of Irish Family History*' *Irish Book Lover*, V, 91, 110, 151, 168, 204, 223 (1913–14); VI, 83, 116 (1914–15).

CRONE, John Smyth, *A Concise Dictionary of Irish Biography*, rev, and enlarged, 1937 [contains some 3,000 five-line biographies].

DARWIN, Kenneth, 'The Irish Records Situation', *Journal of the Society of Archivists*, II, No. 8 (Oct. 1963) [describes the record repositories in Ireland and their contents].

EAGER, Alan Robert, *A Guide to Irish Bibiographical material; being a bibliog. of Irish bibliographies and some sources of information*, 1964.

FALLEY, Margaret Dickson, *Irish and Scotch-Irish Ancestral Research: a guide to the genealogical records, methods and sources in Ireland*, 2 vols, U.S.A., Evanston [1961–2].

FARRAR, Robert Henry, *Irish Marriages ... an index to Walker's 'Hibernian Magazine,' 1771 to 1812, with an appx fr. notes of Sir Arthur Vicars ... of the births, marriages, and deaths in 'The Anthologia Hibernica, 1793 and 1794*, 2 vols, 1897 [75 copies priv. pr.].

GARDNER, David E., Harland, D. *and* SMITH, F., *Genealogical Atlas of Ireland*, U.S.A., Salt Lake City, 1964

HALLIDAY, Bernard, *Ireland and Irish Families: catalogue of special collections of books on Ireland and collections of MSS, 1500–1850, relating to principal families of Ireland ... mostly from the collection of the Rev. J. Graves*, 1904.

LEADER, Michael, 'Irish Records', *Genealogists' Magazine* XII, 512, 540 (Sept, and Dec. 1958).

LIMERICK, 'Farrar's Limerick Directory, 1769', *Irish Genealogist*, III, No.9 (Oct. 1964) [a reprint of the first Limerick directory].

MACLYSAGHT, Edward, *Irish Families: their names, arms and origins*, 1957.

MACLYSAGHT, Edward, *More Irish Families*, 1960

MACLYSAGHT, Edward, *Survey of Documents in private keeping*, 1st ser. *Anal. Hib.* No. 15, 1944 2nd series by John F. Answorth and Edward Maclysaght, *ibid.* No. 20, 1958.

O'BRIEN, A., *An Index of Deaths and Marriages from the Waterford Mirror, 1800-1843.* [In preparation: for Fellowship of the Library Association of Ireland – to be published shortly].

O'BRIEN, George Augustus Thomas, *The Economic History of Ireland in the Eighteenth Century*, [1918].

PENDER, Séamas, *A Guide to Irish Genealogical Collections*, 1935. [*Analecta Hibernica*, VII].

PHAIR, P. B., 'Guide to the Register of Deeds', *Analecta Hibernica*, XXIII, 257 (1966).

SADLEIR, Thomas Ulick, 'Ulster Officer Records', *Genealogists' Magazine*, VI, 434 (June 1934).

YOUNG, Arthur, *A Tour in Ireland, with general observations on the present state of that kingdom made in the years 1776, 1777 and 1778*, 2nd ed. 2 vols, 1780.

Chapter 20. Welsh Records

DAVIES, Trefor Rendall (compiler), *A Book of Welsh Names*, 1952.

Dictionary of Welsh Biography (400–1940), 1959.

HALL, Hubert, 'Welsh Local Records: details and classified topographical list', *Transactions of Hon. Cymmrodorion Society*, pp. 16–24, 1914–15.

JONES, E. D., *The Department of MSS and Records in the National Library of Wales*, 1947 [repr. from the *N. Lib. of Wales Journal*].

JONES, E. D., 'Material for the Genealogist in the National Library of Wales', *Genealogists' Magazine*, XIV, 313 (June 1964).

JONES, Francis, 'An Approach to Welsh Genealogy', *Transactions of the Hon. Soc. of Cymmrodorion* (Session 1948), 1949.

Lewis's Topographical Dictionary of Wales, 1849.

MEYRICK, Samuel Rush, *Heraldic Visitation of Wales and part of the Marches between the years 1586 and 1613*, 2 vols, 1846 (from the MS of Lewis Dwnn).

NICHOLAS, Thomas, *Annals and Antiquities of the counties and country families of Wales*, 2nd ed., rev. and enlarged, 2 vols, 1875.

WILLIAMS, David, *A Short History of Modern Wales*, 1961.

WILLIAMS, William Retlaw, *The Parliamentary History of the Principality of Wales ... 1541–1895, comprising lists of representatives with biographical ... notices of the members*, 1895.

Chapter 21. The Dominions, the U.S.A. and Other Countries

BALLEINE, George Reginald, *A Biographical Dictionary of Jersey* [1948].

BIRD, Jack, 'Some Sources for French Genealogy and Heraldry', *Genealogists' Magazine*, XIII, 237 (Dec. 1960).

BIRD, Jack, 'Some Sources for German Genealogy and Heraldry', *Genealogists' Magazine*, XIII, 143 (March 1960).

CAMAJANI, *Count* Guelfo Guelfi, 'Some Sources for Italian Genealogy', *Genealogists' Magazine*, XIV, 66 (Sept. 1962).

CUNNINGHAM, J. R., 'The Genealogical Work of the Latter-Day Saints', *Genealogists' Magazine*, XIV, 369 (Sept. 1964).

DAVIES, C. E. S. 'Tracing Ancestors and Constructing Family Trees ... Pt. I. Enquires to make in Australia', *The Ancestor*, Dec. 1962 [Quarterly Journal of the Genealogical Society of Victoria, Australia].

FAHY, T. G., 'Genealogical Research in the Netherlands', *Genealogists' Magazine*, XIII, 366 (Dec. 1961).

FAHY, T. G., 'Some Sources for Dutch Genealogy', *Genealogists Magazine*, XIV, 24 (March 1962).

FELTHAM, John *and* WRIGHT, E., *Memorial of 'God's Acre'; being monumental inscriptions in the Isle of Man*, 1868 [from a MS mainly copied in 1797, representing some 2,000 inscriptions and ed. by W. Harrison].

Dictionary of New Zealand Biography, 2 vols, 1940.

FOTHERGILL, Gerald, *American Emigrants: How to trace their English Ancestry*, 1908 [being Vol I. of *Some Special Studies in Genealogy*].

GRAY, Nancy *and others*, 'Compiling a Family History: A guide to procedure and use of Australian records', *Descent*, II, iii, 84 (1965).

GUILLET, Edwin Clarence, *The Great Migration: the Atlantic Crossing by Sailing Ships since 1770*, 2nd ed., 1963.

JOSEPH, Anthony P., 'On Tracing Australian Jewish Genealogy', *Genealogists' Magazine*, XIV, 425 (Dec. 1964) [although particularly dealing with Jewish ancestry, much of the information is equally applicable to Australian genealogy in general].

KAMINKOW, Jack *and* KAMINKOW, Marion (editors), *A List of Emigrants from England to America, 1718–1759 ... transcribed from records at the Guidhall, London*, 1964. [not incl., in Lancour's *Bibliography*].

LANCOUR, Adlore Harold, *A Bibliography of Ship Passenger Lists, 1538–1825*, 3rd ed. (of Passenger lists of ships coming to North America, 1607–1825) rev. and enlarged by R. J. Wolfe, with a list of passenger arrival records in the national archives, by F. E. Bridgers, New York, 1963.

LANGTON, C., 'Records and Record Searching in Jersey', *Genealogists' Magazine*, V, 314 (June 1931).

LAWRENCE-ARCHER, James Henry, *Monumental Inscriptions of the British West Indies ... with genealogical and historical annotations etc.*, 1875

LIVINGSTON, Sir Nöel B., *Sketch Pedigrees of some of the Early Settlers in Jamaica ... with a list of the inhabitants in 1670 etc.*, 1909.

MOORE, Arthur William, *Manx Names ... with a preface by Professor Rhys*, 2nd ed., rev., 1903.

NICHOLSON, Cregoe Donaldson Percy, 'Some Early Emigrants to America', *Genealogists' Magazine*, XII – XIII 'March 1955 to Dec. 1960).

PAYNE, James Bertrand, *An Armorial of Jersey: an account, heraldic and antiquarian, of its chief native families with pedigrees, biographical notices etc.* [issued in parts and incomplete], 1859–65.

PINE, Leslie Gilbert, *American Origins*, New York, 1960. [Gives information of sources in most European countries].

PUBLIC ARCHIVES OF CANADA, *Tracing your Ancestors in Canada*, 1966 [This booklet is reprinted in the *Genealogists' Magazine*, XV, 293 (Dec. 1966)].

PUGH, Ralph Bernard, *The Records of the Colonial and Dominions Offices*, 1964 [Public Record Office Handbook 3].

RABINO di BORGOMALE, H. L., 'Genealogical Research in France', *Genealogists' Magazine*, X, 1 (Sept. 1946).

SERLE, Percival, *Dictionary of Australian Biography*, 2 vols, Sydney, 1949.

WALLACE, William Stewart (ed.), *The Macmillan Biography of Canadian Biography*, 3rd ed. rev. and enlarged, 1963

Chapter 22. Various Other Sources

BERNAU, Charles Allan, *The Genealogy of the Submerged*, 1908 [Vol III of *Some Special Studies in Genealogy*]

'Bibliography of Lists of Apprenticeships,' *Genealogists' Magazine*, VII, 18 and 74 (March and June, 1935).

BURGESS, Frederick, *English Churchyard Memorials*, 1963

COLBY, Reginald, 'The Bryant Index', *Genealogists' Magazine*, X, 488 (March 1950).

GUILDHALL LIBRARY, *London Business House Histories: a handlist* [1964].

HABAKKUK, Hrothgar John, 'Marriage Settlements in the Eighteenth Century', *Transactions of the Royal Historical Society*, XXXII (1950).

KETCHLEY, C. P., 'Apprentices – Trade and Poor', *Amateur Historian*, II, 357 (June–July 1956).

MATTHEWS, William, *British Autobiographies*, Univ. of California, U.S.A., 1955.

MATTHEWS, William, *British Diaries: an annotated bibliography of British diaries, written between 1442 and 1942*, 1950 [Diaries in MS are recorded, with author index].

TRINICK, Michael, 'A Country House Index', *Genealogists' Magazine*, XI, 89 (Sept. 1951) [*The Bryant Index*, see also under Colby, Reginald].

UNWIN, George, *The Guilds and Companies of London*, 2nd ed., 1962 [includes bibliog. of printed works on the different guilds of London additional to those in his 1908 edition].

Chapter 23. Places of Search: I. The Society of Genealogists

CAMP, Anthony John, 'Collections and Indexes of the Society of Genealogists', *Genealogists' Magazine*, XIII, 311 (June 1961)

Guide to the Library of the Society of Genealogists, [mimeographed] 1965.

PERCY-SMITH, Hubert Kendall, 'The Headquarters of Genealogy in Britain', *Amateur Historian*, I, 70 (Dec.–Jan. 1953).

Chapter 24. Places of Search: II The Public Record Office

FINES, J., 'Documents in the Public Record Office: III The Early Chancery Proceedings', *Amateur Historian* VI, 254 (Summer 1965).

GALBRAITH, Vivian Hunter, *An Introduction to the Use of the Public Records*, repr. with corrections, 1952

GALBRAITH, Vivian Hunter, *Studies in the Public Records*, 1948

Guide to the Contents of the Public Record Office, rev. and extended (to 1960) from the Guide by the late M. S. Giuseppi, F.S.A., 2 vols, 1963: Vol. 1. Legal Records, Vol. 2. State Papers and Departmental Records [the official guide, pub. by H.M.S.O.].

HECTOR, L. C., 'Genealogy in the Public Records', *Genealogists' Magazine*, VIII, 57 (June 1938).

JOHNSON, Charles, *The Public Record Office*, 1932 [S.P.C.K. Helps].

LATHAM, R. L., 'Interpreting the Public Records' [various articles], *Amateur Historian*, I, 5, 47, 77, 112, 155 (Aug. 1952–May 1953)

NEWTON, K. C., 'Reading Medieval Local Records', *Amateur Historian*, III, 81 (Winter 1956–7).

PUBLIC RECORD OFFICE, *Information for Readers*, 1963 [a 4 pp. useful pamphlet].

Record Publications (Sectional List No 24) 1965. [See under Chapter IX, *Government Publications*].

Virginia State Library, *The British Public Record Office: history, description, record groups, finding aids and materials for American history with special reference to Virginia*, Richmond, Virginia, U.S.A., 1960 [a useful account in 178 pp. from the U.S.A. point of view].

Chapter 25. Places of Search III. The British Museum and other Libraries

Dopson, Laurence, 'The John Rylands Library, Manchester', *Amateur Historian*, II, 202 (Aug.–Sept. 1955).

Gilson, Julius Parnell, *A Student's Guide to the MSS of the British Museum* [S.P.C.K. *Helps for Students of History* No. 31], 1920.

Hamilton-Edwards, Gerald Kenneth Savery, 'The Burnet Morris Collection at Exeter', *Genealogists' Magazine* XIV, 180 (June 1963).

Hepworth, Philip, *Archives and Manuscripts in Libraries, 1961*, 1962.

Historical Manuscripts Commission, *Record Repositories in Great Britain: a list prepared by a joint committee of the Hist. MSS. Com. and the British Records Assoc.*, 1964

Irwin, Raymond *and* Staveley, Ronald, (editors), *The Libraries of London*, 2nd, rev. ed., 1964.

Jones, Philip Edmund *and* Smith, Raymond, *A Guide to the Records in the Corporation of London Records Office and the Guildhall Library Muniment Room etc.*, 1951.

Jones, Philip Ernest H., 'Genealogy and the City of London Records', *Genealogists' Magazine*, XI, 134, 167 (Dec. 1951, March 1952)

Redstone, Lilian Jane *and* Steer, Francis William (editors), *Local Records: their nature and care*, 1953.

Rye, Reginald Arthur, *The Libraries of London: a guide for students etc.* 3rd ed. 1928.

Smith, Francis Raymond S., 'The Guildhall Library in War and Peace', *Genealogists' Magazine*, X, 175 (June 1948)

Wagner, *Sir* Anthony Richard, *The Records and Collections of the College of Arms*, 1952.

Wallace, A., 'Genealogical MSS in the Newcastle-upon-Tyne Reference Library', *Genealogists Magazine*, XIV, 194 (Sept. 1963).

Chapter 26. Genealogy and Heraldry

BOUTELL, Charles, *English Heraldry*, rev. by C. W. Scott-Giles and J. P. Brooke-Little, 1965.

BURKE, *Sir* John Bernard, *The General Armory of England, Scotland, Ireland and Wales*, 1884, repr. 1962.

CHILD, Heather, *Heraldic Design*, 1965.

DENHOLM-YOUNG, Nöel, *History and Heraldry, 1254 to 1310: a study of the historical value of the Rolls of Arms*, 1965.

FOSTER, Joseph, *Grantees of Arms named in Docquets and Patents between the years 1687 and 1898, preserved in various MSS* ... ed. by W. H. Rylands, 2 vols, 1916. [Harleian Society Vols 67 and 68].

FOSTER, Joseph, *Grantees of Arms named in Docquets and Patents to the end of the 17th century, in the MSS. preserved in the British Museum* ... *and elsewhere, alphabetically arranged etc.*, ed. by W. H. Rylands, 1915 [Harleian Society, Vol. 66].

FOSTER, Joseph, *Some Feudal Coats of Arms from Heraldic Rolls, 1298–1418*, 1902.

FOSTER, Joseph, *Two Tudor Books of Arms: being Harleian MSS. 2169 and 6163*, 1904 [De Walden Library].

FOX-DAVIES, Arthur Charles, *A Complete Guide to Heraldry*, rev. ed. repr. 1961 [still the best general work on English heraldry].

GATFIELD, George, *Guide to Printed Books and Manuscripts relating to English and Foreign Heraldry and Genealogy*, 1892.

GAYRE *of Gayre and Nigg*, Robert, *Heraldic Standards and Other Ensigns*, 1959.

GODFREY, Walter Hindes, assisted by *Sir* Anthony Wagner, *The College of Arms* ... *being the 16th and final monograph of the London Survey Committee*, 1963 [contains biographies of the heralds and their coats of arms].

INNES of Learney, *Sir* Thomas, *Scots Heraldry*, 2nd ed., rev. and enlarged 1956.

JOUGLA DE MORENAS, Henri, *Grand Armorial de France*, 6 vols + 1 Suppl., Paris, 1934–52 [*Les Editions Héraldiques*, later *Société de Grand Armorial de France*].

LYNDSAY, Sir David, *Facsimile of an Ancient Heraldic Manuscript emblazoned by Sir David Lyndsay, Lyon King of Arms, 1542*, 1878.

MATHIEU, Rémi, *Le Système Héraldique Français*, 5th ed., Paris, 1946.

MONCREIFFE of that Ilk, Sir Rupert Iain Kay, *bart. and* POTTINGER, Don, *Simple Heraldry, cheerfully illustrated*, 1953 [amusingly written and illustrated and full of sound accurate information on the subject].

MOULE, Thomas, *Bibliotheca Heraldica Magnae Britanniae: An Analytical Catalogue of Books on Genealogy, Heraldry, etc.*, 1882.

NATIONAL ART LIBRARY, Victoria and Albert Museum *Classed Catalogue of Printed Books; Heraldry*, 1901.

PAPWORTH, John Woody *and* MORANT, Alfred William Whitehead, *Ordinary of British Armorials, reproduced from the original edition of 1874:* intro. by G. D. Squibb [and] A. R. Wagner, 1961.

PAUL, Sir James Balfour, *Heraldry in Relation to Scottish History and Art*, 1899.

PHILLIPS, Sir Edward *and* MORANT, James, *Catalogue of the Library of the Heraldry Society*, 1963.

PINE, Leslie Gilbert, 'Family History from Heraldry', *Amateur Historian*, I, 238. (Oct.–Nov. 1953).

REYNOLDS, John, *A Display of Heraldry of the Particular Coat Armours now in use ... in the six counties of North Wales*, 1739 [24 pp. containing about 60 coats of arms: a facsim. of this ed. has been published].

RIETSTAP, Johannes Baptist, *Armorial Général*, 2nd ed. rev. and augumented, Gouda, 1884–7 [see also below under Rolland, Victor].

ROLLAND, Victor *and* ROLLAND, Henri, *J. B. Rietstap: General Illustrated Armorial*, 3rd ed. [Plates illustrating the text of *l'Armorial général* de J. B. Rietstap] 6 vols [1954].

ROLLAND, Victor *and* ROLLAND, Henri, *Supplément à l'Armorial général* de J. B. Rietstap [vols. 1–5 by V. Rolland; vol. 6 by Henri Rolland], 6 vols, Paris, 1904. *Table du Supplément, etc.*, Lyon, 1951.

ROGERS, Hugh Cuthbert Basset, *The Pageant of Heraldry: an explanation of its principles and its uses today ... with an introduction by Col. H. A. B. Lawson, Rothesay Herald and Lyon Clerk*, 1955.
SCOTT-GILES, Charles Wilfred, The Romance of Heraldry, 1951.
SETON, George, *The Law and Practice of Heraldry in Scotland*, 1863.
SMITH, Christopher J., 'Funeral Hatchments', *Amateur Historian*, II, 138 (Apr.–May 1955).
STEVENSON, John Robert Horne, *Heraldry in Scotland, incl. a Recension of 'The Law and Practice of Heraldry in Scotland' by the late George Seton*, 2 vols, 1914.
STODART, Robert Riddle, *Scottish Arms: being a collection of Armorial Bearings, 1370-1678*, 2 vols, 1881.
SUMMERS, Peter G., 'A Survey of Hatchments', *Genealogists' Magazine*, XII, 443 (March 1958).
WAGNER, *Sir* Anthony Richard, *Heraldry in England*, 1949.
WAGNER, *Sir* Anthony Richard, *Historic Heraldry of Britain*, 1939.

Chapter 27. Genealogy and Biography

The main sources for biography are mentioned in this bibliography under Chapters IX and X. It should also be noted that the British National Bibliography since it began publication annually in 1951 in its section on biography (920) gives all biographies published in each year. See also the author's article in the *Genealogists' Magazine* XV, 68 (June 1965) on 'Genealogy and Biography'.

Chapter 28. Further Back

BERESFORD, Maurice Warwick, *The Lay Subsidy Rolls: Pt i. 1290–1334: Pt ii. After 1334: The Poll Taxes of 1377, 1379 and 1381*, 1963.
Bibliography of British History, 3 vols, 1933–51. 1. Tudor period, 1485–1603; 2. Stuart Period, 1603–1714; 3. Eighteenth Century, 1714–1789.
BOWLER, *Dom* Cyril Hugh, *Recusant Roll No. 2. (1593-1594): An Abstract in English*, 1965. [*Recusant Rolls of the Exchequer, temp. Elizabeth I*].

CARR, A. D., 'Short Guides to Records No. 12: Deeds of Title', *History*, Oct. 1965 [incl. inform. on Bargain and Sale, Lease and Release and Fines].

CHIBNALL, Albert Charles *and* WOODMAN, A. Vere (editors), *Buckinghamshire Village*, 1965 ['Study of the feudal and economic development of a village from Norman times to the 19th century ... from little known documents in the Public Record Office with local and private records'].

CHIBNALL, Albert Charles *and* WOODMAN, A. Vere (editors) *Subsidy Roll for the County of Buckingham, anno. 1524,* 1950 [Bucks. Record Soc., Vol. 8].

CHIBNALL, Marjorie (ed.), *Select Documents of the English Lands of the Abbey of Bec*, 1951 [Camden Soc., 3rd Ser., Vol 73].

CLAYTON, Muriel, *Catalogue of Rubbings of Brasses and Incised Slabs, Victorian and Albert Museum*, 1929.

CORNWALL, Julian, 'A Tudor Domesday: the Musters of 1522', *Journal of Society of Archivists*, III, No. 1 (April 1965)

ELLIS, *Sir* Henry, *Introduction to Domesday Book*, 2 vols [includes index of tenants in capite, of under-tenants and of persons of the time of Edward the Confessor, with biographical and genealogical notes on landholders].

EMMISON, Frederick George, *Archives and Local History*, 1966

FARRER, William, *Honors and Knights' Fees*, 3 vols, 1923 [attempts to trace descent of tenants of these, 11th to 14th centuries].

FURNIVALL, Frederick J., *The Fifty Earliest English Wills in the Court of Probate, London*, A.D. *1387-1439 ... copied and edited from the original registers in Somerset House by F.J.F.*, 1882, repr. 1964. [Early English Text Soc.]

GARRETT, R. E. F., 'Chancery and Other Proceedings', *Genealogists' Magazine*, XV, 97, 139 (Sept. and Dec. 1965).

GOODER, Eileen A., *Latin for Local History: an introduction*, 1961 [intended for use with B. H. Kennedy's *The Shorter Latin Primer*].

GROSS, Charles, *Sources and Literature of English History from the Earliest Times to about 1485*, 2nd ed., 1914.

HALL, Hubert (ed.), *A Repertory of British Archives Pt I:
England*, 1920. [R. Historical Soc.].

HASSALL, William Owen, *Wheatley Records*, 1956.

HECTOR, Leonard Charles, *The Handwriting of English Documents*, 2nd ed., 1966

HONE, Nathaniel J., *The Manor and Manorial Records*, 3rd
ed. 1925 [includes a bibliog.].

HOSKINS, William George, *Local History in England*, 1959
[one of the most useful books, with a valuable bibliog.
Does not include Wales or London, which the author
explains require separate books].

LATHAM, Lucy Clare, *The Manor*, 1931 [Historical Assoc.
Leaflet No. 83].

LATHAM, R. E., 'Coping with Medieval Latin', *Amateur
Historian* I, 331 (Apr.–May 1954).

McGUINESS, Mary, 'Inquisitions Post Mortem', *Amateur
Historian*, VI, No. 7 (Spring 1965).

MARTIN, Charles Trice, *The Record Interpreter: a collection
of abbreviations, Latin words and names used in English
Historical Manuscripts and Records*, 2nd ed., 1910.

MONUMENTAL BRASS SOCIETY, *Portfolios*, 1894–1914, and
1935 onwards: *Transactions*, 1887–1914, 1935—

POWICKE, *Sir* Frederick Maurice *and* FRYDE, Edman Boleslav,
Handbook of British Chronology, 2nd ed., 1961 [useful for
regnal years etc.].

PURVIS, John Stanley, *The Archives of the York Diocesan
Registry*, 1952.

RYE, Walter, *Records and Record Searching: a guide to the
Genealogists and Topographer*, 2nd ed., 1897.

RYE, Walter, *Norfolk Records: being an index to four series
of Norfolk Inquisitions: The Tower series; the Chancery
or Rolls series; the Exchequer series, the Wards and Liveries
series*, 1892. [Norfolk and Norwich Arch. Soc.].

RYE, Walter, *Scandinavian Names in Norfolk*, 2nd ed., 1920

SHEEHAN, Michael M., 'A List of Thirteenth-Century English
Wills', *Genealogists' Magazine*, IX, 259 (March 1961)

SHERWOOD, Leslie, 'The Court Baron', *Amateur Historian*,
II, 374 (June–July 1956)

STEPHENSON, Mill, *List of Monumental Brasses in the British
Isles, with appendix by Ralph Griffin*, 1964

Tomlins, *Sir* Thomas Edlyne, *The Law Dictionary . . . defining and interpreting the terms etc.*, 3rd ed., 2 vols, 1820.

Torr, V. J., 'Brasses and the Monumental Brass Society', *Amateur Historian*, I, 159 (Apr.–May 1953).

West, John, *Village Records*, 1963

Williams, J. Anthony, 'Short Guides to Records No. 11 Recusant Rolls', *History*, June, 1965.

Williams, William Morgan, *The Sociology of an English Village: Gosford, Cumberland*, 1956 ['of general value for methods and materials involved in the study of the recent history of a community', W. G. Hoskins].

Chapter 29. Searching in the United States

American Society of Genealogists, *Genealogical Research Methods and Sources*, Washington, 1960.

Bennett, Archibald F., *Finding your Forefathers in America*, Salt Lake City, 1957.

Bennett, Archibald F., *A Guide for Genealogical Research*, Salt Lake City, 1951.

Bureau of the Census, *Transcriptions of the 1790 Census of the United States*, 12 vols, Washington 1909.

Busby, Gladys *and* Fish, Evelyn, *Practical Research in Genealogy: a compilation of Genealogical research data*, Mesa, 1955.

Curry, Cora C., *Records of the Roman Catholic Church in the United States as a source for authentic genealogical and historical material*, National Genealogical Society, U.S.A., 1935.

Daughters of the American Revolution, *Is that Lineage right? A training manual for the examiner of lineage papers, with helpful hints for the beginner in genealogical research*, Washington, 1958.

Doane, Gilbert Harry, *Searching for Your Ancestors: the how and why of Genealogy*, 3rd ed., Minneapolis, 1960.

Durrie, Daniel S., *Bibliographia Genealogica Americana: an alphabetical index to American genealogies and pedigrees contained in state, county and town histories, printed genealogies and kindred works*, 3rd ed. rev. and enlarged, Albany, 1886 [Supplement 1888].

Forbes, Harriette Merrifield, *Gravestones of Early New England and the men who made them, 1653–1800*, U.S.A., 1927.

Gardner, David E. *and others, A Basic Course in Genealogy*, Salt Lake City, 1958.

Kirkham, E. Kay, *A Survey of American Census Schedules: an explanation and description of our Federal census ennumerations 1790–1950*, Salt Lake City, 1959.

Long Island Historical Society, *Catalogue of American Genealogies*, Brooklyn, N.Y., 1935.

Munsell's Genealogical Index, *Index to American Genealogies and to Genealogical Material contained in all works such as town histories, county histories, local histories, historical society publications, biographies, histories, periodicals and kindred works*, 5th ed., rev., improved and enlarged, Albany, 1900 [Supplement 1900–8, Albany, 1908].

Public Health Service Publications, No 630A, *Where to Write for Birth and Death Records*, 1958; No. 630B, *Where to Write for Marriage Records*, 1958; No. 630C, *Where to Write for Divorce Records*, 1958 [the above are obtainable from the Superintendent of Documents, United States Government Printing Office, Washington, 25 D.C.].

Rider, Fremont J., ed., *The American Genealogical Index*, 48 vols, Middletown, Conn., 1942–52.

Rider, Fremont J., *ed., The American Genealogical Biographical Index*, Middletown, Conn., 1952— [*in progress:* a continuation of the preceeding].

Stetson, Oscar Frank, *The Art of Ancestor Hunting*, Brattleboro, 1936.

Stevenson, Noel C., *Search and Research: the Researcher's Handbook: a guide to official records, and library sources for investigators, historians, genealogists, lawyers and librarians*, rev. ed., Salt Lake City, 1959.

United States National Archives, *Guide to the Records in the National Archives*, Washington, 1948 (National Archives Publication No. 49–13).

White, David, *Reference Manual for Genealogical Research*, [Penllyn], Pa., 1954.

Chapter 30. Writing It Up

INDEX

Hurst, 57
Hyamson, A. M., 118

Immigrants, 121
Importance of Being Earnest, The, 9
Index Ecclesiasticus, 81
Index to Genealogical Periodicals (U.S.A.), 199
India, index of persons connected with, 172
India Library, Commonwealth Office, 108
Inn, neighbouring local, 45
Inns of Court, 82
Inquisitions Post Mortem, 194
Institute of Army Historical Research, 100
Insurance company records, 165
Inventories, P.C.C., 63
Iolanthe, 173
Ireland, 140–7; Betham extracts, 142–3; Chester refugees, 145; Chief Herald, 143, 186, 187; civil registration, 30, 141; Church of Ireland Representative Body, 143, 144; Four Courts, destruction of, 140; Friends Meeting House, Eustace St., 143; funeral certificates, 143; grants of arms, 143, 186; heraldry in, 186; marriage licences, indexes, 143; *Memorials of the Dead*, 147; National Library, 145; Ossory marriage licences, 143; Prerogative Court of Armagh, 142; Prerogative marriage licences, 143; Public Record Office, 140, 142, 145; Quakers, 143; Quaker records, 52; Register of Deeds, 144, 145; registration of Protestant marriages, 30, 141; R. Irish Academy, 145; Trinity College, Dublin, 85, Library, 145; will and administrations, 142
Irish Genealogical Society in Great Britain, 146
Irish Memorials Association, 147
Irish newspapers, 146; in British Museum Newspaper Library, 146
Irish Record Office, Dublin, 140, 142
Irish records, 140–7

'Jewish Ancestors and where to find them', 117
Jewish Historical Society of England, 118
Jewish Museum, 118
Jewish names, 115
Jewish synagogues, registers of, 52
Jewish wills, 118
Jews, in England, 114–8; Portuguese, 116; Spanish, 115; in U.S.A., 200
'John' Company, *see* East India Company
Jones, Francis, Wales Herald Extraordinary, 151
Judges of England, 83

Kelly's Titled, Landed and Official Classes, 72, 73, 171
Kensington Borough Library, 180
Kirk Session Records, 139

Landed Gentry, see *Burke's Landed Gentry*
Land transfer, 193
Lart, C. E. MSS collection, 120
Latter Day Saints (Mormons), 75; genealogical library, 75; great card file, 201
Lay Subsidy Rolls, 194
Leader, Michael, 146
Lease and Release, 193–4
Leeds Philosophical Society, Proceedings of, 77
Leeson, Francis, article by, 166
Leslie, Canon, 144
Leyden University, 85
Library Associated Record, 28
Library of Congress, 197
Lives of British Admirals, 87
Local History in England, 63
Local knowledge, value of, 44
London, City Chamberlain's records, 164; Corporation Record Office, 180; freemen, 164; livery companies of city, 163–4, 179–80; movement to, 199; parish registers, 179; wills, 179
London Citizens (Boyd Collection), 170
London directories, 180
London freemen, 164
London Magazine, 172, 177

ment in Ulster, 141; Record Office, 140, 145

'North of England Newspapers', 77

Northumberland (Bateson), 73

O'Byrne, W. R., 88, 95, 169, 178

Occupations, reasons for taking up, 208

O'Connell, Basil, 143

Officers of the Bengal Army, 107, 172

Old Northwest Genealogical Quarterly, 198

Ordinary of Scottish Arms, An, 138

Osborne, John, apprentice, 161

Oxford Men and their Colleges, 80

Parish, advantages in personal visit to, 43

Parishes, neighbouring, 45

Parish registers, 39–47; fees for searching, 41–3; during Civil War and Commonwealth, 43; personal examination desirable, 41–3

Parliament, records of members, 86, Namier and Brooke's history, 86

Paul, Sir James Balfour, 70, 208

Paynel family, 11

P.C.C., *see* Prerogative Court of Canterbury

P.C.Y., *see* Prerogative Court of York

Peculiars, 56–7

Pedigree making a skilled job, 26

Pedigrees, chart, 205–6; form of notation for, 207–8; methods of reproducing, 27; narrative, 206–8; reasons for making, 10

Peerage of England (Collins), 70

Pennsylvanian Magazine, 198

Pensions, army widows, 106; for wounds, army, 106, R. Navy, 90

People of the Period, 73

Pepsyian MSS, Catalogue of, 93

Pepys, Samuel, 93

Percy-Smith, H. K., 112

Pereira, Isaac Haim, 116

Periodicals, 74–9

Pershouse, Mann and, 67

Photography, use of, 28

Photostat, use of, 28

Physicians, R. College of, 83, 84

Poland, immigrants from, 121

Prerogative Court of Canterbury, 55–63; printed indexes to, 60, 61, 63, 118

Prerogative Court of York, 55

Present House of Commons, The, 86

Principal Probate Registry, 54–5

P.R.O., *see* Public Record Office

Professional assistance, 63–4

Professional genealogists, 19, 64

Protestant dissenters, 194

Protestants, French, *see* Huguenots

Protestation Oath Rolls, 195

Public Record Office, 33, 34, 50, 174–6; Welsh records, 149

Public Record Office Lists and Indexes XVIII (Admiralty Records), 89

Quaker records, 52; Scottish, 52; Irish, 52; U.S.A., 201

Queen's College, Oxford, 181

Questionnaire, sending out, 21–2

Receipt books, value of, 166

Records and Collections of the College of Arms, 187

Records of Naval Men, (Fothergill), 89, 95

Records of the Roman Catholic Church in the United States, 200

Recusant Rolls, 194

Reflex process, copying by, 28

Richmond (Yorks), Archdeaconry of, 57

Roborough, Lord, 117

Rodney, H.M.S., 17

Rolls Series, 177

Roman Catholics, 48, 194; priests, 81; registers, 48 52; U.S.A., 200

Roth, Cecil, 118

Royal Artillery, records of service, 106

Royal Calendar, The, 83, 172

Royal Hospital, Chelsea, 106

Royal Irish Academy, 145

Royal Marines, 98–9; Attestation Forms, 98; Corps Historian, 99; description books, 98; registers of service, 99

Royal Military Academy, 104

Royal Military College, 104

Royal Naval Biography, 87, 88, 95, 169

Stornoway, I. of Lewis, registers, 125
Story of Scotland, 139
Surgeons, R. College of, 83, 84, 91
Surgeons and Barbers Company, 83
Surnames, advantage of unusual, 32; origin of, 16
Survey of London, 187
Swanzy, Rev. H. B., MSS. collection, 144

Tasmania, civil registration, 152
Test Act, 49, 50
Text and Calendars, 79
Theatrical families, 85; article on, 85
Thomson, T. R., 20, 172
Threadneedle Street Church, 119; library, 119
Times, The, 77, 78, 79, 178; obituary notices in, 189; Palmer's Index to, 77
Tithe apportionment lists, 46
Tithe Commutation Act of 1836, 46
Tithe maps, 46
Tithe Redemption Commission, 46
Tithe Redemption maps, 178
Tontines, 165-6
Tour in Quest of Genealogy, 149
'Tracing Ancestors and Constructing Family Trees', 153
Tradition, family, 22
Tyler's Genealogical Quarterly, 198

Ulster King of Arms, *see* Norroy and Ulster King of Arms
United Services Magazine, 78
United States of America, 196-204; Army, soldiers' pensions, 196; Baptist Church, 200; Bibles, family, 197; Boston Tea Party, 203; census returns, 202; church records, 199; church registers, 199-201; civil registration, 199; Civil War, 196; Confederate Army, 196; Daughters of the American Revolution, 203, archives of, 204; Declaration of Independence, 203; distribution lists, 203; Episcopal Church records, 200; family histories, printed, 197; Great Plains, migration to, 196; guardians, children's, 203; Holland Society, 203; Homestead Act, 196;
Jewish archives, 200; Methodist records, 200; migration to, from Gt. Britain, 154-6; monumental inscriptions, 201; National Archives, 196, 204; National Society of Sons of the Revolution, 198; occupations, 198; Pilgrim Fathers, 200; probate courts, 203; probate laws 203; probate offices, 203; probate records, 202-3; Quaker records, 201; Revolutionary War, 196, 197, 203, soldiers' pensions in, 204; Roman Catholics, 200; Society of Cincinnati, 203; Sons and Daughters of the Pilgrims, 203; Sons of Confederate Veterans, 203; Surrogate's Court, New York, 203; town records, 199; Virginia, tax lists, 202
Universities, matriculation registers, 164
University College, London, Huguenot Library at, 119
University of London Library, 180, 190
Upper Ten Thousand, The, 72

Venn, J. and J. A., 80
Vicar-General licences, 66
Vicars, Sir Arthur, 143
Victoria County Histories, 73, 177
Village Records, 53
Virginia Magazine of Biography and History, 198
Vivian, 67

Wagner, Sir Anthony, 11, 12, 18, 187
Wagner collection, 120
Wales, 148-51; bishops' transcripts, 148; commonest surnames, 150; surnames, 149, 150
Wales, National Library of, 148, 149
Walford's County Families, 72, 171
Welply abstracts, 146
Welsh language, 150
Welsh names, 149
Welsh records, 148-51
Welsh Rolls, 150
Wesley, John and Charles, 50-1
Wesleyan Methodist Magazine, 51
Wesleyan Methodists, *see* Methodists